Praise for *Lea*

This is an exceptional book on leadership. *Leader* ⟨…⟩
stories with laser-sharp questions to prompt you t⟨…⟩
grow your leadership capabilities.

If disaster strikes, pray for Shackleton; if a need for mental stimulation and insightful guidance hits you, then most definitely call for Katy and Emmie!

Will Greenwood, former England rugby international and 2003 World Cup winner

Leader is an outstanding book for anyone interested in becoming a better leader. The principles covered are relevant to everyone: from executive to apprentice, from parents to teachers and coaches, and, in my case, to those involved in delivering healthcare as both a doctor and as a leader of clinical teams.

The book skilfully weaves case studies of leadership excellence through a narrative that concentrates on compassion, empathy and vision to inspire, motivate and develop your team. A useful feature is the thoughtful practical exercises for the reader to reflect upon and put into action.

Leader is easy to read and is perfect for either a twenty-minute dip at bedtime or a leisurely afternoon with a cup of tea. So if you're looking for a great book on leadership, my advice is to read this one.

Andrew Cox, consultant cardiologist and general physician, Frimley Health NHS Foundation Trust and the Royal Brompton and Harefield NHS Trust

In *Leader*, Katy Granville-Chapman and Emmie Bidston show why leadership centred on service, truth, kindness, empathy, generosity, purpose and love is what we need to take us forward through the hardest realities and challenges of life.

Katy and Emmie ground their argument in the latest research and illustrate it with compelling case studies of high-performing teams from the worlds of sport, business, healthcare, technology, politics and education. This is the leadership that powers Google, the All Blacks and the British Army – and is modelled by public figures such as Michelle Obama and Andrew Strauss. But it isn't all about big names. It's about strong character. Examples of servant leadership fill the book, as do practical leadership exercises.

This book doesn't simply introduce a way of leading; it inspires, challenges and guides you to step up and lead in your own context for the good of those around you.

Dr Edward Brooks, Executive Director, The Oxford Character Project

If you're seeking the formula for effective teamwork and eager to improve performance and productivity, then *Leader* is the perfect book for you. Interspersed with fascinating case studies and brimming with practical tips and challenges, it is a treat to dip into or read at length.

Distilling decades of research findings, Katy and Emmie take a fresh look at leadership and talk us through the essential ingredients needed to develop ourselves as great leaders – from the importance of really knowing and caring about our teams, to building and sharing a vision that will inspire and motivate them.

Leader offers a comprehensive and accessible guide to leadership, and I'm now eager to implement what I've learned.

Clare Richards, Chief Executive, the ClementJames Centre

This is exactly the sort of book on leadership we need for the modern world in which we live. Katy and Emmie's writing is clear, engaging and communicates a deep understanding of the human condition – a welcome tonic when an ever-growing body of literature simply adds any adjective before the word 'leadership' and claims to be the great catch-all for success. Instead, the authors ground their message in research from a number of different fields, focusing on the essential ingredients which make for a meaningful relationship between the leader and their people. Their particular focus on values is spot-on.

Packed with numerous case studies, useful exercises and practical tips, *Leader* is a must-read for anyone interested in learning about what it takes to lead with compassion, authenticity and success in the twenty-first century.

James Dahl, Master, Wellington College

To be known, loved and inspired is a basic human need which acts as the fuel for a purposeful, values-driven life. Katy and Emmie have encapsulated this simple yet powerful message as the core of this practical guide for those striving to become better leaders and those who aspire to lead. *Leader* will quickly become a go-to companion for many on this journey.

Mike Buchanan, Chair, International Positive Education Network, and founder of PositivelyLeading

Leader

Know, love and inspire your people

Katy Granville-Chapman
and Emmie Bidston

Foreword by
Sir Anthony Seldon

Crown House Publishing Limited
www.crownhouse.co.uk

First published by
Crown House Publishing
Crown Buildings, Bancyfelin, Carmarthen, Wales, SA33 5ND, UK
www.crownhouse.co.uk

and

Crown House Publishing Company LLC
PO Box 2223, Williston, VT 05495, USA
www.crownhousepublishing.com

First published 2020. Reprinted 2021.

Stars graphic © doozydo – stock.adobe.com.

Extract pages 188–190 © Laura Reesby, 2020.

British Library Cataloguing-in-Publication Data

A catalogue entry for this book is available from the British Library.

Print ISBN: 978-178583486-8
Mobi ISBN: 978-178583497-4
ePub ISBN: 978-178583498-1
ePDF ISBN: 978-178583499-8

LCCN 2020931137

Printed and bound in the UK by
TJ Books, Padstow, Cornwall

For Jeremy, Charlie and Harry.

For Neil, Amelie, Bexie and Megan.

Foreword

What constitutes good and bad leadership has fascinated me all of my life. I grew up in the long shadow of the Second World War. I never ceased to be moved by listening to Churchill's speeches and learning more about him. A good leader. Hitler was ubiquitous in my formative years too, in the school curriculum, in films and in literature. A bad leader, albeit with many of the qualities that good leaders need, including oratory, a vision and the ability to motivate his team. As I grew older, I came to realise that leadership is the magic ingredient that can transform any institution, country, company or college for the better. Or worse.

A vision is essential for a leader, but having a vision in itself is not enough. Hitler, for example, had a profoundly dehumanising and evil vision. Leaders operate in a moral universe. To be a good leader they need to embody goodness. But even a vision and ethics are insufficient: the excellent leader needs to find a vision which is appropriate for the organisation at the moment at which they take command. Coming up with an inappropriate vision explains why one leader could be a great success in one organisation but be utterly baleful in another. The true leader will find a vision which is organic to the organisation they have taken over and true to its traditions, rather than implanting an off-the-shelf generic plan dreamed up by a management consultant. This book takes you through how to create a collective vision that everyone can engage with and feel part of.

When I was headmaster of Brighton College (and, later, Wellington College), I became increasingly excited by the prospect of teaching students and staff about leadership. At the latter institution, I was fortunate to have on my staff Katy Granville-Chapman and Emmie Bidston, the authors of this book. Both of them embodied in their lives at the school, and in their interactions with students and staff, an authenticity and a singularity of vision for leadership that prioritises the flourishing of others.

In schools, it is very clear to students, if not always to the teachers concerned, who has sincerity. Students can see through teachers far more quickly than many realise. Katy and Emmie have that gift of effortless authenticity in abundance, and it informs every page of this book.

I believe that every school student and employee should be taught about leadership – good as well as bad, and the leadership traits which pertain to various situations and those which are task specific. The captain of a nuclear submarine requires many attributes in common with the captain of Aston Villa Football Club, but there will be some skills which are particular to each role. In the right hands, few things are more fascinating to learn about than leadership and the qualities we all need to develop as future leaders.

People who might never be turned on by academic work can become highly motivated and fired up when considering leadership and when they are given leadership tasks. They quickly learn that a good leader does not need to shout, coerce or use fear; it is much more effective to lead with clarity, calm, compassion and character.

The challenges we will face in the future include coping with pandemics, tackling global warming and the climate emergency, and helping to rebuild communities torn apart by globalisation and artificial intelligence. The skills required are far more than intellectual. Very few of the greatest political leaders in Britain have been leading intellectuals. Prime ministers customarily come into Downing Street with aides who have very high IQs and brains the size of planets, but who leave after a few months with their missions incomplete.

The leaders of the future need to be rounded figures. They need to be in touch with themselves, with their feelings, with their bodies and, most importantly, with other people. They need to be principled and have a clear vision about how to build a better world.

This wonderful book discusses these and many other topics, and I cannot recommend it too highly.

Sir Anthony Seldon
Vice-Chancellor of the University of Buckingham

Preface

It could have happened to anyone. It was just unlucky that he was the boss on shift that day. Fifty-four years old and many miles from home. Drawn by the promise of good wages in exchange for the risks that inevitably came with the job. It was meant to be a seven-day tour. It turned into a sixty-nine-day ordeal of darkness and despair.

On 5 August 2010, Luis Urzua found himself trapped thousands of feet below ground with thirty-three other men. The San José gold and copper mine in Chile had collapsed, leaving them imprisoned under tonnes of rock. They were fearful of being crushed to death by further rock falls and had no way to communicate with the outside world. No way to know how long they would need to wait or how long they would need to make the two days' worth of supplies last.[1]

The leadership challenge was enormous. Hungry, scared men started forcing open the food cupboard in their fear and grabbing the little that was there. But their shift manager, Urzua, had a reputation for being protective and loving his team. When he intervened in the situation, they trusted him enough to step back and agree to ration the supplies, living off one teaspoon of tuna and a half-glass of milk every few days. Urzua kept reminding the miners that they were all in this together. They were a team. They ate their meagre rations together in the same spot, at the same time, building a sense of belonging. Every man had a role, everyone had a responsibility. They were all involved and utterly focused on achieving their one goal – survival.[2]

Their first contact with the outside world came after seventeen days, which had left them close to starvation. It was another fifty-two days before they were rescued and finally hoisted, one by one, to the surface. No miner wanted to be transported to the hospital before the last man had been brought out.[3]

... what counts in life is not the mere fact that we have lived. It is what difference we have made to the lives of others that will determine the significance of the life we lead.

Nelson Mandela[4]

Urzua never spoke about his own leadership role during the crisis, although many others praised him. He talked instead about his men, their talents and their welfare. He thanked the rescuers and the health officials. He did everything he could to look after his people. He was the last man to be lifted out of the shaft, merely commenting: 'It's been a bit of a long shift.'[5]

Similar to many other individuals who have faced extreme circumstances and adversity, Urzua exemplifies the fact that some people can step up and become effective leaders in the face of impossible circumstances. Yet many others who encounter challenges struggle to bring out the best in their teams, pulling people apart rather than together and creating a culture of fear and blame.

What exactly is it that good leaders do to enable their teams to succeed? How do they think? How much of their success can be predicted by IQ, talent or temperament? What do the recent advancements in neuroscience and research teach us about effective leadership?

This book reflects our efforts to explore these questions. In the following chapters, we will take you on a journey to meet leaders from multiple different spheres. We will show you how effective leaders enable their people to flourish. These individuals will, at times, appear to go against mainstream views of strong leadership. However, the performance they have enabled has been extraordinary.

Great leaders have become great because they have mastered three key lessons:

> **Lesson I: Know your people.** Great leaders know their team's values and strengths through great listening, powerful questioning and empathy.

> **Lesson II: Love your people.** Great leaders love their team through compassion, service and creating psychological safety.

> **Lesson III: Inspire your people.** Great leaders inspire their team through a clear sense of purpose, optimism and gratitude.

Our journey to understand leadership began before we met. Katy Granville-Chapman served in the British Army, deploying to Iraq, and Emmie Bidston in the Civil Service after graduating from Cambridge with a degree in economics. We saw outstanding examples, in both government and the military, of leaders enthusing and engaging people through compassionate and positive leadership. We also saw examples where poor leadership resulted in the loss of morale and motivation, and had a negative impact on performance and mission outcomes. These experiences sparked in us an insatiable curiosity about what makes a great leader and how to grow leaders who bring out the best in people.

In later years we entered teaching, which is where we met, and our leadership adventure began. This led to us helping to advise and train numerous organisations, including England Rugby and the Civil Service, and eventually to advise the Prime Minister's Office. Katy co-founded Global Social Leaders with Jon Harper, a positive leadership and entrepreneurship programme, which now has participants in 102 countries. Emmie co-founded the Young African Leadership Program, a charity that supports innovative African schools as they seek to support, teach and inspire the next generation of African leaders.

We have worked on leadership within elite sport, with government ministers, army officers, head teachers, Oxford University, charities and countless incredible young people from across the globe. Many of these leaders were already serving their people and helping them to flourish – with outstanding results. However, others were harder to convince. They were suspicious of servant leadership (the idea that the main role of the leader is to serve) and perceived compassion as weak and ineffective. This book is our answer to them, because it's not enough for leaders to lead through their own ego. It's not enough to shout orders based on leaders' own values and ideas. Only by watching, listening and working with others can we get the most out of teams and communities.

This book is also our celebration of all the inspiring young people we have worked with, who have set up social action projects around the world and are already having an enormous impact.

By the time you finish reading this book, we hope you will be reconsidering some fundamental assumptions about leadership and what kinds of leaders create high-performing teams. We have set you challenges to complete individually and also with your teams (so please have a notebook handy while you read). Building on the latest evidence, stories and our own experience, we will help you to become the best leader you can be: a leader who knows, loves and inspires their people.

Acknowledgements

We couldn't be more grateful to our wonderful families, who have made such sacrifices to give us the time to write, and to our friends who have been so inspiring. We are particularly grateful to Martha Owen and Emma Tuck for their awesome editing and Crown House Publishing for giving us this opportunity.

Contents

Lesson I
Know Your People

Introduction to Lesson I

Code name: Project Aristotle. What images spring into your mind? An undercover MI6 mission team creeping stealthily into an insurgent's hide-out? An Enigma-style Second World War crack team working on Nazi codes? Or perhaps a ferociously academic team of classicists sifting through dusty manuscripts?

Project Aristotle was actually the brainchild of Google.[6] Google has always been known for its culture of innovation and its relentless drive to improve performance and productivity. Having spent much of the previous decade considering how to bring out the best in the individuals who worked for the company, in 2012 it turned its attention to creating the perfect team – finding out why some teams stumble and others soar.[7]

The fact that Google is a data-driven organisation means it had both the researchers and the algorithms to analyse gigantic quantities of information, so it threw lots of resources at the question. It employed a team of researchers, psychologists and statisticians who started with a literature review, covering academic journals and books from the last fifty years. They then interviewed and observed hundreds of staff and teams at Google.[8]

They were hunting for patterns, for a formula that would help them to decode the data, for clues as to how the best teams work. Do they communicate in the same way? Use the same strategies? Is it about the intellectual ability or emotional intelligence of the individual members? They kept searching and hypothesising, but even a year into the project they were drawing a blank as to the elusive characteristics of high-performing teams. The data just seemed to be pointing in different, contradictory directions. It remained an enigma.

What they did realise, early on, was that there was very little correlation between the abilities, backgrounds or successes of the individual members of a team and the overall success of the team. They continued to interview more teams and trawl more data for clues.

What gradually emerged was the fact that the most significant predictor of team performance was how the members related to one another – for example, how well they took into account each other's opinions and emotions. Team culture was far more significant than the abilities of the individuals in the team.

This linked back to some work done by psychologists at the Massachusetts Institute of Technology a decade ago, who recruited nearly 700 people, divided them into teams and gave them various tasks to accomplish.[9] They used a well-respected classification of group tasks to help them choose the team activities, which involved solving visual puzzles, brainstorming the uses of a brick, making collective moral judgements and negotiating over limited resources.

They found evidence that teams can have a 'collective intelligence' independent of the average (or best) individual team members' intelligence (IQ). This team IQ is largely dependent on the average social sensitivity of the team and how well they communicate – how well they try to know and understand each other and find positive ways to relate to one another.

As leaders, this research reminds us that our teams are more than the sum of the individuals and that their performance and collective IQ will depend critically on how well we can nourish a culture of authentic interactions and real conversations. Leadership is about helping our team members to be the best versions of themselves and work together in ways that allow creativity, risk-taking and vulnerability. The foundation for this kind of high-performance culture is knowing the people on our teams: what really matters to them, their values and their strengths. We will be looking at how to build these foundations in the next two chapters.

Chapter 1

Speaking Serbian

Case Study: The San Antonio Spurs

The San Antonio Spurs are one of the most successful basketball teams of all time, having won five championship titles (1999, 2003, 2005, 2007 and 2014). The Spurs have been an incredible example of a team with the right culture, organisation and winning strategy. An opponent once said that watching them play was like 'listening to Mozart'.[10] What is the secret of their winning culture? Their leader: Gregg Popovich. Popovich has been the Spurs' coach since 1996 and has been on Fortune's list of the 50 World's Greatest Leaders.[11] Yet on first impressions he doesn't seem like the ideal leader, with his volcanic temper and old-school discipline.

He grew up in East Chicago, Indiana, and started playing basketball at a young age. He enrolled at the United States Air Force Academy and was on the academy's basketball team for the next four years. He graduated with a degree in Soviet studies and served the required five years of active duty in the Air Force, competing in the US Armed Forces' basketball team and touring Eastern Europe and Soviet Russia. He first joined the Spurs in 1988 and became the head coach of the team in 1996.[12]

Popovich's success as the Spurs coach has been a result of the way he has cared about his players. Popovich understands that it is his responsibility to connect with his players, to bring them into the Spurs culture, and to make sure they have a strong relationship with him and the other players. Popovich wants his players to be fully human and he's genuinely curious about them. Will Purdue explains that Pop went much further than other coaches were willing to go: 'They cared about you, but they didn't really want to overextend themselves in case you got cut or got traded … I don't think Pop ever even considered that. He saw you as a human being first and a basketball player second.'[13]

By talking to them about their interests and their life outside the court, he shows the players that he truly does care about them. This interest in their lives creates the foundation for their solid relationship.

Popovich is always trying to connect to his team in different ways: he discussed Argentinian politics and conspiracy theories with Manu Ginobili. He flew to the island of St Croix to get to know Tim Duncan before he started. He talked in Serbian to two of his players to build better relationships.[14]

This is a great example of our first lesson in leadership. If you want to be a leader you must really know your people. Not just know their names, but *really* know them – what makes them happy, what makes them mad, what are their dreams, hopes and aspirations. Consider how amazed Perdue was by how much Popovich wanted to know about the team and the effort he went to in order to connect with and know his players.

One reason that knowing your people matters so much is that, 'When thinking back over their lives and selecting their most important leadership role models, people are more likely to choose a family member than anyone else.'[15] Isn't that incredible? When people were asked to choose their most important leadership models, they didn't pick Nelson Mandela, Mother Teresa or Barack Obama, they picked family members. Because they are the people who know you best and you know too. It is all about positive relationships.

There are a multitude of books on leadership and literally hundreds of thousands of research papers on this subject. If you Google the word 'leadership' you will get about 6 billion results. This suggests that there is a lot of interest in the topic, but also that there is still some uncertainty over both what precisely leadership is and how to develop effective leaders.

However, there is also plenty of agreement in the research. Although we can't claim to have read every research paper and book on leadership, we have given it our best shot and we will introduce you to some of the most robust research as we go along.

Relationships with people are what it's all about. You have to make players realize you care about them. And they have to care about each other and be interested in each other.

Gregg Popovich[16]

The evidence suggests that there are two main areas you need to focus on in terms of knowing your people: knowing their values and knowing their strengths.

What Are Values?

We have asked hundreds of people what they think values are. Here is a selection of some of the answers we have received:

- What matters most to me.

- The things that make me tick.

- Who I am when no one is watching.

- A compass for my life.

- The deepest part of me.

We like to use the metaphor of a stick of rock – if we cut you open, what would be written all the way through you? Professor Noel Tichy of the University of Michigan tells us that your personal values speak to the question, 'Who am I?'[17]

Knowing Your Own Values

There is significant interest from leadership scholars in the value of values for leadership. Understanding what you *really* care about will give you courage in difficult situations and help you to make decisions that are congruent with the kind of person you want to be.

You also need to know your values to be an authentic leader – credibility is considered by many to be the foundation of leadership. Leadership is fundamentally a relationship, so if people are going to follow you, they need to believe in you and trust you: 'If you don't believe in the messenger you won't believe in the message.'[18] People need moral authority in order to lead well, and to do this it is critical that they know their own values so they can align their behaviour consistently with them.

It's not just knowing your values that matters, it is also living them out. Your values provide your compass – they show you where you should be going – but you still need to follow them. That is what is meant by being authentic.

In a well-reviewed leadership book, *True North*, Harvard Business School professor Bill George and Peter Sims argue that the essence of good leadership is being true to who you really are.[19] It begins and ends with authenticity. This means that you must be yourself: if creativity really matters to you, then you need to be creative; if friendship really matters to you, then you need to make sure you have time with your friends; if honesty really matters to you, then tell the truth. Authenticity builds trust. People love leaders they can trust – leaders who are being their real selves.

We often discover our own values during the hard times in life, when a situation makes us angry and we realise that something important to us, some critical need or value, isn't being met.

Case Study: Melinda Gates

Melinda Gates provides a good example of this in her book *The Moment of Lift*.[20] Melinda started working at Microsoft straight after university and she loved the energy, pace and challenge of the company. She was passionate about their dream of democratising computing in a way that would change the world and she adored computer coding. However, there were also aspects of the culture that she found difficult and, after a year and a half, she had reached the point where she was ready to quit. It was just too aggressive, argumentative and competitive for her to thrive. It was all about strength, and you proved your strength by winning arguments and taking no notice of anyone else. No one said well done, thanked each other or celebrated one another's successes.

Melinda knew she was capable of performing and leading in that way if she absolutely needed to, but it wasn't authentic to who she was. The effort of trying to be someone she wasn't was dragging her down and taking the joy out of her work. Yet every time she thought about leaving she was torn by the fact that she loved the company's vision. It was an incredible organisation to be part of and the buzz of ideas was electric.

She decided to see if she could either change the culture or at least be a more authentic version of herself within Microsoft. She needed to start being who she actually was: tough and strong, but also vulnerable, honest and collaborative rather than competitive. She searched for people who were also struggling with the culture and built a team of peers, mentors and role models who would help her to find her voice and her own style of leadership.

As she built an honest, collaborative culture she began attracting the brightest stars in Microsoft to work for her — talented individuals who wanted to work in that environment. She ended up leading 1,700 people within the organisation. She created an atmosphere where everyone could be honest about their strengths as well as their weaknesses, where people worked together towards a bigger goal and weren't trying to prove themselves, where failure wasn't hidden but learned from, and where nobody was pretending.

Learning to lead authentically and be true to her values in such an aggressive culture also gave Melinda the confidence to go on and lead in the non-profit sector. The Bill & Melinda Gates Foundation searches for problems that haven't been solved by either governments or markets; these solutions could be the catalysts for rapid and long-lasting development. Having learned to be vulnerable and honest as a leader in Microsoft, she now deliberately takes risks and doesn't play it safe in philanthropy. She knows that some projects will fail but is prepared to make bets on promising solutions, see which ones pay off and share the results so everyone can benefit.

She says: 'Being yourself sounds like a saccharine prescription for how to make it in an aggressive culture. But it's not as sweet as it sounds. It means not acting in a way that's false just to fit in. It's expressing your talents, values and opinions in your style, defending your rights, and never sacrificing your self-respect. That is power.'[21]

Case Study: Vince Lombardi

Vince Lombardi, legendary coach of the Green Bay Packers American football team, inherited a team that had been at the bottom of the National Football League (NFL) for years. No one saw any way back. Lombardi took over the team in 1959. Two years later they won the NFL, and again in 1962 and 1965, followed by the Super Bowl in 1966 and 1967.

Several biographies have been written about his leadership and there has even been a Broadway show about his life, such is the legend that surrounds him.[22] These reviews of his life all circle back to the same foundation of his leadership – that his success was based on the idea that 'Only by knowing yourself can you become an effective leader.'[23] He understood that you have to know what matters to you before you can lead anyone else. Self-knowledge is critical because we bring who we are as a leader to every interaction – our views, strengths, weaknesses, prejudices, assumptions and values. They affect how we interpret the world and our interactions.

You need to know your own values. From this you develop character and integrity and from these you earn the right to leadership. Lombardi put the value of humility at the core of his teaching – players were taught they were never to get too big to do the small things.

Character rises out of our values, our purpose, the standards we set ourselves, our sacrifice and our commitment and the decision we make under pressure, but it is primarily defined by the contribution we make, the responsibility we take, the leadership we show.

James Kerr[24]

Lombardi's view of leadership was all about becoming a leader from the inside out. As leaders, we are measured on external results and yet these results are often achieved (or not) because of who we are as leaders.

Leaders are made,
they are not born.
They are made by hard
effort, which is the
price which all of us
must pay to achieve any
goal that is worthwhile.

Vince Lombardi[25]

We inevitably lead out of who we are as people, and you can't separate the leader from the person. We therefore need to know ourselves and take responsibility for our own character.

Lombardi was loyal and demanding, expecting his team to have a commitment to hard work, to one another, to sacrifice and to give their best at all times. He held himself to the same standards as a leader. His advice was that great leaders need to be self-aware and know who they are – their values, strengths and weaknesses.

Challenge 1: Hunting for Your Own Values

1   The simplest way to find your own values is to choose your top values from a list like the one on page 14. We would recommend sorting them into four groups by putting either 1, 2, 3 or 4 next to each one using the code:

1 = Not important to me

2 = Important to me

3 = Couldn't live without

4 = Absolutely couldn't live without

Warning: this can be really challenging, so don't think about it for too long!

2   Now take all the values with a number 4 next to them and try to choose just your top two or three from the list.

3   Note them down (with your own definition of the values) and try to find someone with whom you can discuss your values and tell them what is important to you about them.

4   Think of two occasions when you were at your very best. What do they have in common? What were you doing and what were you like?

5   What does your answer to question 4 tell you about your values?

Achievement/success	Independence	
Altruism	Integrity	
Autonomy	Intelligence	
Beauty	Kindness	
Calm	Learning	
Challenge	Love	
Communication	Loyalty	
Competence	Making a difference	
Competition	Open-mindedness	
Creativity	Patience	
Dependability	Peace	
Discipline	Power	
Diversity	Productivity	
Effectiveness	Recognition	
Empathy	Respect	
Equality	Responsibility	
Family	Security	
Freedom	Selflessness	
Friendship	Service	
Growth	Simplicity	
Happiness	Spirituality/faith	
Harmony	Strength	
Health	Trust	
Honesty	Truth	
Hope	Variety	
Humour	Wisdom	

Living Out Your Values: Michelle Obama

Of course, it's not just knowing your values that matters. You also need to live them out. Let's get some advice from someone who has had to live out her values in one of the most public jobs in the world, where every move is scrutinised, former First Lady Michelle Obama. In 2017, she attended the Apple Worldwide Developer Conference (WWDC) for a 'fireside chat' in which she discussed what makes a great leader. She observed, 'You have to know what [your] values are and be honest with yourself about whether you're living those values.'[26]

We all get this wrong sometimes. We can say the right thing and perform well in front of others, but then not live out our values behind closed doors. Sometimes we talk a good game, but what we show to the world is something different from who we really are. This integrity is something that Michelle talks to her children about regularly. She says that values have to be lived out in the spotlight *and* behind the scenes. We need to keep asking ourselves the question, who am I when no one is looking?

Just as our values need to be lived out consistently in front of people as well as on our own, they also need to be lived out consistently with different people, no matter who they are. Michelle argues that a crucial aspect of leadership is living out your values with everyone equally. We need to make sure that we treat people with equal dignity and don't just spend all our energy trying to look good in front of the important people in our lives: 'It's the little things,' she said. 'If somebody is sweeping your office, how you treat them, how kind you are, how much attention you give.'

One of the benefits of being true to your values is that it can really help you to overcome fear. If you know who you are and what really matters to you – what your higher purpose is – then you will be stronger when facing the challenges that life will throw at you as a leader. Michelle faced many challenges and argues that knowing your values provides a foundation to return to when you are faced with fear, shame and challenge, because, she argues, they are 'coming for us all'. Michelle is also really determined to know the people she works with and describes how she likes to start every meeting finding out how everyone is doing – how are their families, their health, their sleep. This level of communication is essential for individuals to feel valued and to know you have their back.

What are Michelle Obama's values? She gave us some clues in her first Democratic National Convention speech back in 2008 when she talked about the way that she and Barack were raised to embrace hard work, to be true to their word and to treat people with dignity and respect regardless of whether they agreed with them.[27]

Michelle believes that leadership is about being compassionate to people from all walks of life and using your leadership to serve others. Before she was first lady she fought injustice as a lawyer, and once she became first lady she fought to help improve the lives of people from all parts of society. An example was launching the Let Girls Learn initiative (to fund girls' education projects tackling everything from leadership to poverty) and the school lunch programme (to provide free and reduced meals for low-income children). Michelle's life story is an example of how staying true to your values can change the world for the better.

> *All of us driven by a simple belief that the world as it is just won't do – that we have an obligation to fight for the world as it should be.*
> **Michelle Obama**[28]

Challenge 2: Living Your Values

1   Look back to your values from challenge 1. At the end of each day this week, ask yourself: what have I done that was in line with my values? What did I do that undermined my values? What was the impact on myself? Others?

2   If someone you admire asked the lowest status people in your work/ team how well you treat them, what do you think they would say? What do you learn about yourself and your values from this?

3   How are your team doing at the moment? (Rate yourself on a scale of 1 to 10 for each member of your team in terms of how well you know what is going on in their lives at the moment (1 being 'not well at all',

and 10 being 'extremely well').) Pick one action to take in the light of this to get to know someone on your team better.

Knowing Your People's Values

The most important job of a leader is to look after and serve their people. It is much easier to do this well if you know what really matters to them. Sometimes you can just ask them to describe themselves – for example, the England football team captain Harry Kane was asked in an interview for the *Times* magazine for three words that sum him up and he replied: 'determined, passionate and caring'.[29]

These are all values, and observing Kane's behaviour would show us that he lives out these values. If we wanted to get to know Kane better, and therefore be able to lead him better, we would also want to ask him what each of those words means to him and for him. Even better, we could ask him how we could support him to live out those values while he was at work and make deliberate efforts to think about how we are behaving with Kane and the decisions we are taking that affect him.

Pep Guardiola (who led Manchester City football club to win the Premier League in 2018 and 2019) is known for understanding the ambitions, values and personality of each of his players. While managing FC Barcelona, Lionel Messi was called up by Argentina to play at the 2008 Olympics, much to the disappointment of his club, which didn't want to risk one of their best players getting injured. Guardiola, however, went against the wishes of the club and supported Messi's value of loyalty, in this case to his home nation Argentina, by allowing him to play at the Olympics because he knew how important this was to Messi.[30] In return, he received incredible loyalty to Barcelona from Messi, now widely considered the best player in the world and who helped the club to win numerous titles in the following seasons.

Another example of honouring your people's values was a leader for whom we both used to work. He would say, 'Never say no to a school nativity play', as a way to remind himself and his leadership team about how critical it is to consider what is important to people when making decisions. If someone asked to miss work for their child's nativity play, he would need a very strong reason to say no because family is clearly one of their values. If you cross that value, you undermine someone's loyalty and create resentment. If you say yes to their request, then the benefits of commitment and strengthened relationships will far outweigh any cost.

Challenge 3: Honouring Others' Values

1   What have you done to help someone on your team to stay true to their values this month?

2   What more could you do? (Try to think of one specific action to take this month.)

3   Reflect on the impact of this on you and the person whose values you took action to support.

The Research on Values

There has been extensive research on the importance of values in leadership. In summary, the evidence is that knowing your people's values is critical because it allows you to:

- Understand others' choices and behaviour.[31]

- Know how to motivate people.[32]

- Avoid making others angry (by accidently trampling on what is really important to them).[33]

- Deal with conflict more effectively – bringing it back to values and how you can all honour and support each other's values while finding a strategy that can help you to move forwards.[34]

- Win loyalty by honouring others' values.[35]

▨   Create trust by living authentically and being true to your own values –
    building credibility as a leader.[36]

Hunting for Values

You can't always just ask people upfront what their values are; sometimes you must do a bit more digging to find out. You have to channel your inner Sherlock Holmes and employ your best questioning and observation skills. A leader we really admire is Andrew Strauss, former England cricket captain from 2008 to 2012 and director of cricket from 2015 to 2018.

The whole country was blown away by England's incredible, nail-biting victory against New Zealand to win the World Cup in 2019, and Strauss' leadership had been critical in laying the foundations for the victory and helping England to become the top one-day test team. We were therefore keen to investigate his values and find out what mattered to him, so we asked him to imagine that he was at a party for his 100th birthday and all his friends and family are there. What would he want people to say about him?

Apart from saying that they are 'very surprised that I have made it through to this ripe old age,' Andrew told us he hoped they would say the following:

Andrew has never been interested in what is flashy or looks good (hence his dress sense!). He is far more interested in substance. He values loyalty and decency above all other attributes, and has surrounded himself throughout his life with people he knows will be there for him when the chips are down. He, in turn, would like to think that he has been there similarly for his friends and colleagues when they needed him.

Andrew has always been very competitive – anyone who has seen him on the golf course, the tennis court or the cricket field will know that. He has never been interested in winning at all costs though. He has gained a lot of satisfaction from winning but has got almost as much satisfaction from recognising the challenge, making a plan to overcome something and then seeing it through. Sometimes you can do everything right but the result doesn't go your way. That is OK.

Andrew can't abide those who are dishonest or two-faced. He will forgive many sins but he hates being taken advantage of or used for other people's ends.

Andrew has always been keen on creating a harmonious environment. People are important to him, and he believes very strongly that you get the best out of people by caring for them. He has always said, 'It isn't your decision to lead anyone; it is their decision to be led by you.' If you show you care about people, they are more likely to trust you to lead them.[37]

Now read what Andrew Strauss said again and imagine that you are leading him or working in a team with him. Try to answer the following questions:

- What is extremely important to him?

- What makes him angry?

- What does he think makes a good leader?

- Pick three words that you think summarise his values.

Having practised finding Strauss' values, your next challenge is to find your own team's values.

Challenge 4: Finding Others' Values

Exercise 1: Values Cards

1   The method we like the most is to lay out cards around a room with different values on and ask your team members to choose their top two or three. To do this you will need to write down the values from the list in challenge 1 onto cards, or photocopy the list and ask your team to sort them into four groups, putting either 1, 2, 3 or 4 next to each one, using the code:

   1 = Not important to me

   2 = Important to me

3 = Couldn't live without

4 = Absolutely couldn't live without

2   Now ask them to take all the values with a number 4 next to them and try to choose just their top two or three.

3   Depending on your team dynamics, you can either ask each person to share their values and tell you all both what is important to them about those values and what they mean to them (we find that values words can mean very different things to different people) or, if the team dynamic is not yet at a point where people would feel safe enough to share their values (which is something to work on in itself), then you can just chat to people individually about their values.

Exercise 2: Visualisations

Here is another exercise to try as well as, or instead of, the previous one. Pick two or three of the following questions and ask your team to write down their answers.

1   You have been given advertising space the size of a double-decker bus at Piccadilly Circus which will be lit up brightly every evening. What message would you write to the world on your billboard?

2   What drives you crazy? What makes you feel incredibly cross? What is it about the situation that is making you mad? What values have been crossed?

3   You are at a party for your 100th birthday and all your friends and family are there. When your favourite person gives a speech about you, what do they say?

4   You have unlimited funds and a year off. What would you choose to spend it doing?

Once they have written down their answers, you can ask people to share their thoughts and try to spot what is important to them. What does this suggest about their values?

Exercise 3: Spaghetti Test

If you think you've worked out someone's value, you can always check it with them: 'It sounds like [fairness] is really important to you.'

The best coach we know, Iain Henderson, a deputy head at Wellington College, calls this checking process the 'spaghetti test' – you need to see if it sticks. In the cookbook Emmie was given by her parents when she left for university, it explained that the way to see whether spaghetti is cooked is to throw it against the ceiling. If it sticks then the pasta is cooked, if it falls off then you need to keep cooking it!

It's the same with values – just try it out. Say, 'It sounds like [fairness] is important to you,' and if the person smiles, nods and says, 'Yes, absolutely,' you'll know you're right, but if they say, 'Ooh, ahh, mmmm, kind of,' then you need to try again. Either way, you get to know the person better, and that is what great leadership is all about.

Make the Time

Getting to know your people will require a commitment of time, so in that sense there is a cost to putting relationships first. There are other things that you won't be able to get done because you are investing in people instead.

How you make that time for people will differ depending on your setting and who you are as a person – remember, you have to be authentic.

One example of this is the current head teacher of our school, James Dahl, who has made it a priority to have a meal with every teacher and student in the (1,000+ student) school. He has also worked hard to know every student's name and sends a handwritten birthday card to every student and teacher.

Strengths – Why Fish Shouldn't Climb Trees[38]

Once upon a time the animals decided they must do something heroic to meet the problems of a 'new world', so they organized a school. They adopted an activity curriculum consisting of running, climbing, swimming, and flying. To make it easier to administer the curriculum, all the animals took all the subjects.

The duck was excellent in swimming – in fact, better than his instructor. But he made only passing grades in flying and was very poor in running. Since he was slow in running, he had to stay after school and also drop swimming in order to practise running. This was kept up until his webbed feet were badly worn and he was only average in swimming. But average was acceptable in school, so nobody worried about that except the duck.

The rabbit started at the top of the class in running but had a nervous breakdown because of so much make-up work in swimming.

The squirrel was excellent in climbing until he developed frustration in the flying class, where his teacher made him start from the ground up instead of the treetop down. He also developed cramps in his legs from overexertion and then got a C in climbing and a D in running.

The eagle was a problem child and was disciplined severely. In the climbing class he beat all the others to the top of the tree but insisted on using his own way to get there.

At the end of the year, an abnormal frog that could swim exceedingly well, and also run, climb, and jump quite far had the highest average scores and won the school prize.

The moral of this story by George Reavis may seem obvious: let the ducks swim, the rabbits run and the eagles fly. We don't want a school of average ducks. And yet how many of us live our lives focusing on what we can't do, trying to fix our weaknesses and worrying about what we are bad at rather than playing to our strengths?

Everybody is a genius, but if you judge a fish by its ability to climb a tree it will live its whole life believing that it is stupid.

Anon.

There is a great temptation to fix ourselves (and others) by investing time in improving our weaknesses, and yet the research suggests that you will achieve a better performance if you play to your own and your team's strengths.

The Benefits of Focusing on Strengths

Gallup is a large American company which conducts research, collects data and runs opinion polls around the world. It has, arguably, conducted the most extensive research into this area since it began looking at strengths-based development in 2009. Since then it has studied strengths-based practices for 1.2 million employees globally.[39]

Before 2009, most leaders thought that the best results would come from helping people to improve at what they were bad at. Consequently, most managers would spend the majority of their time with their underperforming staff and most feedback was focused on problems and underperformance.

However, having looked at all the evidence available, Gallup concluded that companies which focused more on using their employees' strengths saw better sales, profit and customer engagement. It also compared companies which focused on people's weaknesses and concluded that identifying individual's strengths (and what they do right) and building on them creates more benefit than identifying weaknesses (or what they do wrong) and trying to correct them.

The results were quite surprising and dramatic. In organisations where workers have a chance to 'do what they do best every day', productivity is one-and-a-half times greater than in average organisations. Furthermore, Gallup argue that people who use their strengths every day are six times more likely to be engaged on the job. Yes – you read that right – six times![40]

To check this wasn't an anomaly, and to see if it worked in other sectors, two researchers, Timothy Hodges and Donald Clifton, decided to look at the impact of providing feedback to high-school students on their strengths.[41] One group of students were given feedback on their strengths as well as advice on how to build on and develop those strengths. Compared to the control group of students who had none of these interventions, they had fewer days absent from school, less lateness and higher scores.

Gallup research also shows that the worst thing you can do is ignore your people.[42] The best engagement was from those who felt that their leader focused on their strengths (only 1% were disengaged from their work), the next best was from those whose leaders focused on their weaknesses (22% disengaged), and the worst from those who felt ignored and unknown by their leaders (40% disengaged from their jobs).

This research clearly shows that if you want your team to be engaged, you need to know them and show that you know them! You will get the best results by knowing their strengths and focusing on these, but even if you focused on their weaknesses at least they would feel you know them and care about them – what you don't want is for them to feel ignored.

If you are looking for a team who are engaged and maximising their performance, then you as their leader need to know their strengths and help them use their strengths. CAPP, a strengths assessment organisation, reviewed the literature and came up with ten great reasons to allow people to focus on their strengths.[43] People who use their strengths more:

1   *Are happier.*[44]

2   *Are more confident.*[45]

3   *Have higher levels of self-esteem.*[46]

4   *Have higher levels of energy and vitality.*[47]

5   *Experience less stress.*[48]

6   *Are more resilient.*[49]

7   *Are more likely to achieve their goals.*[50]

8   *Perform better at work.*[51]

9 *Are more engaged at work.*[52]

10 *Are more effective at developing themselves and growing as individuals.*[53]

As well as specific research into strengths, there is also a broader evidence base which comes from the outstanding work by Martin Seligman, former president of the American Psychological Association (APA). Based on decades of work, he has proposed that rather than focusing purely on what is wrong with individuals, we should emphasise what is right. Instead of merely diagnosing pathologies and problems, we should identify strengths and build on them.

During his time as president of the APA, he altered the whole direction of psychology, shifting it to focus on what is life-giving. This movement has become known as positive psychology,[54] and thousands of researchers have now undertaken studies for the application of positive psychology in schools, coaching, the military, businesses and pretty much every area of life. For example, one study showed that parenting teenagers in a way which focuses on their strengths has a significant positive effect on academic achievement, engagement and perseverance.[55]

When you combine all the different benefits listed above, it is clear that there is a significant correlation between people using their strengths, feeling happy and performing well. One study tried to quantify this and concluded that individuals who use their character strengths frequently are eighteen times more likely to be flourishing than those who do not.[56] The more we can do, both to improve how much we are deploying our own strengths and how much those we lead can use their strengths at work, the more joy we should trigger for everyone.

All employees have strengths – the unique combinations of talents, knowledge, skills, and practice that help them do what they do best every day. These strengths provide employees and employers with their greatest opportunities for success.

Susan Sorenson[57]

Many people don't know what their strengths actually are. We tend to see our own weaknesses more clearly than our strengths. It is our mistakes that are emblazoned in our memory from the times we looked stupid, let others down or underperformed, and they tend to be more powerful memories than when we did well. As a leader, you therefore need to help your people to know their own strengths. In the next challenge, there are three different exercises you could try, each of which can be used to discover your own and your team's strengths.

Challenge 5: Finding Strengths

Exercise 1: The Strengths Survey

The Values in Action Inventory of Strengths (VIA-IS) is a tool which was developed by two brilliant psychologists, Martin Seligman and Chris Peterson. Of course, no survey is perfect, but this one is seriously rigorous in its design and took fifty-five scientists three years to develop. What should emerge at the end are your character strengths – the qualities that come most naturally to you. There are twenty-four strengths in the list: creativity, curiosity, judgement, love of learning, perspective, bravery, perseverance, honesty, zest, love, kindness, social intelligence, teamwork, fairness, leadership, forgiveness, humility, prudence, self-regulation, appreciation of beauty and excellence, gratitude, hope, humour and spirituality.[58]

Bear in mind that everyone has all twenty-four strengths to some degree, but the amount differs between individuals, giving everyone a unique character profile. Head to Seligman and Peterson's website (https://www.viacharacter.org) and complete the survey free of charge. Note down your top five strengths.

Exercise 2: Reflective Questions

Another way to find your strengths is to pay attention to how you feel and perform in different situations. Marcus Buckingham, in his book *Go Put Your Strengths to Work*, says we often identify our strengths and weaknesses in the wrong way because we think of strengths as things we are good at and weaknesses as things we are bad at.[59] He argues that we need to reframe this by considering how activities make us feel – strong or weak, energised or drained. In the light of his advice, try answering the following questions yourself and then look for themes in your answers.

- Think of times when you have felt successful. What were you doing and how were you doing it?

- Make a list of things you are drawn to, even if you don't know why.

- Think of a time when you were fully engaged and in a state of flow.[60] What were you doing and how were you doing it?

- When do you feel most energised and fulfilled?

- What did you enjoy doing as a child that you still love now?

- When do you feel most like the best version of yourself?

- Which activities come easily to you, either without trying or because you have picked them up very easily?

In light of your answers, write down what you think your strengths are.

Exercise 3: Asking Others

We can all find it hard to see ourselves clearly – sometimes what we see as our weaknesses others might see as strengths. It is always a good idea to ask your friends, family, co-workers or a mentor to tell you what they think your strengths are. You are looking for patterns or things that you wouldn't have thought of on your own.

Ask other people to give you examples of when you were at your best. Pick individuals from different parts of your life and ask them to describe what you are like when you are thriving. See if there are any patterns between the stories and examples they give you and use these to create a profile of who you are when you are at your best.

Exercise 4: Find Your Team's Strengths

Now repeat at least one of the exercises on pages 28–29 with your team and write down what each of their strengths are.

Case Study: England Cricket Team

'Incredible ... Indescribable ... You couldn't make it up.'[61]

In July 2019, England won the Cricket World Cup Final against New Zealand in the most amazing of circumstances. The victory came after the two teams were tied at the end of their 50-over innings and a penalty shootout-style 'super over' had failed to separate them, meaning they had to be separated on the number of boundaries hit, which turned out to be England. It is only the third such victory for England's sportsmen in any major global sport in almost ninety years of trying. The men now join the women as world champions in this format.

Andrew Strauss is credited with helping to turn around England's fortunes. He inherited a team that had been divided by fiasco and poor captaincy. They had become an embarrassment in 50-over cricket – until July 2019, England had not won a single knock-out match at a World Cup for over twenty years. In 2015, England were destroyed by New Zealand in Wellington, resulting in a humiliating exit from the tournament.[62]

Yet Strauss was the catalyst to transforming this divided team into the world's top one-day test team. He helped to build a culture of excellence, high performance and professionalism, akin to the professional culture seen in Team GB in the 2012 Olympics. He did this by being authentic to himself and his own values and also by playing to his players' strengths.

One of Strauss' values is humility. The morning after England's triumph, he claimed in interviews that he'd only had 'a small role to play'. But as captain and director, he really did move things in a new direction and create the foundations for the incredible World Cup win.

He insisted on good manners and always took a thoughtful, measured approach to problems – thinking and talking it through rationally before coming back with a plan (and then a win!). He required and inspired discipline and honesty in his men, the two traits at the heart of his own game. Such were his leadership skills, he became one of just three England captains to win an Ashes series home and away against Australia.

Strauss would argue that leaders are made and not born. You would not have met him as a young player and assumed that one day he would be England captain. He was not even sure he would really make it as a professional cricketer, and despite twenty-one Test centuries he does not rate himself as a great player. 'Decent, workmanlike' are the words he would use.[63]

He never aspired to captain England. However, he gradually grew in confidence and when he saw the mess England were in at the beginning of 2009, he recognised that he could be the man to sort it out. He set about learning how to lead, reading every book on leadership he could find and growing into the captain England needed. That legacy of humility, hard work and values helped to build the team that won the World Cup.

One story Strauss told us, which really stands out, was how during the Ashes in 2009 he had tried and failed to change the style of two of his opening bowlers to get them to fit into his strategy for the team. The bowlers were both very risk-averse and constantly played it safe, while Strauss was trying to persuade them to take more risks. Whenever he urged them to be more aggressive and riskier, they would approach it with an attitude of 'It will never work', so inevitably it didn't work.

Frustrated that he couldn't seem to get the best out of these players, Strauss called a meeting with the coach and the team psychologist to decide on a new strategy. They agreed that they would stop trying to change the players and instead create a plan which built on their natural dispositions and strengths. Then they would try to leverage those in a way that created success for the whole team. They decided to fully commit to a strategy which centred on the players' preference for playing it safe, containing and putting pressure on the opposition.

England were playing against Australia, and this strategy of containment ended up being perfect against the aggressive Australian psyche. Strauss found that by really understanding and knowing his people, by letting them be themselves and play to their strengths rather than making them change, the team were able to secure a historic victory. It was also a good lesson for him as a leader about the fact that just because someone might be different from you, it doesn't mean they are wrong. He adds: "My advice would be that as a leader you need to build your strategy around your people, not try and force your people to fit into your own plan – then fully commit to it and see it through."[64]

Question Time

You may be feeling slightly uncomfortable at this point and wishing you could grill us *Question Time*-style, so we've put together some questions which you might want answered.

Q.   *Aren't there times when you need to focus on people's weaknesses?*

A.   Absolutely. When a skill is 'job critical' you must help people to improve it. But your success rate in doing so will be much higher if you have also focused on their strengths and given them authentic feedback about what they are good at. One of the essential values of focusing on strengths is to build the confidence required to do the hard work of self-improvement. Confidence can give people the ability to critique themselves, which is necessary for their growth and improvement. (We will address how to have difficult conversations in Chapter 2.) It allows you to say, 'I'm great at leading but lousy at numbers. So rather than teach me remedial math, get me a good finance partner.'[65]

Q.   *Are you saying that I should never think about my own weaknesses?*

A.   No. But try to find a role, or adapt your role, so that it plays to what you are good at. Great leadership requires emphasising strengths while also working on weaknesses. You will find as a leader that many things you are not good at can be delegated – but not everything. If you find that you lack competence in a skill that is essential for your role, then ignoring it could be disastrous and hurt others. The goal isn't a fairy tale; the goal is excellence, and excellence is hard work.

Q. *By focusing on strengths aren't you ignoring all the research on growth mindset?*

A. Good question! The answer again is no. When someone says 'focus on your strengths', it's easy to interpret that as 'just do what you're naturally talented at, stay in your comfort zone and you won't need to try hard'. But that is what is known as a fixed mindset: believing that your talents are innate gifts. It is the exact opposite to a growth mindset, which is believing that your talents can be developed. Carol Dweck, a key proponent of growth mindset, argues that both strengths and weaknesses can be improved, and that people with a growth mindset will normally achieve a higher performance.[66] This happens because if you believe you can improve, you put more effort into improving, which, in turn, helps you to improve. It's not enough to identify your strengths or even use them; you also need to believe that those strengths can be improved. We will look at mindset in more detail in Chapter 6.

Q. *Can't strengths, when they are overused, become weaknesses?*

A. Yes, absolutely – perhaps someone's wisdom is stopping them from allowing others to contribute and develop, or someone's ability to listen really well is preventing them from giving their ideas in meetings. It's important to build trusting relationships within your team so that you can give one another feedback.

Q. *Won't focusing on strengths make people arrogant and give them a false sense of competence?*

A. It shouldn't do because the feedback should be honest and with relevant examples of when they have shown those strengths; if you do this then there shouldn't be a 'false' sense of competence. Arrogance is a separate issue. If it is impacting on the performance of others in the team or on the person who is being arrogant, then this can be addressed once a really positive relationship has been developed.

People can suffer from the Dunning–Kruger effect, a behavioural economics theory which explains how people who are least competent at a task often rate themselves as high performers.[67] This can occur because individuals don't have the knowledge or insight to know better. The danger is that people don't recognise where they need to improve or what excellence looks like, therefore it is important to be honest about areas for improvement too. We will discuss this further in future chapters.

Equally, people can suffer from imposter syndrome, a psychological term describing the fact that individuals often doubt their own abilities and accomplishments and are constantly scared of being found out as a fraud. The term was first used by psychologists Pauline Clance and Suzanne Imes, although it is not an actual disorder.[68] Many of us experience it: you get a place at your university of choice and your inner voice says that probably not many people applied or you were just filling a quota. You get a promotion and then tell yourself that no one else applied for the role. You are sure that at any moment someone will tell you that you really aren't qualified for the job you are doing, despite your experience and qualifications. Having a leader who recognises your strengths can therefore be hugely empowering.

Q. *How should we apply this when giving feedback to staff?*

A. Marcus Buckingham and Donald Clifton have carried out a wealth of research and provided us with four rules for strengths-based feedback:[69]

1 Counter the idea that praise is mainly a tool to make people feel good or to provide the bread for the unpleasant sandwich filling they are about to receive.

2 Don't assume that people know what their strengths are, no matter how obvious they are to you (nor their weaknesses!).

Whilst people remember criticism, they respond to praise.

Laura Morgan Roberts et al.[70]

3 Don't assume that people will absorb the positive feedback you are giving them easily. Just as individuals can find it hard to hear criticism, it can also be difficult to hear praise. This can be because they are worried about becoming complacent – they think it could go to their heads – and they're concerned they may become weighed down with others' expectations.

4 Because of people's resistance to hearing positive feedback, ensure you deliver enough of a dose. Use 360-degree reviews to collect overwhelming data that confirms an individual's strengths.

Case Study: Standard Chartered Bank

One interesting case study of an organisation that has taken a strengths-based approach to leadership is a global bank with 1,700 branches in seventy countries, Standard Chartered Bank.[71] Banks aren't known for doing anything unless it increases profit and improves the bottom line, so you can be pretty sure that they found the evidence on strengths-based development to be compelling.

In 2000, Standard Chartered decided to change its human resource processes and tools to make them more strength focused. It has also concentrated on helping its leaders to recognise and lead according to their team's talents – to notice what people do best every day and provide them with more opportunities to do this. It introduced a new development initiative, the Great Manager Programme, which involves:

- An online strengths-assessment system for staff.

- 'Strength coaches' to support employees as they consider their strengths and develop action plans to improve their effectiveness and apply these strengths at work.

- Help for individuals to understand their talents and then develop them through training so they become world-class strengths.[72]

Although it is empirically hard to quantify results from these interventions, the bank believes that it has been a key differentiator in helping to attract and retain talent as well as driving high performance. Kari Nelson, a manager in Standard Chartered Bank's human resources group, says: 'We believe this focus on strengths has helped contribute to strong financial performance. Since 2000, when the approach was first introduced, pre-tax profits have increased by 251%, and the future continues to look promising.'[73]

This case study is a reminder to leaders in business not just to focus on finding their own and others' strengths, but to also consider how they can change the processes in their companies to more deliberately focus on strengths.

However, even if you can't change the human resource programmes for your team, there are still ways you can help people to use their strengths more. Have a go at our next challenge, which prompts you to find ways to better use your own and your team's strengths (which you discovered in challenge 5).

Challenge 6: Building on Strengths

Exercise 1: Build on Your Own Strengths as a Leader

How can you redesign your role so that you can be the best version of yourself as a leader for your team?

- Where are you at your best in your role and can you do more of that?
- Is there an area that you are not good at, which you could pass on to someone else or do less of?
- Who brings out the best in you and can you spend more time with them?
- What other ideas do you have that will help you to use your strengths more?

Now discuss the answers to the above questions with a colleague, mentor or friend.

Exercise 2: Build on Your Team's Strengths

Meet up with each member of your team to discuss the results from challenge 5 and then help them to redesign their personal job description to build on what they are good at. You are trying, wherever possible, to create a better fit between their role in the team and their best self. This might involve making small changes in the way they work, who they work with or the way they spend their time. Clearly, this has to be done within the constraints of the team – some roles will have more room for redesign than others, but most roles have at least some space at the margins for change. (Where an individual's natural skills can't be used in their current role, this exercise may help them to realise they need to find another team or may give them the confidence to apply for new roles.)

Conclusion

To finish this chapter, let's imagine that you urgently need a life-saving operation and you are given the choice: have the best surgeon in the country helicoptered in to operate on you or let the local hospital team carry out the operation. Money is no object for you. What would you choose?

Most of us would fly someone in, lured by our love of star performers and belief that individual excellence is probably the highest predictor of success. However, you may change your mind when you consider a study by researchers from Harvard Business School in 2006.[74]

Robert Huckman and Gary Pisano looked at more than 200 heart surgeons in forty-two different hospitals and measured their patients' survival rates. After processing data on over 38,000 procedures, the researchers showed that, as expected, patient outcomes improved as individual heart specialists gained more practice and experience. The more experienced 'star' surgeons had the best results.

What was surprising, however, and the twist in the research, was that this improvement in performance only happened at the hospitals where the surgeons did the majority of their work. When the same star surgeons operated away from home, without their usual teams, performance outcomes dropped back down to average.

The research suggests that there is something critical about working in a familiar team. For the surgeons leading those operations, their performance was dependent on bonds with colleagues and the culture, communication processes and routines they had developed together. Individual performance can't be easily separated from team culture. Leaders only shine with the support of their team. Success depends on strong relationships and connectedness.

As a leader, you need to do whatever it takes to really know your team, however much effort is required. We doubt that will involve speaking Serbian for many of you, but you never know!

Summary

- Know your own values.

- Live out your values.

- Lead authentically from those values.

- Know your people's values.

- Honour those values.

- Know your own strengths and play to them.

- Know your people's strengths and play to them.

Most people do not listen with the intent to understand; they listen with the intent to reply.

Stephen Covey[75]

Chapter 2

Listening Like a Trampoline

Case Study: Drive-by Shootings and Prisons

Maria Arpa grew up in North London. The daughter of immigrant parents, she lived in accommodation declared unfit for human habitation. Growing up in poverty with a mum and dad traumatised by war, she knew what hopeless, dysfunctional living looks like – but she wasn't prepared to accept that and repeat the same cycle of deprivation in her own life. Through hard work and a gutsy refusal to accept her lot in life, she managed to work her way out of the desperate circumstances of her childhood.

Her career was extraordinarily colourful. She ran her own business, worked as a stand-up comic while bringing up two children, spent over two decades in marketing and advertising, and trained as a counsellor, a mediator, a Samaritan volunteer and a Reiki Master (which sounds rather like being a Jedi, and actually kind of is – it involves channelling positive energy).

However, she couldn't ever escape her roots or forget the inequality and conflict which had engulfed her community and surrounded her early years. She chose to live in one of the most deprived areas of London and her passion grew for helping people to learn how to communicate in more effective and healthy ways, rather than resorting to hurting one another.

Arpa became convinced that even violent individuals could be changed and helped through mediation – learning how to talk with each other and hear each other better. She began to build a team with a common vision for community engagement and conflict resolution.

From her home in Brent, Arpa watched as gun crime and drive-by shootings became ever more common, even taking place on her road. Then in 2006 came the fatal shooting of a seven-year-old schoolgirl, Toni-Ann Byfield. She was Britain's youngest victim of gangland violence, shot in the back as she ran from a crack dealer who was trying to prevent her from being a witness to another killing.

The nation was shocked. The community mourned. Arpa decided to step up and try to lead cultural change in her community. She established the Centre for Peaceful Solutions, a social change charity with a vision for a society able to live in harmony with its values, without fighting and abuse.[76]

Arpa's personal history was crucial in developing her ability to reach 'hard to reach' people. She developed a tool called the Dialogue Roadmap to help people communicate clearly and build rapport quickly, in order to resolve hostilities. The Centre for Peaceful Solutions was awarded half a million pounds in 2007 which enabled them to work in some of the most disadvantaged areas of London, with gang members, violent offenders and troubled youths.

Arpa didn't try to solve everyone's problems on her own; her strategy was about empowering other leaders within communities to solve their own conflicts. For example, she worked with a club owner in Brent, spending many hours listening to him, learning about his world and training him in the skills of mediation. Then, when a well-liked young man was shot dead in the area and it looked like the killing would escalate into retaliatory attacks, the club owner was able to use his new skills in mediation and listening to defuse the conflict and save lives.

Arpa also developed a deep friendship with a refugee from Iraq. The Muslim woman had been tortured before escaping to the UK and spoke hardly any English. The Centre for Peaceful Solutions helped her become a leader in her own community and develop a programme of family mediation to help resolve cases of domestic abuse.

Arpa is also teaching mediation in prisons. In an interview with *The Guardian*, a prisoner explains how they came from a really tough background where they didn't learn to communicate their feelings or understand about compassion and empathy.[77] These prisoners are now taking part in mediation training at Dartmoor Prison, where inmates are taught how to find a resolution that satisfies both parties and how to identify people's real concerns, needs and values amid the emotion and angry words.

The inmates are learning new ways to communicate. In the interview, Arpa explains that they now have the skills to pause a conversation when it is going in the wrong direction and ask to start again. They know when and how to ask for time to think, rather than rushing in and saying something they might regret. They are also learning empathy and how to see beneath one another's behaviour to the real reasons behind the violence.

One of the senior prison officers at Dartmoor observes that others might judge the new initiative as 'fluffy' or worry that it would undermine respect and the hierarchy, but he says: 'I want to be on a wing where we talk all day. You can be on the one with the alarm going off and people rolling all over the floor [fighting]. This has the potential to be the biggest thing that's happened to the prison service for the last 100 years.'

Arpa has learned over the years that many of the destructive behaviours we see in society, such as the rise in knife crime, happen because people believe they have no voice. Teaching people who feel marginalised and excluded healthy ways to communicate allows them to articulate their needs and challenge decisions in a way that empowers them to be heard. Helping two sides of a dispute learn to hear one another, know one another and empathise with one another can be the key to empowering leaders in communities to reduce violence and create peaceful solutions.

Arpa told us recently: 'While it's true that organisations need good leadership to get things done properly, organisations are made up of human relationships. Human relationships cannot be led and rely on goodwill. Leaders need to get good at human relationships and building goodwill.'

This story encapsulates the amazing power of communication, listening and empathy. Arpa's ability to help people know each other and lead mediation within their communities literally saved lives and reduced violence.

You may not have to lead a dispute between gangs or prisoners, but the skills to know and lead your people effectively are exactly the same whatever your context: listening, asking effective questions, positivity and empathy.

In our twenty years of training leaders, we have never heard anyone say that a leader communicated too much or too well. In fact, one of the most common criticisms of leaders is that they don't communicate effectively enough. And these aren't soft skills – they work in prisons, they are powerful on the streets and they can transform your team.

So, let's get started and learn how to listen like a trampoline.

Listening

A study of doctors and patients asked people in a GP waiting room how many questions they wanted to ask their doctor. Most wanted to ask around four. The number of questions they actually asked? About one-and-a-half. The reason was that, on average, the doctor would interrupt the patient after they had only been talking for eleven seconds and take over the conversation.[78]

We all know how it feels to talk to somebody who doesn't actually listen. You are telling them something that feels really important to you and then you notice that their eyes are glazing over, they are glancing at their phone or gazing off behind your shoulder. Suddenly you run out of things to say and don't want to talk to them any more. You probably end up feeling pretty frustrated, and it's bad for your relationship.

Daniel Goleman, a former Harvard lecturer, calls this lack of listening the 'common cold' of the workplace: tuning out of what a person is saying before we fully understand them – and telling them our opinion too soon.[79] However, it is in moments of complete attention that interpersonal chemistry occurs, according to Goleman. He provides evidence to show that when we are listening with our complete attention, the most fruitful ideas and collaborations occur, and negotiations and brainstorms are most effective.[80] It has also been shown that better listening increases team engagement, trust, feelings of being supported and commitment to the organisation.[81]

We appreciate the challenges that leaders face, with the barrage of emails, text messages, phone calls, meetings and knocks on the door. However, the skill of listening is too critical to leadership for us to make excuses. Goleman argues that poor listening is essentially just a bad habit that needs to be replaced.

So what does good listening look like?

- Non-judgemental.

- Clears away distractions.

- Creates a safe environment where people feel comfortable to talk.

- Eye contact.

- Good body language as a listener – nodding and showing interest.

- Paying attention to the speaker's words.

- Paying attention to the speaker's body language. (When do they smile and seem full of energy? When do they slow down and seem sad?).

- Paying attention to the speaker's energy.

- Listening out for their values.

- Not interrupting or hijacking the conversation.

Abraham Lincoln, arguably one of the greatest US presidents, was noted for his attentive listening. Journalist Francis Fisher Browne observed that as each visitor approached the president, 'he was greeted with an encouraging nod and smile … the President listening with the most respectful and patient attention'.[82]

Luckily, listening skills are not a fixed talent that you are somehow born with (or not). Listening can be taught and practised. Often, just being aware of the importance of listening can be enough to help you pay attention and become a good listener.

That really is the key skill: *pay attention*. You are back to channelling your inner Sherlock Holmes and using all your best deduction skills and incredible focus to work out the meaning behind what others are saying. Pay particular attention to non-verbal cues. Emotion expressed non-verbally may be more telling than the words people speak. Focus on tone of voice, pace of speech, facial expressions and gestures.

Other skills that really help listening are reflecting back by paraphrasing information – along the lines of, 'What I think I heard you say ...' – and asking questions if you don't understand something. It can also help to summarise what you have just heard at the end.

A great example of learning listening skills is our senior deputy head, Cress Henderson. She worked with Maria Arpa (who we met at the start of this chapter) to learn how to listen in order to help people resolve conflicts. These skills proved useful in lots of different situations at the school. For example, when students were feeling frustrated and angry about the censoring of the student-run school magazine, there was a clash of values between the students' value of freedom/autonomy and the teacher's value of respect. What seemed like an unresolvable disagreement was transformed by great listening, so that both sides felt they understood one another better and relationships improved.

Our thinking depends on the quality of our attention for each other, [so] perhaps the most important thing we could do with our life and with our leadership was to listen to people so expertly, to give them attention so respectfully they would begin to think for themselves, clearly and afresh.

Nancy Kline[83]

Challenge 1: Paying Attention When Listening

The only way to get better at listening is to practise. Here are some listening exercises for you to try out.

Exercise 1: Body Language

Next time you have a conversation with one of your colleagues or friends, practise listening really well by having good body language – nod at the right moments, maintain eye contact, lean forwards and keep focusing on the person. Your mind will definitely wander; this is totally normal. When this happens, gently guide your attention back to the person to whom you are listening. Then reflect: how was the conversation? How did it feel?

Exercise 2: Summarise

Next time you have a conversation with a team member, listen attentively to what they are saying and, at the end, summarise what you heard – for example, 'So, you're telling me you had the best game of your life and feel really excited about the tournament coming up – that's so cool!' What impact does this have on the conversation?

Exercise 3: Noticing Energy

Pick a conversation and pay attention to the energy throughout the exchange. Make a comment about it at the end – for example, 'Wow, you seemed really excited when you spoke about your new job!' or 'You really seem low about that incident.' What impact does this have on the conversation?

Asking Effective Questions

The second skill that you will need in order to get to know your people is the ability to ask great questions. Without insightful questions it will be very hard to encourage others to open up to you and for you to begin to know their values and strengths.

There are many different types of questions which are appropriate for a variety of settings. However, in the context of getting to know your team, the best type of questions to use are coaching questions.

You may have come across executive coaches in top businesses or certainly sports coaches on the track and pitch. That is where coaching first emerged as a credible tool for driving improved performance, although it is now widely used in the field of education as well. The job of a great coach is to ask insightful questions that will help someone to become who they want to be and achieve what they want to achieve.

There is a definition of coaching we really like by John Whitmore: 'Coaching is unlocking a person's potential to maximise their own performance. It is helping them to learn rather than teaching them ... we are more like an acorn which contains within it all the potential to be a magnificent oak tree. We need nourishment, encouragement and the light to reach toward, but the oak-treeness is already within.'[84] We love the idea of empowering others to learn and that one of our key roles as a leader is to help them unlock their potential and allow them to flourish like an oak tree.

Great coaching questions have the following characteristics in common:

- They are open – so don't ask a question that has a yes or no answer.

- They aren't trying to steer the person in a particular direction.

- They are short – no one can remember your question if it's too long.

- They are linked to what the person has been talking about – if they are talking about their next hockey match, don't ask them a question about aliens!

- Start with *what* or *how*, not *why* – why questions make people feel defensive (e.g. 'Why did you hit your little sister?').

In the table on page 49, we take a poor question and turn it into a stronger coaching question. As you read through the questions, have a think about which one is likely to help you get to know your people better.

The other important thing to remember about using questions to get to know people is what we call 'start with the heart'. Don't panic, we're not about to get all soppy on you. This has absolutely nothing to do with Valentine's Day or romance. What we mean is that the best conversations for

Original question	Coaching question
Did you enjoy the match today?	What was the best thing about the match today?
Why did you miss the deadline?	What were the obstacles that stopped you from meeting the deadline?
Why did you miss the penalty?	What was happening around you that caused you to miss the penalty?
Why don't you practise more before your next presentation?	What could you do if you want to perform better in your next presentation?
Did you think that meeting was a waste of time?	You seemed disengaged in that meeting – what are your thoughts on it?
Why don't you revise more before your next assessment?	What would doing well in the next assessment make possible?
Why don't you just go to the gym, rather than saying you intend to and then not doing it?	What is important to you about getting fit?
Yeah, I feel like that too when the boss is patronising – why don't you just tell her not to be?	What is it about being patronised that is making you angry? What value is your boss compromising?
So your colleague is really annoying? Mine too. Why don't you just tell him to stop?	What is the most annoying thing he does that you would want to stop?

getting to know others are those that get to the root of what really matters to people and that help you to identify their values.

We know from Chapter 1 that it is crucial to know people's values if we want to lead them well. The other reason it is so vital is that most of us can solve our own problems in life – for example, we know that if we want to get fit we need to go running or go to the gym, we know that if we want to play for the first team we need to spend more time practising, and we know that if we want to get better at public speaking we need to volunteer to do more of it. The thing stopping us is not that we don't know what to do, it is the motivation to make it happen. We often just need to remember why these things are so important to us, so that we can find the motivation to take the next step. When you ask great questions about values, you help people to solve their own problems and find their own motivation.

Here are some more great 'heart' questions that you can use when you are having day-to-day conversations with your team about a project (you could replace 'project' with other activities or matters).

- What is important to you about this project?

- What is it about the project that gets you excited?

- If you achieved the innovation you are hoping to from this project, what would that give you?

- How is this project in line with your values?

- What is possible for you at the moment?

- What do you want most?

For example, Emmie was listening to a friend talk about her upcoming piano exam. She had failed the previous exam and was feeling discouraged and unmotivated, and her teacher was warning that she might fail again. She could have just listened sympathetically, but she decided to use some of the coaching questions above and ask her what was important to her about playing the piano and what excited her about it. As her friend started explaining the purpose behind playing, her face lit up and the energy in the room changed dramatically as she described herself being able to play music at parties and also use it as a way to relax and lose herself during the stresses of life. She left the conversation with renewed motivation and was determined to practise more effectively.

This small example actually points to a bigger truth from the research, which is that as well as getting to know people better through asking great questions, a side effect is likely to be improved performance. In a study by Manchester Consulting, 100 executives from Fortune 1000 companies received executive coaching from six months to one year. The results showed that coaching programmes delivered a return on investment six times the cost of coaching.[85]

Further benefits to the companies were improvements in:

- Productivity.

- Quality.

- Customer service.

- Reduced customer complaints.

- Retaining executives.

- Cost reductions.

- Bottom-line profitability.

Executives also saw improvements in:

- Working relationships with direct reports.

- Working relationships with immediate supervisors.

- Teamwork.

- Working relationships with peers.

- Job satisfaction.

- Conflict reduction.

- Organisational commitment.

- Working relationships with clients.

Overall, the study concludes that executive coaching not only has a lasting impact on the individuals who take part in it but also improves the financial results of the companies they are part of, thus making a compelling case for leaders to invest in coaching programmes in their organisations and develop their own communication skills.

Case Study: Yorkshire Cricket

In 2015, Yorkshire secured their status as the best county cricket team in the country, with a second straight County Championship title, but what was the secret of their success? In *Cricketing Yorkshire*, a Sky Sports camera crew followed the team throughout the 2015 season to find out, going behind the scenes to track their triumphs and failures. The team pointed to the crucial influence of their leader and head coach, Jason Gillespie.[86]

Jason Gillespie was appointed coach in 2011. He took over the team after they had been relegated to Division Two and he was a catalyst for a run of success not seen for years. During Gillespie's first season, the Yorkshire team were promoted again and went unbeaten for the whole season. In his second season, they finished runners-up in Division One. Yorkshire then went on to win the title in 2014 and 2015, and narrowly missed out on a third successive title in 2016.

Within five years, Gillespie had taken Yorkshire from relegation to being the strongest force in county cricket. What was even more surprising was that the success he achieved in 2015 was despite many of his best players not being available because they were playing for the England team.

How did he do it? In the Sky documentary, you see Gillespie using powerful questions throughout. Rarely does he tell a player what to do; instead he asks question after question, building their own capabilities to become the best players they can be.

Gillespie has an uncomplicated, hands-off approach to coaching, with a focus on listening more than talking. He believes that if in doubt it is better to listen rather than feeling you need to say something: 'I've learnt to sit back and observe. You've got two eyes and two ears. You've only got one mouth. I like observing and I've learnt a really important part of coaching. Ask good questions of the players and then, simply, listen.'[87]

Challenge 2: Powerful (Coaching) Questions

1   Rather than trying to solve people's problems for them this week, try listening really intently and then using these two great coaching questions:

- What is important to you about X?

- What do you want most?

2   Try to avoid starting questions starting with 'why' for a whole day. There are times when why questions are very useful, but generally we tend to overuse them. This challenge is about the breaking the habit of using why questions by default.

Positivity

The next skill to practise is positivity.

A study was conducted of sixty top management teams to find out why certain teams performed so much better than others.[88] The teams were categorised into high, medium and low performing based on their productivity, customer satisfaction and 360-degree evaluations of the manager's competence (anonymous feedback from the people who work above, below and alongside a manager). A separate team of researchers, who didn't know the performance ratings, were given the task of observing the teams during meetings and thousands of other interactions.

What they discovered was that the most important factor in predicting successful performance was the ratio of positive statements to negative statements. This was more than twice as powerful as any other factor. Positive statements express appreciation, support, helpfulness, approval or compliments. Negative statements express criticism, disapproval, dissatisfaction, cynicism or disagreement.

For the high-performing teams, the ratio of positive to negative statements in their top management teams was 5.6 to 1, in the medium-performing teams it was 1.8 to 1 and in the low-performing teams it was 0.36 to 1. In other words, in the lowest performing teams, more than three times as many negative comments were made as positive ones. Criticism and confrontation were still present in the best-performing teams but they occurred within a positive context.[89]

Team members in high-performing teams also asked more questions and asked for others' opinions more often (enquiry statements), rather than defending a position or telling other people what to do (advocacy statements). In the low-performing teams, they only had about five enquiries per 100 advocacy statements.

Another key difference was that the low performers were very imbalanced in their focus on self – only three statements per 100 focused on others' perspectives; whereas the high-performing teams were about balanced in statements that focused on their own and others' perspectives.

Measures of connectivity (how often people interacted together, shared information and helped each other) were also much higher for high-performing teams – about twice as high for the high performers in comparison to the low performers. The conclusion seems to be that when people are more connected you get more engagement, more well-being and more performance.

What Does This Mean for Leaders?

We are not saying that we should all don our rose-tinted glasses and ignore the issues. It is just that teams perform better when there are many more positive statements to negative and when criticism is offered in a trusting, positive relationship.

Barbara Fredrikson and Marcia Losada took this research further in 2005 and found that the most effective ratio of positive to negative statements was between three and eight positive statements to every one negative statement.[90]

Interestingly, the importance of positivity has been demonstrated not only in corporate settings but also in the military:

> In environments thought to be even more stoic than corporate America – like the military – leaders who openly express their positivity get the most out of their teams. In the U.S. Navy, researchers found, annual prizes for efficiency and preparedness are far more frequently awarded to squadrons whose commanding officers are openly encouraging. On the other hand, the squadrons receiving the lowest marks in performance are generally led by commanders with a negative, controlling, and aloof demeanor. Even in an environment where one would think the harsh 'military taskmaster' style of leadership would be most effective, positivity wins out.[91]

It also makes a difference in the context of relationships. Professor John Gottman has done some interesting research in this area.[92] He set up a lab at the University of Washington to study marriage. Couples were asked to fill in various questionnaires and also stay overnight in an apartment. The apartment was wired up with cameras and the various interactions between the couples were observed and recorded. The data was collected and Gottman's research team also surveyed the couples afterwards to see which ones stayed together and were happy, stayed together and were unhappy, or divorced. The team then analysed the data to see whether there were any predicting factors in terms of which couples would end up having successful marriages.

The most significant finding was what has become known as the 5:1 rule. Those couples who had a successful, happy marriage had at least five times as many positive interactions compared to negative interactions. If the ratio started to fall below the 5:1 range, the marriage showed signs of trouble.

If the ratio became much worse, the couple was statistically not likely to make it.

There are many other researched benefits to individuals who experience a positive environment. For example, here are the effects on people of experiencing a high level of positive emotions.[93]

- Succumb to fewer illnesses.[94]

- Have better cardiac health.[95]

- Live longer.[96]

- Higher survival rate after a serious illness or an accident.[97]

- Stay married longer.[98]

- Tolerate pain better.[99]

- Improved self-regulation.[100]

- Work harder and perform better.[101]

- Make more money (some estimate as much as 30%).[102]

- More creative.[103]

- Make more efficient decisions.[104]

- Broader and more flexible in their thinking.[105]

- More adaptive and resilient after trials and trauma.[106]

- Engage more in helping behaviours and citizenship activities.[107]

- Build personal resources – competence (e.g. environmental mastery), meaning (e.g. purpose in life), optimism (e.g. pathways thinking), resilience, self-acceptance, positive relationships.[108]

- Better mental health.[109]

Note: it is the frequency rather than intensity of positive emotions that is more predictive of mental health, so experiencing positive emotions frequently is more important to well-being than how intensely you feel the emotions.[110]

Challenge 3: Positivity

Next time you are having a serious conversation, focus on making the person feel safe and confident. Be affirming in your body language and insert some positive comments about what they are saying. The aim is for them to go away feeling more confident, energised and positive. Also practise the 5:1 ratio of positive to negative statements in every conversation today.

Write down your reflections having tried this out.

Case Study: Pep Guardiola

To develop his players successfully, Pep Guardiola puts the emphasis on communication. He is said to dedicate fifteen minutes a day to one-to-one talks with each of his players.[111] Guardiola's emphasis on communication demonstrates how giving orders is not enough; in fact, explaining and focusing on each team member's role is the key to success. 'Pep doesn't just give you orders,' said Gerard Piqué, a Barcelona player previously managed by Guardiola, 'he also explains why.'[112]

Guardiola is always keen to learn about, and from, those he is with. Whether they be an athlete, a groundsman or a politician, he always enters the conversation believing that he has something to learn. He listens with his full attention and asks great questions: 'Pep never stops asking questions – directed not only at others but at himself.'[113]

It was necessary for Guardiola to communicate in six languages when he was talking to his Bayern Munich team. However, all his interactions are full of passion, and when words aren't enough he'll use gestures, hugs and thumbs-up to encourage his team.[114]

Challenge 4: Making Time

Consider Guardiola's example and answer the following questions:

1   How much time do you spend one-to-one with each member of your team?

2   What one thing could you change this week to give you more time to listen to your team? After you have made more time, reflect on what impact it had.

Empathy

If you put great listening together with asking great questions and positivity, you will also have many of the foundations for being an empathetic leader. Empathy is when you can understand others' emotions and respond to people in a way that is helpful for whatever emotion they are feeling.

The Centre for Creative Leadership investigated 6,731 leaders from thirty-eight countries. They found that empathy is positively related to job performance. They also concluded that managers who show more empathy toward their team members are considered to be better performers in their job by their bosses.[115]

Empathy is also great for giving feedback. A 2017 study showed that employees who were paired up with leaders who expressed empathy while giving critical feedback felt better about the exchange than those paired with un-empathic leaders.[116]

We know that some people are more naturally empathic than others, but the good news is that empathy skills can be developed. Brené Brown, in her bestseller *Dare to Lead*, explores five skills of empathy,[117] and we would like to challenge you to develop each of these.

Challenge 5: Empathy-Building

Try to use each of these skills once every day for a week and note the impact you see.

1. See the World As Others See It

This requires putting your own 'baggage' aside to see the situation through another person's eyes. We can't take off our own lenses (in our cases: white, female, southern England), but we can be open to learning as much as possible about what it is like for the other person. To do this, when someone is describing a situation, say something like, 'Tell me more – what are you thinking?'

2. Be Non-judgemental

Judgement of another person's situation undermines their experience and is often an attempt to protect ourselves from the pain of the situation. Brown says that we are most likely to be judgemental in areas where we are most susceptible to shame. For example, you may judge someone who is not able to run meetings efficiently harshly, and this may be an indication that running meetings has caused you pain in the past. To avoid being judgemental, focus your attention back on to the person and what they are saying. That should quieten down the judging story you are telling yourself in your mind.

3. Understand Others' Feelings and 4. Communicate This Understanding

It's really tempting to say, 'Don't worry, it will be fine!' or 'It could be worse …' While these responses might provide some reassurance, what they don't say is: 'It's totally fine to be feeling really frustrated or disappointed.' Instead, it can cause the person to feel ashamed of having negative feelings.

It is also a really bad idea to say, 'I know how you feel.' You *can't* know how someone else feels because you are not them, and it is likely to really annoy them! This also makes the conversation about you and not them.

When you show deep empathy toward others, their defensive energy goes down, and positive energy replaces it. That's when you can get more creative in solving problems.

Stephen Covey [118]

Much better would be to say something like, 'That sounds like a nightmare. Tell me more about it.'

5. Mindfulness

The master of mindfulness, Jon Kabat-Zinn, describes it as 'the awareness that arises from paying attention, on purpose, in the present moment and non-judgmentally'.[119] Mindfulness has become hugely popular in recent years in the western world, although the concept is ancient.

There is no shortage of evidence of the benefits of mindfulness for leaders, although we would recommend that you learn with a qualified instructor or try out some of the online courses and apps. But, to start off, a great way to become more mindful is just to pay more attention to whatever is happening in the present moment. That could be your breath, so get super-curious about all aspects of it and practise slowing your breathing down. It might be something you are looking at, like a tree or flower. It may be movement, like a yoga sequence, a weights session or a run. Or, most relevant for positive communication and empathy, the person you are listening to.

We can almost guarantee that your mind will wander off somewhere else (maybe to the stack of emails you need to answer or when lunch is) – this is totally normal. Don't beat yourself up about it! Just think to yourself, 'Oh, that's an interesting thought,' and then guide your attention gently back to whatever you were wanting to pay attention to.

Being present in the moment and paying attention to whoever you are with will have an enormously positive impact on your relationship.

Trampolines vs. Sponges

We have looked at four skills in this chapter, all of which are critical for great communication: listening, asking effective questions, positivity and empathy. Let's bring all of these together into one of our favourite metaphors about communication: listening like a trampoline.

You may recall from challenge 1 earlier in this chapter that some of the ways to be an effective listener involve remaining quiet, using your body language to be encouraging and paying attention so that you can repeat back to the speaker what they have said. If you did all this you would effectively be acting like a sponge, passively soaking up whatever the other person said. Giving your attention to people in this way can have a really positive impact. But, interestingly, recent research suggests that these passive listening skills on their own are not quite enough. In fact, the evidence shows that 'the best form of listening comes in playing the same role for the other person that a trampoline plays for a child. It gives energy, acceleration, height and amplification. These are the hallmarks of great listening.'[120]

Jack Zenger and Joseph Folkman looked at data on the behaviour of 3,492 participants in a development programme. They had all had 360-degree assessments as part of the process, so they used these reviews to identify those individuals who were seen as the most effective listeners (the top 5%).

They then compared the best listeners to the average of all the rest and created a list of twenty items showing the largest significant difference. They used this to identify the differences between great and average listeners and the things which made them outstanding listeners. Their conclusion was that great listeners have four main characteristics:

1   The best listeners are also the best questioners. At the right moments (which they will find by paying attention) they will ask questions that encourage insight, challenge assumptions and raise awareness. Not interrupting someone is a great start compared to being an awful listener (like the doctors at the beginning of this chapter) but just silently nodding does not prove you are listening either. However, asking a good question tells the speaker you have understood and are interested enough to want more information.

2   The best listeners make the conversation a positive experience. Good listeners make the other person feel supported and give them confidence by creating a safe atmosphere where issues and difficulties can be discussed and where they don't feel judged.

3   The best listeners work as a team with the people they are listening to, rather than competing with them. No one becomes defensive and it is not a competition where you are listening to identify errors in reasoning or logic. Good listeners can challenge, but the person being listened to should always feel the person is on their side and trying to help them, rather than win an argument. Think of it as the difference between a competitive tennis match, where you are trying to score points and win, compared to a rally where your aim is to keep the ball moving between you, bat around ideas and ensure the person you are playing with can reach the ball.

4   The best listeners make suggestions. This is surprising, as sometimes offering opinions and trying to solve other people's problems can make them feel you are not listening or not showing empathy. The researchers concluded from this data that making suggestions is not the problem in itself, it's how you make them. Are they based on what you have heard and the values and strengths of the person you are listening to, or are they just something that popped into your head? Also, people are more likely to accept suggestions from those who listen well.

These findings suggest that good communication requires all the skills we have set out in this chapter: listening, questioning, positivity and empathy. The best conversations are those where ideas can be bounced around, where energy is amplified, where you come out feeling actively supported and able to reach new heights. We want to be more than just sponges for those around us – we want to be trampolines!

As we come to the end of Lesson I of the book, let's finish with a story that brings together everything we have been discussing about the need to really know your people.

Case Study: Leadership Lessons in the Words of a Head Teacher

I am head of a highly successful school full of the most talented, impressive and wonderful teachers and students, but at times I don't feel like a leader. Like many women who are leading, I suspect, I assume that at some point someone will recognise what I have long suspected – that the real experts are elsewhere! That said, I think there may also be something helpful here in terms of leadership. For one thing, I am aware that this is how I feel and I have been open about it many times with my staff and students.

I want to describe an occasion as a head when reflecting carefully on what we needed, taking time to get to know those around me, and being open and honest in my communication helped me and the school to move ahead in leaps and bounds.

I had appointed a new member of staff to my senior team. The candidate was articulate, imaginative and highly convincing in interview. However, when they started, it became clear that they were struggling. They did not get to know their team or the students quickly enough, they had apparently no direction or vision and they were not on top of the administration. Above all, they didn't seem to have the pioneering drive and charisma which we all thought we'd seen at interview.

I was increasingly certain that I'd made a pretty enormous error. We would not renew the contract after the probationary period. But unlike most employees in this situation, this particular colleague did not get angry or defensive. They did not try to excuse or deny or explain away their poor performance, and nor did they suggest that I was wrong in my assessment of their performance to date. They entirely understood why I was disappointed and said that they shared my disappointment.

Time for real reflection and consideration from me. Here was someone I was planning to sack who had behaved with grace, integrity and had the courage to say, 'Yes, I know it's been a muddle so far. But I care and I want to get it right, and I will work incredibly hard to make it so, if you let me.'

So I did. We started to have some real conversations and we started again. I extended the probation, we talked through what they could do and what I could do to help them. I gave practical support but I also found out what values drove them: above all, kindness and consideration, a powerful concern for those around them and a genuine desire to bring out the best in others. Once their self-belief was reinstated, the most phenomenal, creative and exciting imagination emerged, which has given rise to fantastic, game-changing projects and initiatives in my school.

I also learned a critical lesson about my own leadership. Doing the best for the team is not always about doing the most immediate and obvious thing. Leadership can be learned, developed and nurtured, and absolutely should be. And all of this depends on taking the time to really get to know the people you are working with and for.

Challenge 6: Listening, Questioning and Empathy for Performance

▨ Who in your team is currently underperforming or not flourishing?

▨ What could you do to support them so they can be the best version of themselves?

Note: this may take time but the results could amaze you!

Conclusion

Having read the account above from a head teacher, think back to the story about Gregg Popovich at the start of this lesson. He had to have some brutally honest conversations about performance with his team and he could be pretty blunt with the feedback he gave. However, because Popovich had built the foundation of trust and connection with all his players, they could accept, and even welcome, him being very clear and direct with them.

Knowing your people's values and strengths through exceptional listening, questioning and empathy is not a 'fluffy' option. It is the heart of leadership – the foundation that allows for flourishing and high performance.

Spurs assistant coach from 2014, Ettore Messina, has said that the demanding nature of Popovich's personality is based on the care he has for everyone in the organisation. Because he knows his people, he can inspire them to high standards.[121] 'A lot of coaches can yell or be nice, but what Pop does is different,' said another Spurs assistant coach, Chip Engelland. 'He delivers two things over and over: he'll tell you the truth, with no BS, and then he'll love you to death.'[122]

Summary

- Listen intently.
- Ask coach-like questions.
- Make time for your team.
- Practise empathy.
- Build positivity.
- Bring energy like a trampoline.

Love Your People

Influence is determined by how abundantly you place other people's interests first.

Bob Burg and John Mann[123]

Introduction to Lesson II

Imagine we gave you a million pounds to invest. Given that you have limited experience of trading on the stock market, we offer you a choice of two fund managers who will invest your money for you.

Firstly, our equivalent of the Wolf of Wall Street. This fund manager is ruthless. Outstanding with numbers, slickly dressed in a tailor-made suit and with a deliciously high tolerance for risk. They grab each day by the throat and are driven entirely by results and the relentless drive to win. They are happy to trample over people to get where they want to be, grabbing any financial opportunity, even at a cost to others. You might even say they have psychopathic tendencies, sipping their stiff drink at the end of another successful day, as they watch from their twenty-fourth floor corner office as inferior traders scurry around like ants.

Secondly, a different sort of trader. Also outstanding with numbers, but gentler, kinder, caring, more responsible and aware of their own weaknesses. Slightly more dishevelled, having focused on getting the kids up rather than their own appearance, and more considerate of whether their decisions will adversely impact on others. This trader is more likely to be found drinking tea in the canteen with the administrators than sitting in their corner office. In fact, they turned down the corner office in favour of staying in the open-plan area with the rest of their team.

Many of us may buy into the narrative that it is the most ruthless and narcissistic leaders and managers who are the most successful. We have watched Darth Vader's rise to power in the Star Wars trilogies and, like young Anakin, been seduced by the deceptive ease of ruling others via ego and fear. Far quicker and less painful than the slower-paced Jedi training which requires its apprentices to wrestle with their own character and make sacrifices for others.

Psychologists have long been fascinated by 'dark triad' leaders – those who are narcissistic, Machiavellian and psychopathic.[124] These leaders are selfish, domineering and lacking in empathy, but they are also leaders we might consider to be 'strong'. In contrast, compassion and kindness are often seen as weaknesses when it comes to leading others and being successful.

We might think that kindness is important for success in the caring professions – and we don't necessarily like, or agree with, the values of the first trader – but, surely, ruthless trumps kind when success is measured entirely by money? When the share price, profit margin and bottom line are all that count?

Researchers Leanne ten Brinke, Aimee Kish and Dacher Keltner decided to look at the impact of different personality traits on the performance of hedge fund managers in the United States between 2005 and 2015.[125] These managers were dealing with significant sums of money – their firms each managed between US$40 million and US$1 trillion in assets. Success was entirely measured in terms of how much money these hedge fund managers could make.

If ever there were a scenario where financial gain was the priority, whatever the cost in terms of kindness, this was it. However, the results showed the opposite. The more Machiavellian, self-focused and lacking in empathy the managers were, the worse their financial returns. Managers who were significantly less empathic than the average earned 30% less over the course of a decade.

A similar study looking at US senators came to the same conclusion.[126] Senators with low empathy and other psychopathic tendencies received less support for bills they had proposed. In contrast, those who demonstrated humanity, kindness, courage and fairness were more effective at passing legislation.

These two studies should make us rethink any assumptions we have that we need to be ruthless or callous to be successful as a leader. Even in 'non-caring' professions like investment management, these traits won't improve performance; in fact, the studies suggest they may hinder it.

What is the alternative? Love your people. Show them love through kindness, service, gratitude and fearlessness.

Chapter 3

More Southgate, Less Mourinho

Gareth Southgate was born in Watford on 3 September 1970. He loved sport from an early age but was also smart and diligent, spending plenty of time studying. Like many children, he loved playing football with his friends, but he also had to contend with the normal struggles of growing up and was regularly teased for his large nose. He stood out at school sports trials as a multi-talented sportsman who excelled at athletics, rugby and football.[127]

Always known for his large smile and great sense of humour, Southgate doubted whether he would be good enough to make it as a professional footballer and considered journalism for a while. His PE teacher advised him to be a travel agent in case he didn't succeed in sport. However, he was signed by Crystal Palace aged 14 and eventually became captain and led them to the 1993–1994 First Division title. He made his first appearance for England in 1995 and in 1996 was part of the England squad for the Euro 96 tournament.

England were hosting the event and the nation was going crazy – football was finally coming home and 'Three Lions' was top of the charts. And yet the Euro 96 tournament was ill-fated from the start. On a warm-up trip to the Far East, their star player Paul Gascoigne got into a row on the plane with a steward and the pilot threatened to kick them all out in Russia. The match in Hong Kong had been such a shambles that the Football Association didn't issue caps to those who played. In addition, the team were charged £5,000 in damages on their way home, accompanied by ruthless media coverage of their bad behaviour from a wild night out.

England made it to the semi-finals to face Germany and the match went to a sudden death penalty shoot-out. Southgate showed the leadership to stand up and be counted as he took the sixth-spot kick. More experienced players shunned the opportunity. He missed and, in that moment, destroyed England's dreams. He tasted failure: pitied and hated by the nation, commiserated with by the prime minister at the time and immortalised in a Pizza Hut advert with a brown paper bag on his head.

Southgate took on his first managerial role at Middlesbrough Football Club in June 2006 after Steve McClaren had left to take the position as England manager. He was a controversial appointment, with many criticising the choice because of his lack of the required coaching qualifications to manage a top club. After a steady start, Southgate found things taking a turn for the worse and in 2008 Middlesbrough went fourteen games without a win. Relegation was looming and the supporters were soon baying for blood and calling for Southgate's dismissal.

Middlesbrough finished nineteenth and were relegated to the Championship after a 2–1 defeat at West Ham United. It was an all-time low for the football club, their supporters, the players and Southgate. The following season he was booed off the pitch by his own fans, and on 20 October 2009 Southgate was dismissed as manager. It seemed he just wasn't born to be a leader.

> *I live with it every day. People go past and whisper 'that's the guy that missed the penalty'. Such is life – you play for 15 years and people remember 15 seconds of it …*
>
> *I've learnt a million things from the day and the years that have followed it. The biggest thing being that when something goes wrong in your life it doesn't finish you.*
>
> **Gareth Southgate**[128]

However, he didn't give up and later he went on to coach the England under-21s. He was then given his big break when in 2016 he was put in temporary charge of the England team – when Sam Allardyce resigned after only one game due to a scandal. The timing was dreadful for England, with a World Cup on the horizon. As former Premier League striker Robbie Fowler pointed out: 'No one wanted him as England manager … no one believed he had the track record or quality as a coach to qualify him for the job.'[129]

Losing your job is something which will affect anyone's confidence ... it is a blow to the ego ... but in hindsight it gave me a chance to learn and strengthen myself in areas of coaching where I needed more knowledge.

Gareth Southgate[130]

The newspapers described the 2018 World Cup in Russia as a 'doomed mission' for the England team: 'Every England manager's career ends in failure, but perhaps no previous incumbent has been better prepared than Gareth Southgate.'[131]

Yet despite these brutal predictions, England's summer of 2018 will live long in the memory, breaking free from the routine of other years. Weeks of hot, balmy days were boosted by national fervour as the team progressed further and further into the World Cup draw. Against all the odds (and with a statement waistcoat), Southgate led the team to their first World Cup semi-final since 1990. It was the Three Lions' third ever appearance at this stage in a World Cup. Southgate defied the odds and not only gave fans a fantastic summer of sport, but also changed the lives of the players in the team and inspired a whole generation of young footballers to a new vision of football as professional, compassionate and honourable – a far cry from the example of previous England teams.

Southgate's path to the top had been torturous and peppered with failure, but he was learning to lead. By 2018, he had an emotional intelligence that set him apart from football's historical system of hierarchy and dominance. The traditional expletive-laden half-time admonishments were nowhere to be seen. Southgate knew the limitations of such dominant leadership. When players unthinkingly carry out instructions, fearful of their manager, they are less creative, less independent, unable to step up and make good decisions in the pressure of a match. Instead, Southgate led by inspiration, compassion and wisdom. He explained his decisions, got to know his players, asked questions of them and was humble enough to learn from them too.

Southgate didn't demand respect but the team volunteered it. Duncan Watmore played for Southgate at under-21 level and said: 'He was probably the best manager I have played for in terms of how he communicated with the squad. Every time we met up he would come and spend 20 minutes with every single player and find out how they were outside of football and just generally come across as a really nice person.'[132]

Southgate changed the culture of the team; where once it was stuffed with entitled, surly stars, he created a culture that was more humble, more playful and more positive. They appointed a team psychologist who focused on helping the players get to know each other – sharing life experiences, anxieties and truths about their values and what drives them. The aim was to build trust and help them to understand each other better. Southgate has made one-to-one time with his players a priority, which proved invaluable in getting to know their mindsets.

The team are no longer scared of failure, seeing it instead as a useful process for learning and progressing. This gives them the freedom to prepare hard, focus on the things they can control and then enjoy the game.

Yet there is one moment from the World Cup that particularly revealed his character above all others. It was after England had just won its first penalty shoot-out in a World Cup (ever) and, having celebrated with his own players, Southgate went to seek out Mateus Uribe, the Colombian player whose miss had set up the victory, and gave him a hug.[133] This was an amazing act of kindness and a remarkable moment of empathy.

Accolades poured in for Southgate's leadership style after the World Cup. He was awarded the BBC Sports Personality Coach of the Year 2018, and throngs of fans rushed to the shops to buy the famous waistcoat. In a few short weeks, he had become an icon.

Southgate vs. Mourinho

José Mourinho is an iconic football manger. When he first burst on to the football management scene his results were almost unrivalled, including nine years of unbeaten home league games in one stretch, two UEFA Champions League titles and four league titles in different countries. He was a pioneering strategist, constantly reading, studying and trying out ideas. However, if you track his results for the last three clubs he has managed (Real Madrid, Chelsea and Manchester United), you see a pattern of initial improvements followed by sharp declines in performance after the second season.[134] It is as if his leadership style can drive change, but not maintain it.

Mourinho was sacked as the manager of Manchester United at the end of 2018, just three years after he left Chelsea for the second time. Chelsea's board asked him to leave following a series of bad results which left the club not qualifying for the Champions League despite having a team of arguably the best players in the world at the time.

So what was Mourinho's leadership style? He seems to believe in the importance of autocratic, top-down leadership, calling himself 'a special one' when he arrived at Chelsea in 2014.[135] He was renowned in the media for conflict and confrontation – with the press, the players and everyone else he met. He criticised players in public, reportedly leaving them feeling insecure, unsupported and resentful. The constant criticism created friction and fall-outs within the team. Players seemed to respond to this domineering approach initially, working harder out of fear of letting him down. But it wasn't sustainable, and they eventually stopped performing under his dictatorial leadership style and started undermining his authority. His negativity infected the morale of the whole team, dragging it down.[136]

He also displayed a ruthless approach to winning, epitomised in the comment, 'It is not important how we play. If you have a Ferrari and I have a small car, to beat you in a race I have to break your wheel or put sugar in your tank.'[137] When he lost, it brought out the worst in him. The media accused him of being unable to accept failure or take responsibility for defeat. He would lash out and blame others, preferring to be sacked than take responsibility for losing.

People can change, though, and leadership can be learned. When Mourinho took up his new position as head coach for Tottenham Hotspur in November 2019, eleven months after he was sacked by Manchester United, he seemed a humbler and more reflective leader. He claimed that he had used the time to learn from past mistakes and consider who he wants to be as a coach. Rather than referring to himself as the special one, he said: 'It is not about myself at all. It is about my club, my club's fans, my players. It is not about me. I am here to try and help everyone.'[138]

Love Them with Kindness

We want more Southgate and less Mourinho in our leadership, and there is a biological reason for this. Kindness and compassion really are the superpowers of leadership and this is partly associated with the work of a neurotransmitter called oxytocin. Oxytocin was originally recognised because of its purpose of helping the uterus to contract during childbirth[139] and stimulate the let-down reflex in breastfeeding.[140]

However, more recently scientists have discovered that it is also associated with feeling calm and contented and helping people to feel better about life.[141] It is sometimes known as the 'cuddle hormone' because it is released (from the pituitary gland) when you hug someone, but it is also released when you are kind, receiving an act of kindness or even watching someone else being kind.[142]

Experiments have also measured the levels of oxytocin in the blood[143] and saliva[144] and found that oxytocin is related to valuable benefits for both individuals and relationships. Some of these benefits include:

- Pleasant feelings: calm, contentment, warmth, belonging and happiness.[145]

- Inhibits addiction.[146]

- Increased physical health by reducing inflammation.[147]

- Improved memory.[148]

- Improved creativity.[149]

- Better decision-making and analysis.[150]

- Reduces the impact of excessive fear or stress.[151]

- Lowers anxiety.[152]

- Increases generosity.[153]

- Makes forgiveness easier.[154]

- Helps build trust.[155]

Put On Your Own Oxygen Mask First

Which of the stated benefits from oxytocin would make the biggest difference in your own life? Do you need less anxiety? More creativity? Are you physically run down?

This is not a selfish exercise. Sir Anthony Seldon gave a talk at the Ultimate Wellbeing in Education Conference in 2019 about the importance of 'putting on your own oxygen mask first'.[156] Most of us will have heard this instruction given by a flight attendant on a plane before take-off, but Seldon used the analogy to explain the importance of teachers (and leaders) looking after their own well-being.

Tal Ben-Shahar and Angus Ridgeway write that 'the feeling of being happy and fulfilled and the ability to lead – to inspire others and make a meaningful difference – to be so strongly associated as to be virtually inseparable'.[157] Our teams and those we work and live with absorb who we are, not just what we say. If we are flourishing then it is easier for us to be fully present and full of integrity, compassion and love so that we transform the culture around us.

Leaders cast a long shadow by the way they behave. What they do has a significant impact and others often start copying their behaviours. We may try to be kind to our staff, for example, by telling them to get home in time for dinner with their families, but if we never show the same kindness to ourselves and keep sending emails until midnight then that is the culture we will create. As a leader your shadow is long – never underestimate your ability to impact the lives of others.

As we go through this chapter and consider oxytocin, kindness and self-compassion, we want to challenge you to also show yourself self-compassion. As a leader, you are aiming to help your people to flourish, but that can only happen if you flourish too.

Kindness and Performance

Kindness helps not just individuals but organisations. Several benefits to organisations of leaders being kind and compassionate are that they experience lower turnover because employees are more committed to the company.[158] They are also more collaborative and trusting.[159]

In a longitudinal study, Sigal Barsade and Olivia O'Neill concluded that a culture of love and compassion can significantly improve health outcomes.[160] They also surveyed more than 3,000 employees in seven different industries and found that a culture of compassion had significant performance benefits. When people felt cared for and could express emotions and compassion freely, they were happier in their jobs, felt more devoted to their company and were more accountable for their results.

But that's not all. Dacher Keltner, founder of the Greater Good Science Center and professor at University of California, Berkeley, explains that if we see people being kind it makes us feel better, so it uplifts everyone around us. He also says that kindness helps to beat anxiety and depression by making us less self-focused.[161] When we think about helping other people, we gain a new lens or perspective on our own problems and generally feel more positive.[162]

Surprisingly, perhaps, compassionate leaders also appear stronger and have more engaged followers.[163] James Fowler of University of California, San Diego and Nicolas Christakis of Harvard also demonstrated that generosity and kindness are contagious – they spread out as a chain reaction.[164]

Challenge 1: Acts of Kindness

Doing random acts of kindness is an easy and fun way to increase compassion and spread oxytocin. You can do these individually, with your team or with your family. Try to choose a different challenge each day for a week and tick them off, or block off several hours and take time to do something more significant for another person.

- Write a thank-you card to someone.

- Let someone go before you in line at a cafe.

- Volunteer for the task no one else wants to do.

- Plan a surprise party.

- Make someone a drink.

- Bake something for a colleague (or bring in treats if you're not a baker).

- Put your phone away and listen really well.

- Meet up with a friend rather than interacting with them over social media.

- Hug people – touch increases oxytocin and improves your immune system. (But do check they don't mind.)

- What is the kindest thing someone has done for you? Pay it forward and do the same to someone else.

Kindness in Action

You can see the way that kindness is contagious in the outpouring of love for Gareth Southgate after his compassion towards Mateus Uribe following the penalty miss. The hashtag #GarethSouthgateWould began with, '#Gareth-SouthgateWould give you a lift to the airport & wouldn't accept petrol money', and it spread like wildfire.[165] Everyone from Amnesty International to the London Ambulance Service got involved and #GarethSouthgateWould soon shot to the top of Twitter's trends for the UK, with examples including:

- #GarethSouthgateWould butter one slice of toast then use a new knife to butter the second slice to avoid crumbs in the butter.[166]

- #GarethSouthgateWould watch England lose a World Cup semi-final and immediately start worrying about the recycling.[167]

- #GarethSouthgateWould give up his seat for someone who needed it more without hesitation, and offer some of his water while he is at it too.[168]

So how did Gareth Southgate bring kindness back to the heart of English football in 2018?

Danny Rose, the left-back, had been struggling with depression but keeping it to himself and battling on alone. Out of the many people he could have turned to for help (family, psychologist, manager) he chose to call Southgate. Southgate met with him over a meal, talked it through and helped him come to terms with it by going public.[169] 'England has been my salvation and I can't thank the manager and the medical staff enough,' he told the press.[170] Southgate was genuinely interested in his team and their stories. The result was incredible loyalty and dedication from the England players.

The Manchester City midfielder Fabian Delph was delighted to be part of the England squad for the 2018 World Cup, but faced a collision of responsibilities and a clash of values. His wife Natalie was due to give birth on 30 June and Delph considers himself both a team man and a family man. How could he choose between those two values, between playing in the World Cup or seeing his third child arrive? Gareth made sure that Delph could make it home for the birth, even though he missed the tense penalty shoot-out win over Colombia when the Three Lions booked their place in the quarter-finals. And not only did Gareth ensure Delph could get home, but he and the team also gave him more reasons to smile, with a commemorative England football babygro for the newest arrival!

Southgate encouraged families to come out to the hotel during the World Cup, whereas during some tournaments families were kept away because managers thought the players would be distracted. This showed real kindness to the players and their wives, girlfriends and children, and it gained Southgate more loyalty and respect from the players. All of this created a culture of kindness within the team where everyone looked out for each other. It seems that, even in football, the era of yelling, domineering leaders is over.

Southgate had the emotional intelligence to realise this and never bought into the 'dark triad' of ruthless leadership we discussed earlier. Caulfield says that Southgate realised early on in his coaching career that instilling fear wasn't going to work: 'People had this lazy opinion that he's too "nice" and they see kindness as weakness, but it's the most unbelievable strength if you use it in the right way.'[171]

Leadership lies in sacrifice, self-denial, love, fearlessness, and humility.

Vince Lombardi[172]

You now know why kindness is powerful, how oxytocin can improve your team's performance and you have seen how Southgate modelled kindness in his leadership. If you are going to help your team go all the way to the latter stages of the World Cup or improve the returns on your hedge fund (OK – we can't guarantee either of these, but at least this will improve your chances!), then you need to create a culture of kindness which will win loyalty and respect and release oxytocin. And the place to start is with you.

Case Study: 40 Seconds to Save a Life

If the evidence for the importance of kindness in business is compelling, then in terms of healthcare outcomes the scientific evidence is utterly overwhelming. If you are a leader in healthcare, then not only is kindness the superpower of your leadership, it is also the super-drug of your healthcare provision.

After decades of studies, researchers have concluded that when patients feel more cared for by their doctor or nurse they actually get better faster and don't get sick as often.

If patients feel they have been shown empathy, the research shows that:

- If they have a cold it is likely to be shorter and less severe.[173]

- They are more likely to take their medication and listen to their doctor's advice.[174]

- Hospitalisation rates are reduced for diabetics.[175]

- Glucose levels improve for diabetics.[176]

- They will feel less post-operative pain.[177]

- They will be discharged faster after surgery and need 50% less medication.[178]

- Survival rates of cancer patients are boosted.[179]

- There is a reduction in patient anxiety and an increase in peacefulness.[180]

Meta-analyses of clinical studies have even suggested that the patient–clinician relationship is more statistically significant than:

- Using aspirin to reduce the risk of heart attack.[181]

- The effect of giving up smoking on male mortality.[182]

Yet we would not question the health benefits in these instances.

This data is not surprising given the benefits from kindness and oxytocin that we have already discussed: increased well-being, reduced inflammation, lower blood pressure and combatting stress. It also makes sense because if someone genuinely cares for a patient they will work harder, have higher standards, listen better, diagnose more accurately and make fewer mistakes.[183]

In *Compassionomics: The Revolutionary Scientific Evidence That Caring Makes a Difference*, Stephen Trzeciak and Anthony Mazzarelli discuss a study conducted in 2004 which looked at anxiety in cancer patients.[184] The study considered the impact on patients of various interventions and found that when a doctor showed compassion – by visiting the patient and speaking words of support and empathy – there was a significant lowering of the patient's anxiety levels. It was a randomised controlled trial and the intervention took about forty seconds. Trzeciak also considers this finding in his TEDx Talk, 'How 40 Seconds of Compassion Could Save a Life'.[185] Such a small amount of time it takes to be kind; such a profound impact.

Challenge 2: Building Compassionate Teams

Exercise 1

1   With your team, choose two things that provide your group with opportunities to build and strengthen relationships and/or increase their feeling of trust and belonging at work. You may wish to refer to increasing oxytocin levels.

2   Get feedback from at least two members of your team after a month about how successful this was and ideas on what else you could try.

3   We would also advise that you tell a senior leader what you have tried and what feedback you received. This provides you with a great opportunity to lead upwards and teach others about the benefits of compassion and kindness.

Exercise 2

Think about how your organisation's policies and practices can foster greater kindness. For example, our school asks for weekly nominations of staff who have displayed kindness, respect, responsibility, courage or integrity. The nominations are read at the senior team meeting and then the head teacher writes a thank-you card to each person. Other organisations allow employees to give up holiday days to help fellow employees who need assistance, give people days off to volunteer and match any funds that are raised for charity.

Case Study: When the CEO Cleans the Loos

You can see her on her hands and knees, scrubbing the bathroom floor and wiping the dirt from under the loo. A job we would all choose to avoid if we could, but especially given that she is heavily pregnant, cumbersome in movement and inflexible, contorting herself to reach around her prominent bump. You assume she has no choice. Perhaps the reality of poverty has brought her here.

You would be mistaken.

If you had asked around the office, they would tell you in hushed tones that Nanna was the CEO of a thriving Icelandic company, owning Karen Millen, All Saints, Whistles and Shoe Studio shops across Iceland. That this wasn't just a random, one-off act of service – impressive as that would be given how uncommon that level of service is in the business world. That this demonstration of a great work ethic and sacrifice is a glimpse into her whole philosophy of leadership. An approach to business that puts others first, where no one is too important to clean loos, where everyone matters and everyone helps.

Nanna Ásgrímsdóttir trained as a lawyer before making the move into business. A strong-minded, endlessly energetic and principled woman, she was acutely aware of her lack of experience when she started off. Knowing that she needed to surround herself with an outstanding team, she decided from the beginning that she would only employ people who fitted with her values, who were kind and respectful. Easier said than done?

When we interviewed Ásgrímsdóttir, she explained that she would interview new staff in a local cafe, paying attention not just to their verbal responses but to who they were and how they reacted to those around them. Purposely running interviews back to back, she could watch them interact with the next candidate, spotting moments of empathy, compassion or competitiveness. Of course, she made mistakes: the time she broke her own hiring rule by going on a recommendation for two people from another company was disastrous. Both brought with them an attitude of superiority which poisoned the atmosphere of service and kindness Ásgrímsdóttir told us she was trying to create.

As the company expanded, Ásgrímsdóttir stuck to her vision of limited hierarchy and ensuring that every staff member mattered. There was no manager in any store. It was just Ásgrímsdóttir as the owner working between the shops, giving the rest of the staff equal power and influence. She built the business like a family – taking staff with her to choose and buy stock, involving them in decision-making, eating together regularly and inviting everyone's children to work to meet one another. Employees worked with her, not for her – and the careful recruiting, combined with modelling service, grew a culture of positivity and consideration.

Her business was enormously successful and within two years had grown by 500%. Her sacrifices of time and energy actually led to her own success. She knew intuitively what the biological and anthropological evidence confirms – that service really can pave the way to happiness and success. Leadership for her was never about the power but always about the responsibility of caring for others. When Ásgrímsdóttir finally sold the company it quickly lost the family feel and became too impersonal; without the servant leadership and hard work the profits fell rapidly. The staff were no longer willing to give everything to a business that didn't know them, value them and love them in the same way Ásgrímsdóttir had.

When we met Ásgrímsdóttir in Reykjavik, there was evidence of a recent social get-together with the original team. You could feel the emotional warmth towards her as we wandered the city – former employees thrilled to bump into her and introduce her to their children. One employee commented that working at the company was the best time of his life because the people were so kind.

Challenge 3: Serve

1   Do at least one job this week that no one else wants to do (at work or at home). Do it regardless of whether anyone is watching or not. (In our department the coffee cups pile up endlessly and no one likes to wash them up.)

2   What else could you do to model servant leadership?

Ásgrímsdóttir's understanding of leadership is also reflected in the approach of the All Blacks, New Zealand's outrageously good national rugby team. You will meet them in Chapter 5 when we look at the importance of inspiring your people, but it is worth knowing at this point that one of their key mottoes is 'sweep the sheds'. After a major game, while their fans are out celebrating, the All Blacks tidy up the changing rooms: 'Sweeping the sheds. Doing it properly. So no one else has to.'[186] They take responsibility for cleaning up their own space and are humble enough to do the mundane jobs.

Case Study: London's
Grenfell Tower Tragedy

On 14 June 2017, the twenty-four storey Grenfell Tower block caught fire. It took 200 firefighters and forty fire engines nearly twenty-four hours to get it under control. Seventy-two people died in what was one of the UK's worst modern disasters. There was an outpouring of support and charitable donations from the public, but these kind gestures didn't always translate into coordinated care.

One lawyer, Felicity Kirk, went out of her way to try to lead a coordinated legal response for those affected by the tragedy.[187] The North Kensington Law Centre had been inundated with offers of help from across the profession, from law students to partners, and simply didn't have the resources to handle them. Kirk worked with Rebecca Greenhalgh to bring together and organise all the volunteer lawyers. She helped them to set up advice services, clinics and support networks. She organised lawyers to take notes at client meetings, manage press enquiries and provide specialist advice on housing, wills, guardianship and adoption to those in need. Together they were able to help over 150 local households.

Kirk showed great leadership – seeing a need that she cared deeply about, using her own strengths and experience to help meet an aspect of that need, working in partnership with others and being humble enough to serve and do the mundane tasks of arranging rotas and providing office supplies to volunteers. She was later recognised for the role she played in responding to the tragedy at the LawWorks Pro Bono 2017 Awards.

> *The cost of leadership is self-interest.*
>
> **Lieutenant General George Flynn, United States Marine Corps**[188]

Givers and Takers

Why does it matter whether the CEO cleans the loos? We are going to explore the links between success and the sacrificial giving of your time and energy.

Let's start by asking a question. A friend takes you out for coffee and tells you they are interested in finding a job as a nurse but are struggling to get work experience. You have an old friend who works in a maternity unit, but you haven't spoken to her for quite a few years. What would you do?

- Offer to put them in touch with your friend.

- Offer to put them in touch but then ask for advice on your own problem.

- Don't tell your friend about the contact at the maternity unit; after all, you haven't seen her in ages and it would be time-consuming and awkward.

How you answer these kinds of questions reflects whether you are what Adam Grant refers to as a giver, taker or matcher. Grant is the author of *Give and Take*,[189] and in his book he describes these three reciprocal styles:

1. Takers are people who always put their own needs first and are interested in getting as much as they can from any interaction, while giving as little as possible. You probably hate these people – never sharing ideas with you, taking credit for what you have done in meetings, pushing ahead to get the best positions and resources.

2. Givers are people who love to give, regardless of what they get back. Their main thought is always about what they can contribute and how they can help. They will give you the last tea bag, let you copy their lecture notes so you can have a lie-in, allow you to push into the queue in front of them, stand up so you can sit down and tell everyone that the success was entirely down to you – even if it wasn't. We all love givers.

3. Matchers are people who want an interaction to be balanced. They care about fairness and they will give as much (or as little) as they get.

They will also take as much or as little as is taken from them. Most people are matchers.

From an ethical point of view, most of us would probably agree that it is better to be a giver. We can see how it makes the world a better place. Mother Teresa was obviously a giver and she had a great impact. But realistically we can't all be clones of Mother Teresa, and you might also have some concerns that being too giving could result in your kindness being abused and you getting trampled on. Let's see what the evidence shows.

Grant did experiments and gathered data from salespeople in North Carolina and conducted research into medical students in Belgium and engineers from San Francisco.[190] The data included questionnaires and interviews to determine who was more likely to display tendencies of taking, giving or matching, which was then plotted against different measures of success. In the sales teams they used revenue as the measure of success; in the medical schools they assessed students' grades; and in engineering firms they looked at the number of jobs completed, technical reports drafted, hours logged and drawings produced. They also considered efficiency, errors, deadlines met and money spent per job.

The evidence was mixed. In fact, it was slightly confusing and even contradictory. The worst-performing medical students were those who loved to help others the most, who spent their time helping everyone else on the course, explaining the concepts and running out of time and energy to complete their own assignments. The same was true in engineering, where the lowest productivity performers were mostly givers. In sales, givers brought in two-and-a-half times less annual sales revenue than the average, too concerned about doing what was best for their customers to sell aggressively.

However, the best performers – the star performers – were not the takers. It was also the givers. The sales personnel who made the most revenue were those who went out of their way to help others and serve them and give with no strings attached. The same was true for the engineers and medical students. The engineers who produced the most technical drawings and reports, who made the least mistakes and were the most productive, were also the ones with the highest giving scores.

The givers had both the highest and lowest performance in medical school, engineering and sales. The takers and matchers were in the middle of the distribution. Why is that? Well, takers often don't make it to the top because of their inability to build strong relationships and the fact that the matchers will take from them and knock them down too. However, the matchers will give generously to the givers and support them in their success. Givers build quality relationships and make the people around them happier.

But what explains the contradiction of high and low performance givers? The contradiction is partly explained by the timescale. Grant makes it clear that givers are much more likely to succeed in the long run, as compared to the short run. Although givers start off with lower sales revenue and medical school scores, after a year in sales, the highest revenue goes to those same givers, and by the end of medical school, the top grades belong to the students who are most motivated to help others.

It is also influenced by motivation – you can't be a giver in order to get. People will see through that; you have to give authentically because you love people. It is that genuine service motivated by love that will build quality relationships, open doors to more opportunities and networks, engender loyalty and build a better reputation over the long term. Being motivated to help others will also help you to find purpose and energy and weather the hard times. All this gradually builds the foundation for success.

Equally important is the fact that when givers do succeed and become star performers, they bring others up with them. Rather than succeeding at the expense of others, they lift others up, so it isn't lonely at the top!

In terms of performance, which givers rise to the top and which ones get trampled on and left behind? It seems that it is possible to give too much, allow people to take advantage of you and burn yourself out. The givers who rise to the top are strategically generous – they put other people first the majority of the time, but they find a way to do this while also meeting their own needs and objectives.

Grant suggests some top tips for being a successful giver:

- A 'five-minute favour' rule, where you look for high-impact ways to help that don't have too high a personal cost.[191]

- 'Pay it forward' – ask others to pass on the favour so that your giving impacts more people.[192]

- Beware the takers and don't give them too much. If you feel that people are taking advantage of you, do what Grant calls 'generous tit-for-tat'– that is, be generous (but not a pushover) and match their taking when necessary.[193]

- Remember that your energy, time and money are important for those you care about. When you are wise with your giving and protect yourself from takers, you are also giving to those you love. For example, Grant mentions a study of new MBA graduates who were negotiating their starting salaries for a job. Givers walked away with much higher pay deals when they were reminded that their income would have a significant impact on the well-being of their family or when they pretended they were negotiating on behalf of a good friend they had recommended for the job.[194]

If givers are the most successful over the long term, can you learn to be a giver? Absolutely! We all have the capacity to give and take and demonstrate both in different circumstances and relationships. But you can start to give more by considering what you have to offer that can help others in terms of knowledge, time, contacts and skills.

Challenge 4: Becoming a Successful Giver

1   Aim for three five-minute favours this week – reflect on the impact.

2   Discuss the benefits of giving with your team, then together consider whether there is anything you can do individually or as a group to pay forward favours you have received.

3   Where do you need to be more giving to those you care about and love? Think about one thing you could do to be more giving to those most important in your life this week.

Case Study: Lacrosse Superstar

Here is a great example of a teenager giving strategically in a way that enabled him and those around him to succeed.[195]

A young high school student, Stephen, stood out for being exceptional at lacrosse. Coaches from colleges across the United States would turn up to his school games to watch him play, and soon colleges were competing aggressively to sign him up for their team, offering sports scholarships to lure him to their campuses.

Stephen was particularly interested in one college whose team was headed up by John Brubaker (Coach Bru). However, he refused to sign up, saying he would prefer to wait until the following spring before making a binding commitment to anyone. Coach Bru agreed to keep the scholarship option open for him until the spring.

Throughout the rest of that season, recruiters from all over the country came to watch Stephen's games, hoping they could win him over. Finally, he agreed to sign up with Coach Bru, who asked him why he had waited so long to make up his mind. This is what Stephen said: 'Coach, I don't know if you've noticed, but a lot of colleges come to see me play each week. Most of my teammates weren't getting scholarship offers or even being recruited earlier this year, but now they are.'

Stephen recognised that by not committing to a particular team, all the coaches who were scouting him would continue to come and watch him play. This meant they would also get the opportunity to see how good some of his teammates were too. Had he signed early, the coaches would have ended their visits and his teammates wouldn't have been signed up.

What a great example of being a giver and a servant. A star performer who, by giving, lifted others up with him. At an age when people can often be inward-looking, this young man was being a true leader and already thinking of how to bring the best out in others.

> *But among you it will be different. Whoever wants to be a leader among you must be your servant.*
>
> **Matthew 20:26**

Case Study: Private Michelle Norris

At 11.06pm, C Company of the First Battalion Princess of Wales's Royal Regiment left camp on a search operation in Al Amarah, Iraq. The soldiers soon found themselves under heavy attack from a well-organised Mahdi army force of over 200.[196]

Private Michelle Norris was a combat medic and only 19 years old. They were out all night and the attacks intensified, with shots coming from all around them and constant reports over the radio of more fighting. As dawn crept up, it looked as if Private Norris and her company would make it out unscathed. But then a report came over the radio that one of their Warrior tanks was trapped in a ditch with a hostile crowd gathering around it. Immediately her team turned their tank around and set off to help. As they drew closer, she started to hear things bouncing off their own Warrior, little pings and dings. It sounded like kids throwing stones, but then she heard the turret getting hit and knew it was bullets.

Amid the noise of the tank and the bullets, she could sense that something was wrong and yelled up to check everyone was OK. They weren't. A sniper had shot the vehicle commander, Colour Sergeant Ian Page, in the face. The only way Private Norris could reach him was to climb out of the vehicle and onto the top.

With no concern for her own safety and the sniper still out there, Private Norris climbed out of the vehicle and scrambled over the top to administer first aid through the commander's hatch. The area was teeming with armed men, grenade attacks continued and the sniper kept firing shots at her. She continued to administer first aid until they eventually managed to get Colour Sergeant Page to the nearest helicopter evacuation point. He survived and recovered well.

Despite the fear and shock she must have felt, the 19-year-old immediately and without hesitation remounted the Warrior and returned to the battle for the remainder of the operation. When they finally returned to camp, she and the gunner helped to clean the large amounts of blood and human tissue from the turret. She refused to let someone else carry out this traumatic task.

Perhaps the most remarkable thing about this story is that, within the army, it's actually not particularly remarkable. Every soldier Katy has had the privilege of serving with would have done exactly the same thing.

Do the young men and women who join the army have a bravery gene that the rest of the population don't have?

Conclusion

Simon Sinek considered the question of whether leaders are born or made in his talk 'How Great Leaders Inspire Action',[197] one of the most popular TED Talk presentations of all time. He has also written a book called *Leaders Eat Last: Why Some Teams Pull Together and Others Don't.*

Sinek argues that it is not that people in the army are better, kinder or braver than those in business; it is the culture that is different. In the army everyone has each other's backs – trust, cooperation and sacrifice are drilled into training, taught and rewarded. 'In the military, they give medals to people who sacrifice themselves so that others may gain,' says Sinek. 'In business, they give bonuses to people who sacrifice others so that they may gain.'[198]

The motto of the Royal Military Academy Sandhurst, where all army officers go for a year to be trained, is 'Serve to lead'.[199] This view of leadership as being about sacrifice and looking after your people is deeply embedded in military personnel. Sinek had a conversation with a Marine Corps general who explained that when they go in to eat, the marines line up in rank order, with the most senior person at the back of the line and the most junior person at the front. The juniors eat first and the officers eat last. That is how they see leadership: not as a title, but as a responsibility for others.

We love the title of Sinek's book, *Leaders Eat Last*, because it so clearly encapsulates the simple truth that leadership is about putting others first. It's about loving your people. This is something we can all do as leaders. We can also create a culture where others will want to do the same.

'We call them leaders because they go first, because they take the risk before anybody else does, because they will choose to sacrifice so their people will be safe and protected,' says Sinek. 'The natural response is that our people will sacrifice for us.'[200]

Summary

- Create a culture of kindness rather than instilling fear.

- Serve to lead.

- Create an ethos of service.

- Be a wise giver.

- Eat last.

Chapter 4

More Shackleton, Less Scott

It is not the critic who counts; not the man who points out how the strong man stumbles, or where the doer of deeds could have done them better. The credit belongs to the man who is actually in the arena, whose face is marred by dust and sweat and blood; who strives valiantly; who errs, who comes short again and again, because there is no effort without error and shortcoming; but who does actually strive to do the deeds; who knows great enthusiasms, the great devotions; who spends himself in a worthy cause; who at the best knows in the end the triumph of high achievement, and who at the worst, if he fails, at least fails while daring greatly, so that his place shall never be with those cold and timid souls who neither know victory nor defeat.

Theodore Roosevelt[201]

Love and courage are inextricably combined. The word courage has a Latin root, *cor*, which means heart. To love your people sacrificially will take incredible courage on your part: you will need to be fearless about failure in your own life and the lives of others and create a culture of fearless communication.

*A coward is incapable
of exhibiting love;
it is the prerogative
of the brave.*

Mahatma Gandhi[202]

Shackleton vs. Scott

Just over 100 years ago a great race was taking place. A race that has been immortalised in books, documentaries and films. A race that required immense courage and placed huge demands on its leaders. A race that revealed men's true characters and inspired generations of new adventurers. The race to the South Pole.[203]

On 14 December 1911, the Norwegian explorer Roald Amundsen and his team became the first to reach the South Pole. Weeks later the British explorer Robert Scott and four of his men also arrived, too late to win the race and so exhausted that they tragically perished on the horrific journey home. In August 1914, a further expedition left the UK for the Antarctic. This was the British Imperial Trans-Antarctic Expedition under the leadership of Ernest Shackleton. He planned to cross Antarctica from a base on the Weddell Sea to McMurdo Sound, via the South Pole, but the expedition ship *Endurance* became trapped in ice.[204]

Both Scott and Shackleton's lives and leadership were defined by brutal Antarctic journeys and both of their most famous expeditions failed. Scott failed to be the first to reach the South Pole. Shackleton failed to cross Antarctica – in fact, his team never even set foot on it. Both have gone down in history as models of unflinching determination and courage.

The key difference, however, is that Shackleton managed to bring all twenty-seven of his men home alive, against all the odds and after 634 days of incredible suffering. There has been heated debate about the causes of Scott's tragic end and how Shackleton defied the odds to make it back, but their leadership was certainly a key component.

In both men's diaries you can read of the brutal journeys they made and catch glimpses of their very different styles of leadership. In Scott's diaries and accounts of his leadership, you see a man confident in his own ability and decision-making.[205] He preferred to make decisions alone, without the advice or counsel of his team, rarely explaining the logic behind his choices to others. He had a strong emphasis on hierarchy – the team were expected to obey without asking questions. He was not interested in their views or ideas. This comes across clearly in his resistance to taking advice from others about the best way to travel across the terrain. He ignored those with more experience who advised using dogs and sleds and instead chose untested motorised sledges and ponies. The motorised sledges consequently broke and the ponies died in the harsh conditions and had to be fed to the few dogs they took with them.

Towards the end of his journey, Scott comes across as depressive and endlessly critical of himself and his team. Although they stayed together physically until the end, there is little sense of emotional togetherness. Scott failed to overcome the despair in his own mind and heart or find a solution to the diminishing supplies and deteriorating health. A leader in science, determined to keep collecting specimens as they struggled on, but less of a leader of men.

Shackleton was a different sort of leader.[206] His diaries and letters have the benefit of being edited after he returned safely from the expedition, but even so, the tone is entirely different. There is an air of positivity and optimism amid the desperate circumstances they were facing. There is a cheerfulness even after the *Endurance* is crushed by ice and sinks, leaving the men stranded on the ice with three small lifeboats, several tents and few supplies. Shackleton knew at that point that the battle for survival he was facing was not just against the treacherous conditions externally, but also the internal battles against fear, hopelessness and disengagement. He managed this by maintaining routines, order and regular interactions of the team. He knew that he needed to model optimism and energy in all he said and did. His own mindset would be crucial for the well-being and survival of his crew. When they were finally marooned on Elephant Island, with barely anything to eat and little chance of rescue, there are records of them laughing, of silly anecdotes and of banjo concerts amid the suffering.

Shackleton forged extremely strong bonds with his team. He was empathic to what his men were going through and skilled at dealing with conflict. He got stuck in with the day-to-day chores of the expedition, his service creating an atmosphere where hierarchy and rank were less important than individual strengths and abilities. He wanted to know what they were thinking and feeling, and this created a bond of unity. Shackleton's team worked together against enormous odds, even selflessly dividing their last rations.

After realising there was no way they could all leave Elephant Island, Shackleton left twenty-two of his men on that bleak and barren rock with only two upturned boats made into a shelter – nicknamed 'the snuggery'. He took five men with him on a small boat and sailed more than 800 miles to the island of South Georgia to get help. Defying all probabilities, they made it to land and across a perilous mountain range to find help at a small whaling station.

Even then it looked like it would be impossible to get back and rescue the other men from Elephant Island. Shackleton's first three attempts failed and he had to turn back as the pack ice threatened to trap and crush them, as it had done to *Endurance*. But there was no way Shackleton was abandoning his men. They tried a fourth time and were finally successful. Four months after leaving Elephant Island Shackleton made it back for his stranded men. They had all survived. As he wrote to his wife: 'Not a life lost and we have been through Hell.'[207]

Shackleton understood that a leader's primary role is to look after their people and keep them safe, whatever it takes. He had a deep sense of loyalty to his fellow crew members. His men knew this and that is why they followed him and gave their best to him. That hope, unity and the belief he instilled in them were crucial to their survival.

Scott was still an amazing explorer, admired and revered for his determination. But if you were going to choose someone to lead you, it would be worth taking the advice of Antarctic explorer Sir Raymond Priestley, who said in his 1956 address to the British Association: 'Scott for scientific method, Amundsen for speed and efficiency but when disaster strikes and all hope is gone, get down on your knees and pray for Shackleton.'[208]

Fearless Leading

Fearless leading is about not being afraid to fail; instead, it is about having the courage to take responsibility. It is about loving your team by being vulnerable and honest, and creating a culture in which people aren't scared to speak up and be themselves.

When teams and organisations are fearful, bad stuff happens. This might include people hiding mistakes, blaming one another rather than taking responsibility, not speaking up, a lack of challenge and creativity, cover-ups and being too scared to take risks because no one wants to be judged if they fail. There is a focus on short-term results to make the bosses happy, even at the expense of what is better for the team in the long run.

However, when teams feel safe, all sorts of good things happen: people take risks because they are not scared of making mistakes, they stick their neck out for one another, they are brave enough to talk about and try out their crazy ideas, so are more innovative and creative. People speak up and challenge one another. People talk more honestly so more ideas get shared. People admit mistakes so they are fixed faster and everyone learns from them and improves. People grow more.

Think back to Project Aristotle, when Google spent two years trawling through about fifty years' worth of academic papers and also investigated their own teams, striving to answer the question of what makes certain teams succeed. After a lot of scratching of heads and finding contradictory patterns, they finally spotted two group norms that were present in nearly every highly successful team: 'conversational turn-taking' and 'social sensitivity'.[209]

They concluded that by creating a culture of conversational turn-taking (good listening and questioning between your team) and social sensitivity (empathy), you create a psychologically safe work environment. The Project Aristotle researchers therefore regarded psychological safety as by far the most important trait of a high-performing team. As Paul Santagata, head of industry at Google, observes: 'There's no team without trust.'[210]

Fearful Teams

Seven astronauts were launched into space on 16 January 2003, and the world waited expectantly to see what they would discover. The *Columbia* mission's dream was to further the United States' space research programme, conducting experiments which would advance humanity's understanding and add to the legacy of knowledge and scientific applications the space programme had already provided. However, on 1 February 2003 at 9am, something went tragically wrong. The re-entry was disastrous and all seven astronauts died.[211]

No astronaut goes into space without knowing the risks – it is a perilous job that requires great courage. It is dependent on teams of skilled engineers, mathematicians, physicists and computer scientists. What made this event particularly tragic is that potentially it could have been avoided. If the culture at NASA had been different, they would have been forewarned of the danger and able to launch a rescue mission.

One of the engineers, Rodney Rocha, who had watched the launch of the *Columbia*, had major concerns that something wasn't right. He had glimpsed what he thought could have been a chunk of foam breaking off from the Space Shuttle and hitting the wing of the orbiter. He wasn't completely sure – the screen he was watching on and the recordings he had access to didn't have high definition and it was hard to make out clearly. But he was pretty sure that something had gone wrong. The only way to be certain would be for Rocha to access satellite photos, which were not available to him at his rank. He passed the concern upwards, looking for help to access the images. His boss told him it was unnecessary.

A meeting took place between senior managers a week later and the issue was discussed briefly, but it was not taken any further and no satellite images were requested to check for problems. Rocha wasn't at the decision-making table, but he sat on a chair at the edge listening. He said nothing, despite his continued misgivings.

Rocha was correct. A piece of foam had dislodged from the main shuttle and made a hole in the wing of the orbiter, leading to the disaster. Had NASA obtained the satellite imagery and realised what the problem was in advance of re-entry, there is a chance they could have saved the astronauts. So why didn't Rocha speak up at the meeting? Why didn't he insist that they check out his concerns and obtain the images?

In a news interview Rocha said, 'I just couldn't do it. I'm too low down.'[212] It sounds like he just wasn't brave enough or wasn't fearless enough. In fact, what he says betrays a culture of hierarchy that made it almost impossible for those lower down the ranks to speak up. It wasn't psychologically safe for people to voice their concerns – and the consequences were disastrous.

Amy Edmondson, Novartis Professor of Leadership and Management at the Harvard Business School, has been researching the importance of psychological safety in teams since 1999. She has received many awards, including being recognised four times by the biannual Thinkers50 global ranking of management thinkers (and being honoured with the Talent Award in 2017). Edmondson has written many books, our favourite of which is *The Fearless Organization: Creating Psychological Safety in the Workplace for Learning, Innovation, and Growth.*[213] She has looked at lots of different examples of companies and teams which didn't have safe cultures, where people were fearful of speaking up, and she shows the consequences of this.

For example, the car manufacturer Volkswagen, known for its iconic Beetle, has had to pay over US$20 billion in the United States alone in terms of fines and compensation because it cheated government emissions tests, which resulted in it selling cars which were emitting nitrogen oxide pollutants up to forty times higher than permitted. This was partly a greedy pursuit of profits at the expense of integrity and the environment. However, it also happened because of a culture of fear and intimidation within VW, a culture where there were exacting deadlines and a constant threat of redundancy for those who didn't meet them. No wonder no one spoke up.[214]

The airline industry is generally known for being very good at learning from failure. Every plane is equipped with a black box, which records what is going on during a flight, and after any accident the black box is collected and dissected so that mistakes can be learned from. It is one of the reasons that air travel has such an outstanding safety record. However, one of Boeing 747s' deadliest crashes was in 1977 and came about because of a lack of safety in their culture. The flight was from the Canary Islands and the problem occurred because the captain had misunderstood instructions from air-traffic control. The co-pilot knew the captain was wrong, but felt unable to speak up.[215]

Fearless Teams

Contrast VW's culture of hiding problems with Toyota, which has a process allowing any worker who sees a problem to stop the production line. It's called the 'Andon cord' and empowers workers to stop production as soon as they think there could be a fault.

In his book *The Culture Code*, Daniel Coyle retells the well-known story of Google's beginning when it was in a head-to-head race with Overture to dominate the search engine market. Google was the underdog in this race, with far less expertise and resources than Overture, which was making millions of dollars in profit and had recently had a billion dollar IPO (initial public offering of shares). It was a David versus Goliath kind of fight. But we know that Google won, and the turning point came when one of the Google engineers saw a note that the company's founders had pinned up in the staff kitchen stating what was currently wrong with their search software. They knew what the problem was, but they didn't have a solution.

Google already had a culture of frank discussions and energetic debates over ideas, projects and strategies, so when this engineer from another part of the company saw the problem pinned up in the kitchen he was intrigued. It wasn't part of his job description, but he worked through the night and over the weekend and found a solution. His fix made all the difference to their search software and the following year Google's profits went from US$6 million to US$99 million. Meanwhile Overture's culture was one of bureaucracy and competitive internal competition, everyone fighting for status and position, and every idea stuck in an endless cycle of committees. Coyle summarises the story by suggesting that 'Google didn't win because it was smarter. It won because it was safer.'[216]

Or consider the movie industry, a particularly brutal environment where most producers have only an occasional hit and success is entirely determined by the number of viewers. Amy Edmondson describes how the success of the second of Pixar's Toy Story films was due to the director's ability to take on-board harsh feedback, fail, rewrite and keep trying.[217] Pixar Animation Studios created what it called a 'Braintrust', so that everyone could give constructive feedback about the films in a non-defensive, safe environment. Pixar has had seventeen major box office hits in a row.

Ed Catmull was the president of Pixar at the time. He tried to create and maintain a safe environment where honest and critical feedback was expected and welcomed. He modelled this, regularly telling people about the mistakes he had made, showing the way as a leader so that others knew he was fallible too and that failure was OK. He demonstrated humility and curiosity when things went wrong in his own life and set up systems and processes to make it easier for people to give movies critical feedback. He is clear that there is no way to excellence without going through the bad and the boring along the way, learning from it and making it better.

Psychological Safety – the Research

The anecdotal evidence supports the idea that creating an environment where people feel safe to speak up and make mistakes is a powerful way to love your people and improve performance. But what does the research show?

Amy Edmondson came across the concept of psychological safety while conducting a study to see whether better hospital teams make fewer medication errors. This was during the early 1990s when there was growing concern over medical mistakes in hospitals. It seems obvious – surely, the better teams make fewer mistakes. However, Edmondson looked at the data and found exactly the opposite: the best teams were making the most mistakes.[218]

She put forward a new hypothesis: the best teams were not making more mistakes than the others, they were just reporting the most mistakes because they were more willing to admit to them. This led to Edmondson's influential paper, 'Psychological safety and learning behavior in work teams'.[219] Over the two decades since, there has been a plethora of research showing that psychological safety can make not just teams but entire organisations better.

Edmondson defines psychological safety as 'a shared belief held by members of a team that the team is safe for interpersonal risk-taking … a sense of confidence that the team will not embarrass, reject or punish someone for speaking up … it describes a team climate characterised by interpersonal trust and mutual respect in which people are comfortable being themselves'.[220]

The reason is that every time we avoid taking the risk of speaking up because we are fearful of the damage to our self-esteem or social esteem, and every time we avoid admitting a mistake or trying something new, we deprive our teammates and ourselves of opportunities to learn, improve and innovate.

When Edmondson interviewed nurses in underperforming hospital units, who didn't report mistakes, they described the culture as 'unforgiving': 'heads will roll if you make a mistake, you're treated like a child or put on trial'.[221] Instead, people would hide mistakes and cover them up, which meant no one would learn and the safety record would never improve. It sounds a bit like Scott's expedition to the Antarctic, when he wouldn't take advice or listen to the people who said the ponies wouldn't cope in the snow.

Gallup also did some research for their *State of the American Workplace Report* which showed that just three in ten US workers strongly agree that their opinions seem to count at work. They estimated that by moving that ratio to six in ten employees, organisations could reduce staff turnover by 27% and increase productivity by 12%.[222]

Another key researcher in this area is neuro-economist Paul Zak. In 2001, he derived a mathematical relationship between economic performance and trust.[223] His studies show that compared with employees in low-trust companies, those in high-trust companies report less stress, fewer sick days, more engagement, more satisfaction with their lives and less burnout. Because of these factors, employees in high-trust teams or businesses are 50% more productive.

In the early 2000s, Zak began measuring brain activity and conducting various neuroscience experiments to find out how to create a culture of trust. He found that the amount of oxytocin produced by participants was a strong predictor of how trustworthy and trusting they would act during the experiment.[224] Participants were asked to choose an amount of money to give to a stranger via a computer transfer in the knowledge that the stranger would decide whether or not to share the cash. The stranger could be trustworthy and share the money with the sender, or not. Zak measured oxytocin levels by drawing blood from participants' arms.

He then spent a decade investigating the relationship between oxytocin and trust further, conducting experiments to work out what inhibits or encourages oxytocin. He even went to the rainforests of Papua New Guinea to find out if the relationship between oxytocin and trust is cultural or universal. It is universal. So, when you increase oxytocin in your teams (using the challenges in Chapter 3), you are also increasing safety.

Knowing your people, building strong relationships, showing kindness and service all link together to create psychological safety. Neuroscience experiments by Zak and his team suggest that when people build deeper relationships at work, their performance improves. A Google study similarly found that leaders who 'express interest in and concern for team members' success and personal well-being' outperform others in the quality and quantity of their work.[225] Loving your people is the right thing to do intrinsically, but research also shows us that it is great for performance.

In *The Fearless Organization*, Edmondson summarises safe/high-trust teams as having:

- Less stress.

- More creativity.

- More energy.

- Higher productivity.

- Fewer sick days.

- More innovation.

- More engagement.

- More life satisfaction.

- Less burnout.
- Happier lives.
- Better performance.

Which of these benefits does your team need most at the moment?

Challenge 1: Fearless Leading

1   Think of a time when you felt really safe, trusting and trusted in a team. Write down what made you feel safe, trusting and trusted.

2   When have you felt the opposite – unsafe, untrusted and unable to trust? Write down what caused these feelings.

3   Write down two things in your leadership you could change to ensure your team feel safe, trusted and able to be trusting.

Top Tips from Amy Edmondson

Amy Edmondson provides us with some key ideas to enable us to create psychological safety:[226]

1   **Don't mention psychological safety!** Edmondson says that referring to safety might suggest a comforting atmosphere where everyone thinks, 'Oh, we're just fine and everything's going to be great.' Edmondson tells us that actually psychological safety isn't about everyone just being nice to each other; instead, it is about creating an environment of mutual respect. This includes:

- Being open with people.
- Being direct.
- Feeling safe enough to take risks.
- Being happy to say 'I messed that up'.

- Being willing to ask for help when you're in over your head.

2 **Embrace the challenge (because others aren't doing it yet).**
Edmondson says that psychological safety isn't the norm in teams because it's not easy and goes against our natural impulses. It is more instinctive for people to remain silent, to keep their ideas to themselves and to avoid speaking up. It feels safer and ensures they won't look foolish in front of others, especially in a hierarchy where they want to be sure that those higher up will receive what they say positively. It is exactly because it does go against our instincts that psychological safety is powerful when we achieve it, and pursuing it can give your team a real competitive advantage.

3 **Set the stage.** According to Edmondson you need to get everyone on the same page, with common goals and a shared understanding of what they are up against. This will differ depending on the task. For example, a team looking for a cure to a disease will need to be prepared to fail repeatedly before they find the solution. The process is inevitably one of creativity, trials, mistakes and learning. Taking risks and exploring is crucial. In contrast, a luxury car manufacturing process may need perfection, so leaders must frame the work by warning workers of the need to catch and rectify tiny deviations before the car moves on down the assembly line.

4 **Invite engagement.** Edmondson recommends that you remind people of why you need them to speak up and take risks. Try talking about the uncertainty or complexity out there and the fact that their voice might make the difference. You are creating a compelling and logical case for their voice. She advises us to ask people directly: 'what are you seeing out there? I need to hear from you. What ideas do you have? What help can I offer?'[227]

5 **Listen and learn.** Edmondson says that once you have asked people to share their thoughts, it is critical that you listen and are genuinely interested in what they then have to say, especially if it is threatening or uncomfortable. Leaders need to have situational humility – to acknowledge that they don't have all the answers and they need

input from others. Leaders need to keep learning from their team and beyond, and to model this.

6   **Create blameless reporting.** Edmondson stresses that there needs to be a blameless reporting policy to enable people to be encouraged (and even rewarded) for bringing forward their own and the organisation's failings. When failure is reported, leaders need to help their team members to look forward and work through the options for next steps.

For the Cynics

If you are feeling slightly cynical, you may be wondering about the Ubers and the Apples, firms which don't seem to be that high trust or psychologically safe and yet have phenomenal profit margins and share prices.

The evidence is definitely there of a robust correlation between psychological safety and learning and performance. However, that doesn't mean you can't have high performance without it. There are other variables that will impact performance – like a great strategy, brilliant product or awesome marketing. But these companies are performing well despite the lack of safety, not because of it. Imagine how much more successful they might be if they created a fearless environment where the brilliance and creativity of all the staff could be engaged.[228]

Challenge 2: Building Psychological Safety

Firstly, self-rate how safe you think your team is at the moment (out of 10, with 1 being 'not safe at all' and 10 being 'extremely safe'). Consider:

▨   How often people challenge ideas and each other.

▨   Whether people admit mistakes.

▨   Whether people show vulnerability.

▨   How good they are at questioning one another and ideas.

You could also ask individuals directly how safe they feel and how you could increase their feeling of safety. Write down the numbers you have collated.

The challenge now is to increase that number over the coming month. Here are a few things to try:

- Emphasise your own vulnerability in meetings more often. Remind people that you don't have all the answers and that what you are trying to achieve is complex, therefore you need to hear all their voices and ideas.

- Start asking more questions – for example, what are you seeing from where you are? What ideas do you have? What help can I offer?

- Listen to what they say. Maybe keep a journal of people's ideas and comments so you don't forget.

Tigers and Amygdala Hijacks

The reason that creating a fear-free culture is so important has to do with what is going on in our heads biologically and chemically when we are scared. To understand it fully, we need to be neuroscientists. OK, that might be asking a bit too much, but it does help to have some understanding of how the brain works.

The brain is made up of different parts. The limbic system deep inside the brain generates powerful instinctive emotions, like fear and excitement. Some scientists see it as a very ancient part of the brain – the part where our primitive 'animal urges' come from. Linked to this is the amygdala – our emotional control centre. These older parts of the brain take over the newer parts of the brain if any threat (physical or psychological) is perceived and activate the fight or flight response.

This works well when there is a real threat (like a tiger), but it can cause problems when wrongly activated. To give you extra strength to run or fight, your body diverts energy from other areas, including the brain, which means you get worse at making decisions, remembering, being creative, learning and being kind to others. (No one really needs to be kind or creative in the face of a great white shark: survival is the only thing that matters.)

When someone feels threatened or scared, the neocortex (where rational thought as well as empathy take place) can get hijacked by the ancient reptilian brain. This is sometimes called an 'amygdala hijack'. As a leader, you need to know when you or your team members are having an amygdala hijack.

Our brain can see a bad piece of feedback, a small mistake, a negative comment or a poor decision by a referee as a life-or-death threat. The amygdala, the alarm bell in the brain, then ignites the fight or flight response, hijacking higher brain centres. This 'act first, think later' brain structure shuts down perspective and analytical reasoning. Just when we need it most, we quite literally lose our minds. While that acute stress response may save us in perilous situations, it handicaps the strategic thinking needed during difficult conversations or stressful circumstances.

This primitive reaction helps to explain why psychological safety is both essential and fragile – especially in volatile, interdependent environments where we really need clear strategic thinking.

Success in today's workplaces doesn't depend on the fight or flight response, but on another system – the broaden-and-build mode. This allows us to develop collegial relationships and solve complicated problems. Research on the broaden-and-build theory was conducted by Barbara Fredrickson at the University of North Carolina.[229] She found that positive emotions like trust, curiosity, confidence and inspiration broaden our perspectives and actions, as well as building intellectual, psychological, social and physical resources. When we feel safe we become more open-minded – we can discard automatic responses and look for creative solutions.

Amygdala Hijacks Today

Owen Farrell, the England rugby captain since 2018, described to the *Times* newspaper his need to remain calm with officials after he fell out with referee Tom Foley during Saracens' defeat by Exeter Chiefs on 22 December 2018.[230] He became frustrated and spoke rudely – a classic amygdala hijack. An irritated ref snapped 'Enough!' before, in the second half, awarding a penalty against Farrell's backchat. Exeter's 31–13 win ended Saracens' twenty-two-game unbeaten run and meant they replaced Farrell's team as Premiership leaders. To be the best England leader he can be, beyond monitoring his rugby skills, Farrell has also worked hard on his composure – keeping calm and learning to deal with those amygdala hijacks.

Another classic example is the French footballing giant Zinedine Zidane's headbutt during the 2006 FIFA World Cup Final. It was due to be Zidane's final tournament after eighteen years of professional football. His career had included fifteen trophies and he was considered by many as football's best technician, the iconic midfielder. However, in the 108th-minute of the final between France and Italy he succumbed to a moment of madness and in front of 28.8 million viewers he headbutted the 6'4'' Italian centre-back Marco Materazzi in the chest after he provoked him. Zidane was sent off the pitch ten minutes before the looming penalty shoot-out and France lost the World Cup to Italy on penalties 5–3. He said afterwards, 'I apologise to football, to the fans, to the team. After the game, I went into the [French] dressing room and told them: "Forgive me. This doesn't change anything, but sorry everyone."'[231] As a player he was known for his elegance and class, and yet he finished his career humiliated and embarrassed. Such is the consequence of a high-profile amygdala hijack.

Challenge 3: Taming the Amygdala

Before

You can be better prepared for a hijack by practising mindfulness every day; when you find yourself in a stressful situation, it will be easier to turn on the mindful part of your brain. See the empathy-building challenge (challenge

5) in Chapter 2 for ideas on how to learn to be mindful, although we recommend finding a qualified teacher.

During

Unless you are Yoda or the Dalai Lama, you are still likely to experience amygdala hijacks occasionally. You will know you have been hit by one if you experience a strong emotional reaction that seems to come from nowhere and that you later realise was disproportionate.

You can expect to take up to three or four hours to return to normal, but here are some things to try during a hijack:

- Name the emotions as you are experiencing them (in your head!).

- Breathe deeply from your stomach.

- Focus your attention on one aspect of the environment (e.g. a tree you can see out of the window or the light in the room).

- Try counting in your head (this works even better if you count in another language or count backwards).

- Excuse yourself from the situation if it's really bad.

After

You can reduce the risk and severity of future hijacks by doing a quick post-mortem. Ask yourself:

- What exactly triggered the strong reaction – was it that a value was being transgressed?

- What emotions did you feel? Name them as accurately as possible.

- What did you feel physically – shaking, heart racing, queasiness?

- What were your thoughts at the time?

- To what extent were your thoughts accurate?

- Was there another way to view or think about the situation at the time that would have led to less of a response from you?

You should also try to avoid triggering a fight or flight response in others. When you approach a difficult conversation where there is the potential for conflict, try asking, 'How could we achieve a mutually desirable outcome?'

Fearless Failure

Failure isn't a disaster; in fact, it is sometimes needed for success and leadership. The Wright brothers declared that flying was possible and nearly killed themselves trying to make it happen. But they learned from their failures and failed forward, becoming the fathers of man-powered flight.

You need to accept the fact that you are going to fail if you are going to do your best work, and you need to make sure that everyone on your team knows that too. You need to free yourself and your team from the shackles of perfection.

As the author of the incredible Harry Potter series, J. K. Rowling is worth US$1 billion, has sold over 500 million copies of the Harry Potter books and has received lots of awards for her work. She is the ultimate success story. And yet there is a hidden story behind her achievement. She came from a family where her imagination was seen as 'an amusing personal quirk that would never pay a mortgage, or secure a pension',[232] and she struggled considerably before becoming one of the world's most successful writers. Her marriage had failed, she was jobless and poor, and she was writing in cafes while she and her daughter lived on benefits. She sent the manuscript for *Harry Potter and the Philosopher's Stone* to twelve different publishers, who all refused to publish it, before finally sending it to Bloomsbury, who did. Luckily for us she didn't give up after the first rejection, or the second, or the third.

J. K. Rowling was fearless in failure and has some good advice for us all:

> *It is impossible to live without failing at something ... You will never truly know yourself, or the strength of your relationships, until both have been tested by adversity. Such knowledge is a true gift, for all that*

it is painfully won, and it has been worth more than any qualification I ever earned.[233]

Myshkin Ingawale is one of the founders of an Indian medical engineering and design company called Biosense Technologies.[234] In a TEDx Talk, Ingawale discusses how he was travelling near Mumbai one summer and was shocked by the number of mothers dying during childbirth from internal bleeding due to undiagnosed anaemia.[235] The deaths were completely preventable. In most cities in India, a woman can easily have her blood tested for anaemia and can be prescribed folic acid and iron tablets. But the machines to test the blood are expensive and require technicians to run them, making the process slow and unaffordable for many rural health centres.

Ingawale wanted to come up with a cheaper, easier solution to test for anaemia. He wanted to design something simple enough for the local health workers in India to use, something with no needles (so there was no medical waste) and which could be carried easily from village to village. Ingawale got a team of people together and they built it.

It didn't work.

So they tried again and again and again. They built it thirty-two times. And now it does work! It is a mobile phone-sized device that can measure haemoglobin, oxygen and pulse rate. It takes about twenty seconds and can help to diagnose anaemia at the point of care. The machine is now being used across India by organisations like the Indian Council of Medical Research, and is saving lives. It is helping to achieve Biosense Technologies' bigger vision of increasing access to healthcare everywhere. Ingawale could have given up after the tenth or twentieth time, but he didn't. Failure was a necessary step to achieving success.

Richard Branson is sometimes referred to as the 'rebel billionaire'. He has earned that nickname from his bold business decisions and crazy hobbies (such as jumping out of planes). Yet despite being super-successful and rich now, his life has had lots of ups and downs. When he dropped out of high school at age 16, having struggled with dyslexia, his headmaster said, 'Congratulations, Branson. I predict you will either go to prison or become a millionaire.'[236] Branson's headmaster was right on both counts: by the end of the first year of Branson's first business venture, he was in jail for selling records without paying tax to the UK government.

Going to prison was one of the best things that could have happened to him, though, because he realised that he wanted to live the rest of his life more honestly. Branson learned that 'crime doesn't pay and there are no short-cuts, in business or in life'.[237] Before he went to prison he was simply thinking about ensuring his business survived; by the time he left he was thinking big and for the long term. He launched lots of businesses; some failed and some succeeded, but he is now a billionaire entrepreneur.[238]

And the list goes on and on: Abraham Lincoln, Steve Jobs, Walt Disney, The Beatles. Leaders in their field who pushed through failure, failed forward and kept going. Try this next challenge to build your own failing-forward muscles.

Challenge 4: Failing Forward

As a leader you are going to fail, so let's think about how to fail better – how to fail forward.

1   When have you been able to bounce back after a failure?

2   What enabled you to bounce back and be resilient – what resources did you draw on?

3   What did bouncing back from the failure give you (perhaps more confidence)?

4   What did you learn from this failure?

5   How have you applied, or could you apply, this learning in your leadership?

6   What could you do to enable your team to bounce back better?

*For this thing that
we call failure is not
the falling down but
the staying down.*

Mary Pickford[239]

Case Study: General Motors and Mary Barra

Mary Barra became the first woman to run a major car manufacturing firm when she took over the leadership of General Motors (GM) as their CEO in 2014. GM has more than 200,000 employees and it was going to be a challenge. However, it proved to be even more challenging than she had anticipated when, within days of taking on the leadership of the company, GM discovered that one of the ignition switches from their 1990 car models was faulty. The result had been over 120 deaths and nearly 300 injuries.[240]

Finding herself leading a company in the middle of a crisis that could easily destroy them, Barra had to make some tough decisions. She recalled more than 30 million vehicles in 2014 and also decided to change the entire culture. Her first step was to ensure that everything was brought out into the open and dealt with honestly before the public. She immediately notified the regulator of the fault – a big step given that GM had first detected the problem in 2001.

She also wanted an independent inquiry, so hired a former US attorney, Anton Valukas, to look into the causes of the crisis and report back on how such a catastrophic failure had happened. He had previously investigated Lehman Brothers after the firm's 2008 collapse. Valukas produced a devastating report blaming the failures on the fact that GM had a toxic culture which meant that staff were afraid to question one another, concerns were ignored and complaints were bogged down in bureaucracy before being dismissed.

Barra's next step was to get rid of some of the needless rules and empower employees to speak up. She told her employees at a meeting in 2014: 'I never want to put this behind us. I want to put this painful experience permanently in our collective memories.' She also set up a 'Speak Up For Safety' phone line so that any concerns about the safety of vehicles could be reported immediately and dealt with straight away.

The way Barra stepped up and showed fearless leadership, acknowledging mistakes and empowering staff to have their say, changed perceptions of the company. Incredibly, GM had record sales in her first year as CEO, despite the recall scandal.

In 2018, Barra told Andrew Ross Sorkin of *The Times* that the ignition scandal had changed her view of leadership. 'We have 200,000 employees at General Motors – they want to do the right thing,' she said. 'Just make sure they know you want them to do the right thing.'[241]

Challenge 5: Safe to Speak

1   Consider whether there are any obstacles to your team being able to voice their concerns. Write down any thoughts you have.

2   What will you do to remove these obstacles?

3   What action will you take to ensure your team know you want them to do the right thing?

Creating a Culture of Fearless Failure

As leaders, if we want to create a fearless culture for our teams – one in which they will be creative, innovative, challenge each other and speak up – then we need to embrace failure. It is not enough as a leader to embrace failure for yourself; you also need to allow others to fail and learn, fail again and keep trying.

Gareth Southgate could talk to his team about failure with real authority and authenticity, and he also had a team psychologist called Pippa Grange to give them some really good advice. She emphasised in an interview with *The Guardian* how it is only through trying that we achieve success, but that trying actually often ends in failure. She advises us all to learn from our failures and encourages us to 'keep those dreams and goals alive'.[242]

This links to advice from another sport performance consultant Andy Barton, who says in the same article: 'Often, it's the spin you put on things.' You can choose to see things differently. England players in the past would talk about the dread of taking a penalty, as if it was the worst thing you could possibly do. But you can rethink the idea of a penalty from a threat to an opportunity.

You need to choose the way you see failure, problems and criticism. You need to choose which glasses you are going to wear: you can see failure as a cue to try harder or you can see it as a sign that you don't have the ability to succeed. Your choice. As the old saying goes, we don't see things as they are; we see them as we are.

Yet if it is that easy, why don't more organisations manage to create a safe culture? Amy Edmondson suggests that it is because most of us have learned over time that admitting failure means taking the blame. Leaders are often reluctant to respond constructively to failure in case it results in laziness and people stop striving for excellence. They are concerned that if employees aren't blamed for failures, it might create a sloppy environment where people don't try their hardest and mistakes multiply. Yet this view is based on a false dichotomy. As Edmondson observes, 'a culture that makes it safe to admit and report on failure can – and in some organizational contexts must – coexist with high standards for performance'.[243]

This becomes clear when you consider the fact that individuals might fail for multiple different reasons – everything from tiredness to misunderstanding, positive risk-taking or deliberate malpractice. When asked by Edmondson to guess how many of the failures in their organisations are truly blameworthy, leaders generally answered between 2% to 5%. But when asked how many were *treated* as blameworthy, they said 70% to 90%. It is no wonder that many failures aren't admitted to or learned from.

Edmondson concludes that leaders should stop worrying that they will be too soft on employees who make mistakes: 'This common worry should be replaced by a new paradigm – one that recognizes the inevitability of failure in today's complex work organizations. Those that catch, correct, and learn from failure before others do will succeed. Those that wallow in the blame game will not.'[244]

Challenge 6: Learning from Failure

Not all failures are equal. The reason for each failure and the consequences of it will differ enormously. As a leader, you therefore need to consider carefully the kinds of mistakes that are made and the context-specific solutions. However, here are some general ideas you can try.

1   As a team, discuss the kinds of failures that can be expected to occur in your context. (This will be very different depending on whether you are involved with routine production, complex operations, playing on a sports team or involved with something creative.)

2   When someone voices a concern, admits a mistake or tells you some bad news, celebrate their honesty rather than getting cross with them. Then work out how to fix it and learn from it.

3   Be clear about what acts are blameworthy. (People feel safer if they know what the red lines are that they must not cross.)

4   Encourage opportunities for people to experiment and reflect.

5   Work together to devise a team saying which can encourage and remind you all to learn from failure.

6   Try adding a meeting agenda item encouraging people to share their failures and celebrate what they have learned from this.

7   Keep asking your team questions. Yale professor Ingrid Nembhard and Amy Edmondson found that intensive care unit medical directors who asked frequent questions created more psychologically safe workplaces, which in turn developed more learning and quality improvement in their teams.[245]

Facing the Gremlins

If you are going to lead fearlessly and embrace failure you will encounter some challenges, so we need to introduce you to someone. Someone whose voice you may recognise, even if you don't know what he or she looks like. Someone who may be holding you back from being the best you can be. You need to meet your gremlin.

Most of us have a gremlin that lurks in trees, hides behind the goalposts, jumps out in the office, shouts from the crowd and distracts us from reaching our dreams. And the gremlin loves to show up whenever you do something hard, when you aim high or when you leave your comfort zone.

You might be about to volunteer to take the next penalty, give a major presentation at work or challenge someone higher up the ladder. Your gremlin will jump out and say, 'Wait! What if you fail? What if everyone laughs at you? What if you look silly? You'll have no friends. You'll be rubbish. Don't try. Stop!'

You can spot your gremlin by listening for when you hear yourself say:

- I should have …
- I can't do …
- I'm not good enough …
- I won't be able to …
- I'm not lucky enough …

Growth Mindset

One way to combat your gremlins and become more fearless in failure is to have what experts call a 'growth mindset', a term famously used by Carol Dweck in her book, *Mindset: The New Psychology of Success*.[246]

People with a growth mindset believe that success is more about effort than talent and that you can always get better at something. You can increase your intelligence through reading and hard work, improve your football skills through practice or become a better leader through learning and trying out ideas. People with a growth mindset also embrace feedback (even negative feedback) because it is a chance to improve.

Years of research has shown that the brain is not fixed (like an Xbox which once created has a limited amount of memory space) but is much more malleable – more like a muscle which gets stronger the more you exercise it.[247] Or like an artificially intelligent robot that can adapt its learning and beat a reigning chess champion. If you deliberately practise something again and again, your brain makes new neural pathways and you actually change your brain. Failure really is an opportunity to learn and improve.

Here are a few tips to help you change your mindset:

- Don't think, 'Did I win or lose?' Think, 'Did I make my best effort?'

- Rather than imagining our heroes as being born different from us, think of them as relatively ordinary people who made themselves extraordinary.

- Don't rest on your current abilities or feel helpless about your current level. No matter what your ability is, effort is what ignites that ability and turns it into accomplishment.

- When you feel discouraged about practising something, try picturing your brain forming new connections as you meet the challenge and learn.

- Keep alive the passion for stretching yourself.

What you see and what you hear depends a great deal on where you are standing. It also depends on what sort of person you are.

C. S. Lewis, *The Magician's Nephew*[248]

Challenge 7: Failing Forward

We recommend you try asking yourself these questions before asking them to your team:

- What has been your biggest failure so far?

- What did you learn from it?

- How could you see it differently? (Which glasses do you want to look at it through?)

- What is the opportunity in the failure?

- What is your current dream/goal?

- What is the biggest challenge to making it happen?

- What is your gremlin saying about it?

- What do you want to say back to him/her?

- How could you approach that challenge with a growth mindset?

- What will you do next to create a 'black box' mentality in your team, where failures and mistakes can be constructively debated and learned from?

Case Study: Fearless Healthcare

There were enormous challenges facing healthcare provision in most countries even before the COVID-19 outbreak, with ageing populations, rising expectations, expensive new technologies and stretched government budgets. Those challenges have now been amplified. As people around the world have come to show greater appreciation for healthcare workers, the pandemic has not only highlighted the courage of health workers but also the staff and equipment shortages and the desperate need for good leadership.

The culture of medicine has developed from a mindset of individual expertise, where the training and expertise of clinicians has been the most crucial variable in patient outcomes. However, as healthcare has evolved, interdependence and teamwork have become increasingly important. Accident and emergency and urgent care centres are reliant on excellent communication skills as a team of triage nurses, doctors, managers and other professionals interact to meet patient needs. Simple jobs, such as blood tests and scans, can require half a dozen different clinicians, often working in isolation from one another and focused on making their own department run smoothly, rather than making the procedure work efficiently. Increasing incidences of chronic disease require interactions between GPs, hospitals, occupational therapists, physiotherapists, hospices and other specialists. Individual expertise is one jigsaw piece in a larger context.

In an environment where clarity of communication can have life-or-death consequences, psychological safety is key. Yet healthcare professionals are often fighting against a culture where status differences between doctors and nurses have prevented individuals from speaking up. People are often reluctant to ask questions or challenge – for instance, by questioning a medication order. Where fear of litigation has created a blame culture, this is the antithesis of safe.

Julie Morath, chief operating officer of the Children's Minnesota Hospital, was concerned about this and so began a programme called SAFE to try to create a culture where staff could discuss medical errors in an environment conducive to learning rather than blame.[249] This was a brave thing to do: people were scared that the more the hospital admitted mistakes, the more it would be open to legal challenges and litigation. However, she was determined to do what was best for the patients and staff in the long run. Her goal was for a better long-term safety record, even though that would mean more reporting of mistakes in the short term. The only way to achieve that would be if people stopped accusing individuals and casting blame, and instead recognised the interdependence of staff and the collective responsibility for learning from mistakes and problems and improving.

According to Amy Edmondson, Morath attempted to reframe how healthcare professionals in the hospital viewed their roles, emphasising the interactions between their different jobs and the ways that working together could prevent harm.[250] She broadcast the message that healthcare is a very complex system, and complex systems are, by their very nature, error-prone. She wanted people to know that some mistakes were inevitable, but that the important thing was to work together and collaborate across clinical groups to catch and correct errors and improve health outcomes.

She started asking everyone questions about how they could improve patient care, in a way that wasn't about allocating blame. She asked questions such as, 'What have you seen this week that could have been safer for our patients?' or 'Think about your experience last week with your patients. Was everything as safe as you would like it to be?'

She changed the lens through which everyone was viewing patient care. It was no longer about being good enough, avoiding things going wrong and litigation; instead, it was about constant improvement. If someone made a mistake she didn't attribute blame. She would ask, 'Was everything as safe as you would like it to be?' It was an 'aha moment'. Her office became a confessional. People were lining up to come in and say, 'No, it isn't as safe as I'd like it to be.' She was constantly asking for people's views and ideas.

There are bad outcomes and risks in hospitals from omitting to take action or try new things for patients, just as there can be risks from trying something and making a mistake. Morath wanted hospital staff to feel trusted as experts and to try what they thought was best for patients without fear. She instigated 'blameless reporting' and also changed the way the hospital communicated with patients and their families when mistakes were made. Rather than taking the advice of lawyers and never admitting blame or giving information away, they moved to a policy of full disclosure.

None of this was an excuse to let deliberate malpractice or incompetence go unchallenged. But a culture of fear meant lessons were not being learned. Many mistakes were failures of communication or collective processes that, when brought into the light, could be prevented and learned from.

> *Leader = Anyone who takes responsibility for finding the potential in people and processes and who has the courage to develop that potential.*
>
> **Brené Brown**[251]

In summary, Morath was fearless in loving her patients and staff, and showed great courage in pushing back against the status quo and legal advice to create a safer environment for everyone.

Fearless Communication

You may remember that one of the questions that the research on strengths raised for us was about underperformance. What happens when people have significant, job-critical weaknesses? Now that you have worked on your listening, questioning and empathy, and developed a culture of kindness and service, we can come back to that question. Because really knowing your people will mean that you know their weaknesses as well as their strengths, which will entail some potentially difficult conversations. By really loving them, those conversations will be a lot easier.

Brené Brown, a research professor at the University of Houston, has spent the past ten years studying vulnerability, courage, authenticity and shame. Her team conducted interviews with various senior leaders and asked them a single question:

> *What, if anything, about the way people are leading today needs to change in order for leaders to be successful in a complex, rapidly changing environment where we're faced with seemingly intractable challenges and an insatiable demand for innovation?*[252]

Surprisingly, there was significant crossover between the majority of the answers, and a clear theme emerged: the need for braver leaders.

They continued the research and interviewed the leaders again to investigate why courage was so important and what the barriers to it were. Ten barriers came up in these discussions, but the issue of greatest concern was the avoidance of tough conversations.

Brown and her team felt that too many people lacked the courage and skills to give honest, productive feedback. The result of this avoidance was lower levels of trust and engagement, poorer performance and an increase in damaging behaviour, such as talking behind people's backs, backchannel communication, gossip and a lack of integrity.

We absolutely must not avoid hard conversations as leaders; we must embrace them. That is the only way to create fearless environments where people can speak up, challenge one another and feel safe to fail and learn.

In *Dare to Lead*, Brown suggests that we change our lens on difficult conversations and think of them as a 'rumble' (an old US word for a skirmish, scuffle or street fight). If you have watched *West Side Story*, you will recognise the language (although, in fact, the only overlap with *West Side Story* is the call to have courage when you face a potential conflict). Brown is not trying to get us to be aggressive, but rather to acknowledge that these exchanges will be scary and we will require courage. But courage and fear are not mutually exclusive; they go hand in hand in most tricky discussions.

To turn a difficult conversation into a rumble, you need to choose to show up to the conflict with a commitment to listen intently, show bravery in accepting your own impact and role, and be fully present and committed to serving one another and the work you are trying to achieve, rather than protecting your own reputation. You will also need to use a coaching approach to encourage the person to help you understand – for example, by saying 'Tell me more …' and 'Help me to understand …'[253]

The other crucial lesson from Brown's work on hard conversations that we all need to remember is a simple but profound statement: 'Clear is kind. Unclear is unkind.'[254] Research suggests that many of us avoid awkward conversations because we don't want to hurt other people, when arguably the opposite is true. When we are not clear and straightforward with people, we are actually being unkind to them.

If we hide the truth from people or only give them half the story in order to protect their feelings (in fact, we are often protecting our own feelings), it is unkind. Talking about people behind their backs rather than telling them to their faces is unkind. Having expectations of people which you never directly tell them is unkind. Clear is kind. Unclear is unkind.

If you have completed the challenges in this chapter, then you have already started to develop the core skills you will need in order to be fearless in conversations: listening, effective questions, empathy and positivity. Your aim is to create a culture where you can talk to people honestly and where they can also do the same to you. You want them to give you feedback about your own performance and impact and also to tell you when something goes wrong.

Imagine someone comes to you and says, 'My work is really delayed, it's not going to plan and I can't meet the deadline.' This is dreadful news for you as their leader and your instinct will be to be angry, disappointed and accusative. You will want to ask all those 'why' questions: why didn't you do it earlier/try this/fix this? It's OK to be disappointed, that is a real emotion, but not to get angry – because that is going to make the person feel unsafe, so they won't tell you the next time something goes wrong.

A helpful response is to thank them for telling you – after all, you now have some forewarning so you know what to expect and have time to prepare – and then find out what help they need to get back on track. That is the outcome you both want.

If the individual has messed things up, they probably feel awful about it already. We are all human and we all make mistakes. The best way forward (assuming this isn't a regular slip-up) is simply to help them work out how to get back to where they want to be. Find out what they need: support, time, training, coaching. You are looking to offer support in the short run for this project, but also to equip them in the long run so they don't make the same mistake again.

Brown also suggests looking at the problem 'next to each other', rather than 'across from each other'.[255] It is much safer to consider a problem together as a team, instead of asking an individual to fix it on their own.

The Magic Formula for Difficult Conversations

You may have already realised that, unfortunately, there is no quick-fix or magic formula for having difficult conversations with people. These conversations always take place in the context of relationships, so the more you know and love your people, the better chance you have of turning those discussions into something positive over the long term. A brilliant head teacher we know reminded us of this when he told us the following story:

> *A long-standing colleague had been in post for many years, and it was proving challenging getting him to realise that for his own benefit, and that of his students, it was time to stand down. For a year, I dealt with the situation as his line manager without much success. I finally decided to change the venue for our meeting and spoke to him as a friend and as someone who knew how he worked. I was also able to talk to him openly about my own experiences having come out of a similar role. It was taking that step of vulnerability and honesty that made the difference, and I don't think I could have done that successfully without knowing him as deeply as I did. I made the decision to be entirely me, rather than a line manager, and it seemed to work immediately. He has subsequently let me know that this was one of the most important 'meetings' of his life, and he is now thriving.*

Challenge 8: Fearless Communication

The next time you need to broach a difficult conversation, try following these steps and reflect on how it goes. Think about the impact of each step – did it work for you? If so, what worked well and what didn't work so well?

- Start from the philosophy that everyone wants to do their best.

- Ensure the person feels safe – this may take time. What is your role in this?

Truly human leadership protects an organization from the internal rivalries that can shatter a culture. When we have to protect ourselves from each other, the whole organization suffers. But when trust and cooperation thrive internally, we pull together and the organization grows stronger as a result.

Simon Sinek[256]

- Replace blame with curiosity to avoid creating an amygdala hijack.

- Listen extremely well – be curious and try to learn.

- What is their (and your) core purpose? Are they or can they be aligned (e.g. helping students to learn if you're a teacher, creating more innovative products)?

- Aim to connect the person to their values, passions and purpose.

- Describe a situation instead of evaluating it.

- Identify objective consequences or personal feelings rather than placing blame.

- Suggest acceptable alternatives instead of arguing about whose fault it is – explore these together and engage them by coming up with solutions.

- Remember that clear is kind, unclear is unkind.

- Rumble!

Conclusion

Fearless leadership matters enormously. It can literally save lives, as we saw in the story of Shackleton's self-sacrifice and as Katy has seen countless times in the army, where leaders bravely go headfirst into conflict and always come back for their troops. But even in a corporate setting like Google, which hires incredibly bright, self-starting individuals, psychological safety was still the biggest predictor of success. Fearless leadership matters: unsafe environments hold people back, while safe environments untap their talent and ideas and enable them to flourish.

If you are a leader, you have a responsibility to create a high-trust environment with a clear direction. It's not about being soft or easy; fearless leaders hold others accountable, embrace the difficult conversations (but without micromanaging them) and treat people like responsible adults.

Summary

- Be courageous by being vulnerable about your own limitations.

- Create a culture in which people aren't scared to speak up and be themselves.

- Beware the power of your amygdala.

- Change your lens on failure.

- Don't listen to the gremlins.

- Learn from mistakes – discuss them and fail forward.

- Be clear to be kind.

- Be brave.

Inspire Your People

Introduction to Lesson III

Researchers at the Massachusetts Institute of Technology conducted an experiment where they took a whole group of students and gave them various challenges.[257] These consisted of activities like physical tasks, memorising digits, working out word puzzles and solving spatial problems. There were three different levels of reward to help motivate the students: small monetary rewards for decent performance, larger rewards for better performance and big prizes for the top performers.

The results were surprising. As long as the task involved only mechanical skill, bonuses worked as most of us would expect: the higher the pay, the better the performance. However, once the test called for even basic cognitive skills or creativity, a larger reward actually led to poorer performance. To check the result wasn't an anomaly, the researchers recreated a similar experiment in Madurai, rural India. They offered three different groups 4, 40 or 400 rupees per game for scoring highly. They found that once again those offered the highest incentives performed the worst in every challenge area – physical skills, creativity and memory.

These results have been replicated over and over again. For simple straightforward tasks, which require no creative thought, extrinsic incentives (such as money) work exceptionally well. If you offer people more money to dig ditches, they will dig more ditches. The more you pay people to do easy mechanical tasks, the better they perform. But in situations where individuals need to solve complex tasks and use creative thinking, extrinsic motivators don't generally work. In fact, it often makes things worse. The reason is that using 'carrots' in leadership can diminish intrinsic motivation, crush creativity, crowd out social behaviour, encourage shortcuts and foster short-term thinking. Edward Deci, a behavioural scientist, looked at 128 experiments over three decades and concluded that performance-contingent rewards significantly decrease intrinsic motivation.[258] When you focus on short-term results, you do so at the expense of long-term motivation.

Several studies show that paying people to exercise, stop smoking or take their medicines produces fantastic results at first, but these changes in behaviour don't last. The healthy behaviour disappears once the incentives are removed.[259]

Warning: we are not saying that money doesn't matter or implying that paying a living wage isn't incredibly important. But as Dan Pink explains: 'Money is a motivator at work, but in a slightly strange way. If you don't pay people enough they won't be motivated. What's curious is there's another paradox here, that the best use of money as a motivator is to pay people enough to take the issue of money off the table. Pay people enough that they're not thinking about money, they're thinking about the work.'[260]

It is critical for leaders to motivate their teams so that together they can achieve their best. So, the question we want to answer in this lesson is, if financial incentives don't work as a motivator, how do leaders inspire their people to excellence?

Chapter 5

Lessons from a Small Island

Case Study: The All Blacks

Possibly the most successful sporting team of all time are the New Zealand rugby team: the All Blacks. If you look at their results from around 1900 until the present day, they have an incredible win rate of about 77%.[261] No other elite team can compare with this remarkable achievement.

But in the mid-2000s they had lost their way, both in terms of the behaviour of the players and their scores. The 2003 World Cup had not gone well, and they hadn't actually won the tournament since 1987. In 2004 they suffered a comprehensive defeat to South Africa (26–40). The loss was bad enough but what followed was worse – the players got way out of hand and were drinking too much. The culture was all wrong. Wayne Smith, assistant coach at the time, said: 'I don't want to be involved with the All Blacks if it is going to be like this.'[262]

The start of the journey to re-establishing the team's success came after this low point. A new management team was established with the complex task of working out what the problem was and then healing and rebuilding the All Blacks from the inside.

They returned to Auckland and had a three-day meeting where they set the goal to become the most dominant rugby team in the history of the world. Over the course of those three days they made some big decisions about what things were unacceptable and asked themselves some big questions about who they wanted to be: 'What is the meaning of being an All Black?' 'What does it mean to be a New Zealander?'[263] A team of ten players were given the autonomy to meet every Sunday for six weeks to agree on the standards that were to become the defining principles of the team. They agreed that they wanted a fresh culture that placed the emphasis on individual character and personal leadership. Their mantra was 'Better people make better All Blacks'.[264]

They wrote their standards and mottoes in what became known as the 'Black Book':

> *Understand the privilege.*
>
> *No one is bigger than the team.*
>
> *Leave the jersey in a better place.*
>
> *Live for the jersey, die for the jersey.*
>
> *It's not enough to be good, it's about being great.*
>
> *It's an honour not a job.*
>
> *Front up – or get lost.*
>
> *Your purpose is to add to the legacy.*[265]

This vision was (and is) powerful. The humility, expectation and responsibility that it brought lifted their game and helped to make them the best team in the world. By looking back at their roots and their values to rediscover what was most important to them, they changed the narrative they told about who they were and reconnected with what they cared about.

The Maori way of life is about understanding what has come before you and understanding that your moment of fame will be to uphold the culture and pass it on. By reminding themselves that there was a story and vision beyond the now, beyond the pitch, they gave themselves something worth playing for.

The result? Two consecutive Rugby World Cup titles in 2011 and 2015.

Purpose is the deepest dimension within us – our central core or essence – where we have a profound sense of who we are, where we came from and where we're going. Purpose is the quality we choose to shape our lives around. Purpose is a source of energy and direction.

Richard Lieder[266]

Meaning and Purpose

We would like to introduce you to two concepts that, when harnessed, will help your team to thrive: meaning and purpose. Meaning is connecting with what you care about. Purpose is knowing that what you do matters. The All Blacks' battle for identity in the 2000s is an impressive example of purpose-driven leadership.

In 2016, LinkedIn and Imperative partnered to answer some interesting questions about meaning in a global survey.[267] The survey involved over 26,000 people in forty different countries and using sixteen different languages. The results were consistent in virtually every country and industry studied, and showed a correlation between feeling a sense of purpose and feeling satisfied at work.

People who have a sense of purpose are statistically more satisfied at work. And people who are more satisfied at work perform better, both individually and as teams. Happier teams also attract more talent, so there is a positive upward spiral of better performance in the future. Have a look at the following list of all the positive impacts that a sense of purpose can have in comparison to being in an environment without purpose:

Great companies must have a noble cause. Then it's the leader's job to transform that noble cause into such an inspiring vision that it will attract the most talented people in the world to want to join it.

Steve Jobs[268]

- Better physical health.[269]

- Reduced risk of death.[270]

- Better sleep.[271]

- Higher life satisfaction.[272]

- Longer life.[273]

- Greater well-being.[274]

- More likely to feel fulfilled at work and in life.[275]

- Higher profits.[276]

- Increases student performance and motivation.[277]

- Critical for attracting millennials to work for a company and retaining them.[278]

Case study: DTE Energy

As an example of the remarkable impact that purpose can have, let's look at the story of DTE Energy.[279]

When Gerry Anderson first became the president of DTE Energy (a large American producer of gas and electricity), he did not believe in the power of higher organisational purpose. He was extremely dubious about how much it mattered; it just didn't fit into his economic understanding of the firm.

But after the financial crisis and recession of 2008, Anderson knew that he needed to change something or the business would be in trouble. He wanted his employees to work harder and be more productive, yet DTE employees were not very engaged. People were underperforming and not being the best versions of themselves, and they weren't using their intelligence and creativity to improve DTE. Anderson knew that he needed a more committed workforce, but didn't know how to get one. He had tried to shake things up by providing training, changing incentives and giving managers more control, but the results had been disappointing.

He went on a visit to another company which ran call centres, on invitation from one of the board members, Joe Robles. Working in a call centre can be pretty dull: it requires no qualifications and involves making phone call after phone call. Anderson expected to see bored individuals going through the motions. Instead he watched positive, fully engaged employees going the extra mile to make customers satisfied.

When Anderson asked how this could be, Robles answered that a leader's most important job is 'to connect the people to their purpose'. Employees at the call centre all took part in a four-day training programme when they joined and made a promise to provide extraordinary service to the people from whom they took calls.

This was then reinforced and discussed with employees at all levels, who were asked questions and shared ideas about how to fulfil their purpose. Before 2008, Anderson would have rejected the idea of higher purpose as superficial, pointless rhetoric. But he had run out of his own ideas and was beginning to question his premisses and beliefs about leadership, so he was open to new ideas.

When Anderson returned to DTE's head office, he made a video that expressed DTE's higher purpose. DTE provides energy, so he needed to connect that energy to what it was being used for and the difference it was making. The video showed DTE's truck drivers, plant operators, office workers and many others and portrayed the impact of their work on the wider community – the hospitals, schools and factories that needed the energy DTE provided.

The first group of employees to see the video gave it a standing ovation. Some of them even cried because they had never before seen how their work connected to the greater good of society. They had never articulated or envisioned the meaningful contribution that their roles had. DTE now had a purpose: 'We serve with our energy, the lifeblood of communities and the engine of progress.'[280]

And they didn't stop there. The company's leaders devoted themselves to backing that purpose. It wasn't just a slogan but was woven into everyday interactions, training programmes, meetings, conferences and also specific culture-building activities, such as film festivals and sing-alongs. Even that wouldn't have been enough if DTE's leaders hadn't really believed in the purpose themselves, but because employees concluded that the purpose was authentic, a transformation began to take place. Engagement scores rocketed. DTE received a Gallup Great Workplace Award for seven years in a row (as of 2019).[281] Financial performance improved too: DTE's stock price more than tripled from the end of 2008 to the end of 2017.

Challenge 1: Find Your Why

The objective for this challenge is to work out the clear 'why' for your team. To find out what your 'noble cause' is. We suggest you do this in three stages.

1. People

Get as many people from your company or team together as possible. Depending on the size of your team this could be over dinner or in smaller focus groups, or you could collect stories and ideas. (It might make a difference if you can eat together while you discuss this.) The more people involved, the better because it will increase engagement and make it more likely that people will buy into your purpose.

2. Questions

You need to ask numerous questions. What these questions are will depend on what your team does. Here are some suggestions:

- What is the purpose of our team?

- Why do we exist?

- Who benefits from what we do?

- How do they benefit?

- In what ways does our team make society better?

- What are the ripple effects we have on other people and teams?

- If we didn't exist, what would be missing?

- If we won an award in the future, what would we win it for and what would people say about us?

- If we were the best team we could possibly be, what would we achieve? Why is that important?

As you and your team consider the question of how your jobs contribute to society, you may want to consider the UN Sustainable Development Goals for inspiration.[282]

3. Learning from Others

Have a look at the mission statements of other organisations and discuss as a team which of them excites you most and why. Here are some to get you started.

- Making doing good, doable (We Organisation).

- Capture and share the world's moments (Instagram).

- Reach for new heights and reveal the unknown (NASA).

- Bring inspiration and innovation to every athlete in the world (Nike).

- Accelerate the adoption and everyday use of reusable products (Chilly Water Bottles).

- Accelerate the world's transition to sustainable energy (Tesla).

- Changing business for good (Virgin Unite).

- To make natural, delicious, food and drink that helps people live well and die old (Innocent).

- The happiness of all its members, through their worthwhile and satisfying employment in a successful business (John Lewis).

Building a Purpose Statement

A vast amount has been written about the importance of having a vision and a mission which will inspire and uplift your team.[283] The literature on leadership tends to distinguish between the mission and the vision. The difference can often be confusing as there is so much overlap, so we are just going to focus on how to create a purpose statement.

Your purpose statement needs to paint a picture of where your team is heading – sometimes called a 'north star'. You need to set out where the company or team aspires to be and where you want a community, or the world, to be as a result of your services.

To create a purpose statement you need to answer the question of why your team or organisation exists. Leadership expert Simon Sinek, in his book *Start with Why*, points out that many leaders focus on *what* they do, whereas great leaders (whether that is Nelson Mandela, Martin Luther King Jr or successful companies such as Apple) focus on *why* they do it.[284] They focus on the why, the how and then the what, rather than the other way around.

As we have seen in the stories of the All Blacks and DTE Energy, it is the bigger purpose, the why, that motivates people to give their all for their teams. A major study of ethical work by Howard Gardner, Mihaly Csikszentmihalyi and William Damon showed that those doing what they call 'good work' – defined as 'work of expert quality that benefits the broader society' – consistently show high levels of job satisfaction.[285]

In order to work well, your purpose statement therefore needs to be:

- Visible – see yourself on the top of the mountain.

- Future-looking – at least five years.

- Audacious – think big.

- Descriptive – a single statement.

But, most importantly, your purpose needs to make you want to get out of bed in the morning and give your best to making it a reality!

Imagine what would happen if every person was connected to purpose at work – to a job that mattered to them, their company, and the world. Imagine how much more productive and successful they'd be. Think of what we could collectively accomplish.

You have the power to make work more meaningful. We can all create engagement and inspiration – by connecting purpose with work.

LinkedIn and Imperative[286]

Challenge 2: Create a Purpose Statement

1   Using the thoughts from challenge 1, write down all your ideas for a purpose statement for your team.

2   You then need to test it by asking:

  - Is it visible? According to Simon Sinek in his video 'Why Leaders Eat Last', we are visual animals and very dependent on our eyes, so a vision needs to be something you can all envisage and imagine.

  - Is it long term? About five years tends to be the suggested length of time.

  - Is it audacious? It needs to be challenging and inspiring.

  - Is it short and memorable?

  - Does it have social impact?

3   Now do the t-shirt test on your statement:

  - Would your purpose fit on a t-shirt?

  - Would you feel proud to wear it?

  - Would all your team wear it?

  - Would the people you serve be inspired if they saw your team wearing it?

  - Would they want to buy one?

Once you have a purpose statement that you all believe in, you will have to think about how to make it real. We will consider that in the following case study and the next challenge.

Case Study: PepsiCo

Indra Nooyi has been consistently ranked among the world's 100 most powerful women.[287] The former CEO of PepsiCo (2006–2018) made her name by turning it into one of the most successful food and drink companies in the world – with an 80% growth in sales under her leadership. Nooyi is one of only a small number of female CEOs of Standard and Poor's 500 Companies and has led over 26,000 employees.

When Nooyi started as CEO she created a new mission for the company: performance with purpose. This purpose included making healthier foods, protecting the planet and empowering people. For example, while many companies were focusing on new flavours, she concentrated on reducing the salt and fat content in classic products. PepsiCo also developed a 'Good for You' food category and Nooyi made strategic mergers with brands which produced healthier food options (such as Naked Drinks and Quaker Oats). She also employed PepsiCo's first ever chief scientific officer and director of global health policy to help develop their ranges.[288] She also focused on improving the company's environmental impact – for example, their potato farmers decreased water consumption by 50% in five years.[289]

In terms of empowering staff, Nooyi was keen to create a culture where everyone could bring their whole selves to work. She believes that this kind of culture is good for staff but also good for performance because it attracts talent, increases retention and enables creativity. Practically, it involved giving staff more autonomy to solve their own problems (for example, by developing a new recycling and upcycling process in Arkansas) and coming up with new crisp flavours and products (seaweed in China and cuttlefish in Thailand!).[290]

During her time as CEO, PepsiCo also improved their employee benefits such as flexitime, day-care centres and generous maternity and paternity leave. This is all part of Nooyi's passion to ensure that the company has a valuable impact on the world and people's lives through the normal course of business. This includes empowering women – for example, by building gender-segregated factory floors in Saudi Arabia so they can hire women while still abiding by the country's strict gender regulation policies.[291]

One story about Nooyi that stands out is when she visited India to see her mother. During her stay, visitors congratulated Nooyi's mother on her daughter's success as CEO. This made Nooyi reflect on the power of gratitude and the fact that parents rarely get recognition for the children they raise. Nooyi took action and wrote more than 400 letters to the parents of her leadership team, saying thank you for the role they had played in raising them. Some of her senior team reported back, 'My God, this is the best thing that's happened to my parents. And it's the best thing that's happened to me.'[292]

Nooyi's purpose for PepsiCo of making a valuable impact in the world was incredibly broad, but it wasn't just about paying lip service to corporate social responsibility. She believed in the purpose and worked it out in specific actions, key decisions and appointments. Her success models the power of providing a clear sense of purpose, empowering your people to reach it and saying thank you.

Challenge 3: Making Your Purpose Real

1   What actions can you take to show that your purpose is not just a string of words? Note them down.

2   Which of these would have the most impact on your team? On the wider community?

3   Choose one action to discuss further with your team.

In Discussion with Amy Edmondson, Adam Grant and Amy Wrzesniewski

If we could invite three experts onto the couch for a breakfast TV show and interview them about purpose, we would choose Amy Edmondson, Adam Grant and Amy Wrzesniewski. We didn't manage to get them together on TV for an interview, but we did ask each of them what their advice would be on helping your team find a sense of purpose and meaning.

Amy Edmondson

We introduced you to Amy Edmondson in Chapter 4. She advises that finding your purpose might not mean changing career, but rather thinking about how the work you are already doing makes a positive contribution to society.

You might be tempted to think that this was enormously dependent on your choice of career. That nurses, firefighters and charity workers, for example, would easily connect their jobs to a greater meaning, whereas hedge fund managers and accountants might find it harder. Remarkably, this is not the case. In fact, finding a sense of purpose is far more about how you view your job than what your role actually is. This is exemplified by the well-known story of the bricklayers.

> *Three bricklayers are asked, 'What are you doing?'*
>
> *The first says, 'I am laying bricks.'*
>
> *The second says, 'I am building a church.'*
>
> *The third says, 'I am building the house of God.'*
>
> *The first bricklayer has a job. The second has a career. The third has a calling.*[293]

The third bricklayer has found a sense of purpose. Edmondson has examined the impact of purpose by looking at the performance of cardiac surgery teams as they learned a new system for operating on hearts. It was an ideal situation to examine why some teams perform better and learn faster than others, because the surgical teams used the same protocols and technology and received the same training programme for the new procedure. She looked at 660 patients across sixteen medical centres.[294]

If you had to pick out which team would perform the best, you might have looked at which surgeons had the most experience or which teams had the most impressive educational backgrounds. Surprisingly, these were not the determining factors of high performance. It was the teams which focused on (a) how much the new procedure was helping the patients, (b) how their role was contributing to the success of the operation (whatever role that was) and (c) the excitement of doing something new in medicine that significantly outperformed teams which had more impressive education and experience.

The most successful teams also felt psychologically safe to question each other, even if they were the most junior individuals, because they all felt valued members of the group – another factor that enhances how meaningful people find their work.

These results have been shown time and time again. In a different experiment, some students were asked to reflect on the purpose behind what they were studying.[295] Incredibly, this small action led them to double the amount of time they spent studying for an upcoming exam. They worked harder on tedious maths problems (even when given the option to watch entertaining videos instead) and their reports and grades improved.

When we asked Amy for her top piece of advice on finding purpose, she said: 'The key is to ask, and try to answer, the question of why what we do matters – the purpose question.' That purpose question has been at the forefront of many of our minds during the COVID-19 pandemic. People have striven to connect to a higher purpose: neighbours have mobilised community support, artists have found new ways to create and inspire, small business owners have sacrificially cared for their employees and customers, and parents have embarked on new adventures in home education.

Adam Grant

Adam Grant has been recognised both as Wharton Business School's top-rated professor for seven straight years and as one of the world's ten most influential management thinkers.[296] We asked him, what three things would you advise a leader to do to help bring more meaning and purpose into their team members' working life? Here is what he suggested:

1   Ask them about the most meaningful project they have ever worked on and what would make their current work more meaningful. (This is all about identifying core values – see Chapter 1 for other ideas on how to find out about your team's values.)

2   Highlight who benefits from their work and make sure they have a chance to meet, and receive direct feedback from, those people.

3   At staff meetings, invite people to share stories about the ways the team has made a difference in the lives of others.

Another piece of advice is to see if you can connect the parts of your job (or your team's jobs) that don't feel meaningful to a core value. For example, Grant says that answering emails can seem trivial, but when he remembers that it is connected to one of his core values (responsiveness) it takes on a new meaning. Instead of focusing on the boring aspects of replying, his attention shifts to the meaningful act of helping.

Amy Wrzesniewski

Another top tip is to 'craft your job' so that you spend more time doing things that align with your values. Amy Wrzesniewski, a Yale professor specialising in finding meaning, recommends thinking about how you can change your current work in small but meaningful ways to enhance its connection to your core values. She calls this 'job crafting'. You can get your boss involved in this and you can help your team to do this too; if you get it right, you're pretty much guaranteed to improve their performance.[297]

Wrzesniewski suggested to us (and she writes extensively about this in Jane Dutton and Gretchen Spreitzer's *How to Be a Positive Leader*[298]) that there are three aspects of your job that you can redesign: your tasks, your relationships and your thoughts.

1   Task crafting. You can adjust the time you spend on certain tasks and redesign aspects of your role that are flexible. Think back to Chapter 1 and ask yourself, 'What are my strengths?' and 'How can I use these strengths better?' So, if you have a keen attention to detail you might take on more operational tasks, or spend time sharing your more detailed input with colleagues and let others tackle the big picture.

2   Relational crafting. It is important, where possible, to dedicate your energy to forming meaningful connections with others and spend less time in situations that drag you down. For example, in a 2003 study, Wrzesniewski and her colleagues instructed hospital cleaning staff to interact with patients and families in kind and nurturing ways. Although this was outside the official scope of their jobs, it strengthened their sense of meaning and purpose at work.[299]

3   Cognitive crafting is very similar to Amy Edmondson's advice. It is about changing your perspective on the things you already do. For example, a shop assistant in Starbucks doesn't just brew coffee; instead they might consider how they bring customers joy as they start their day. Even when you can't see a positive way of reframing a task, you can try to view it as a learning opportunity and be curious about what you can gain or learn from it. One study found that when people are motivated by curiosity, rather than fear or obligation, they feel more satisfied about their accomplishments.[300]

Three decades of research suggests that people who engage in job crafting are more satisfied with their jobs, perform better, experience greater happiness and are less likely to take days off or quit.[301] If your manager isn't too keen to chat about meaning and purpose, you could get a group of colleagues together for a communal activity that feels meaningful, which will also increase your sense of purpose. For example, as part of Katy's PhD research, she asked schools to come up with different ways to boost their well-being, and they suggested some brilliant ideas that also increased their sense of meaning at work. One group of teachers decided to coach each other, which connected with their values of building positive relationships, caring for others and service. In another school, teachers identified kindness, community and generosity as their values and then decided to set up a scheme of anonymous random acts of kindness. They shared stories of these secret kindness missions on a WhatsApp group.

Challenge 4: Connecting with Purpose

1   Meet each member of your team and ask them about the most meaningful project they have ever worked on and what would make their current work more meaningful.

2   Invite somebody who has benefitted from your team's work to talk at a meeting.

3   At your next staff meeting, invite people to share stories about the ways that the team has made a difference in the lives of others.

Case Study: *Ubuntu*

Owen Eastwood is a world-leading performance culture expert and former South African fast bowler. He is also a former lawyer and has worked with the world's elite teams in different sports and organisations, focusing on transforming their culture.[302] He has worked with the South African cricket team, Manchester City and Chelsea Football Club, the England football team, the military command group of NATO, the Scotland rugby team, top investment banks and accounting firms.

A pretty impressive CV! What is intriguing is that none of these organisations could be described as 'fluffy'. Quite the opposite; they are brutally competitive environments where performance is everything and results are immediately measurable in score lines or share prices. If Eastwood's advice didn't impact on performance, if it was just a 'nice' added extra, he wouldn't have been employed. Eastwood suggests that high-performing teams are 'vision driven': 'They convert their sense of purpose into a compelling vision – of what success looks like and how they can achieve it – which, in turn, drives the strategy and the design of the team culture.'[303] Crucially, they also connect their vision to their authentic beliefs, heritage and history. It is this purpose that provides a pathway to leaving a legacy.

Eastwood put this into practice when working with the South African cricket team, the Proteas, in 2008. When he began working with the Proteas the side was at number four in the world rankings. Eastwood helped them discover their 'why' – what the South Africans call their 'ubuntu'. According to James Kerr, 'Ubuntu means we send out ripples from us to the wider community: our actions affect everyone, not just us.'[304] You therefore need to be the best you can be in order to enable the community around you to improve. You play for something greater than yourself.

On 28 August 2012, with ubuntu as their mantra, the Proteas became the first team to be world number one in all three formats of the game. When Morne Morkel retired in 2018 (having become only the fifth South African bowler to reach 300 Test wickets), he

> *He who has a why to live for can bear almost any how.*
> **Friedrich Nietzsche**[305]

looked back and reflected on the powerful effect that Eastwood's work had had on the whole team. He believed it was the catalyst for transforming their culture because 'it connected people to their own challenges and the high-performance culture created a sustainable winning environment'.[306]

Challenge 5: Job Crafting

The objective of this exercise is to bring more meaning into your own and your team members' roles without actually changing jobs. Meet up with each of your team individually and ask them:

- How do the various parts of your role benefit others and enhance their well-being?

- How can you prioritise the parts of your role that help others or are meaningful?

The purpose of life is not to be happy. It is to be useful, to be honorable, to be compassionate, to have it make some difference that you have lived and lived well.

Ralph Waldo Emerson [307]

- Think about which parts of your job are least meaningful. How could you connect these parts of your job to your values?

- What small changes could you make to your role which would allow you to spend more time doing things you find meaningful?

Case Study: KPMG

As an example of the remarkable impact that purpose can have, let's look at the story of KPMG.[308] KPMG is a very large firm, employing over 200,000 people, specialising in tax, audit and advisory services. They basically inspect the finances of other large companies. Doesn't sound that exciting, does it? Certainly not as meaningful as being a doctor, a firefighter or a marine biologist saving turtles. However, they decided to do some investigations into the impact of purpose on their employees and what they found was interesting.

Getting their leaders to talk about purposeful work had a significant impact on their employees' sense of company pride and work satisfaction, and how long they stayed at the company, but how did they do it? How did they take what on the surface looked like a pretty boring set of operations and persuade people who worked there that it had a higher purpose?

- They conducted hundreds of employee interviews.

- They produced corporate posters and a 'We Shape History' video.

- They invited employees everywhere to share their own stories of purpose-driven work. The results exceeded all expectations: they collected more than 40,000 stories. These stories were then featured in a 'higher purpose' initiative.

- The firm taught the power of purpose to their leaders.

People began to see their work differently. They weren't just auditing or sorting out tax; they were, for example, making important research in the Antarctic possible through the financial advice they gave the National Science Foundation.

Weaving Purpose into Every Day

Once you have your purpose statement, the challenge is to ensure that it seeps into the culture of your entire organisation, that it is written in your DNA, that people buy into it. In the story of KPMG, they did this in multiple ways – videos, interviews, films, meetings and campaigns.

This might seem slightly over the top, slightly corny, even off-putting. However, if it is authentic and embodied by the leader then it can be transformative. In order to weave your purpose into the whole culture, you need to name the specific behaviours and characteristics you want people to embody to reach that purpose. This might be in the form of mottoes, catchphrases or maxims.

In *The Culture Code*, Daniel Coyle describes some incredibly successful restaurants in New York run by Danny Meyer. Some of their catchphrases are: 'athletic hospitality', 'loving problems', 'finding the yes', 'making the charitable assumption' and 'we take care of people'.[309] As a leader, Meyer is very intentional about embedding his catchphrases and priorities throughout all of his restaurants.

This may seem like a simple set of rules, but research has shown that they can stimulate complex and intricate behaviours. They are more than just mottoes; they act as powerful reminders that enable us to make quick decisions when faced with different scenarios. This is similar to the way honeybees operate – they are able to run complex operations from a set of simple rules. Many top leaders focus on creating purpose and key behaviours, and then permeating the environment with things that link the two. The All Blacks did this when they wrote their Black Book.

Coyle refers to research done by *Inc. Magazine*, which asked executives at 600 companies to estimate the percentage of their employees who could name their top three priorities. The executive predicted that 64% would be able to name them. When *Inc.* asked the workforce, only 2% could.[310] Don't worry about being over the top – you need to over-communicate priorities. Paint them on the walls, drop them into conversations and meetings, test them regularly.

Stories are also powerful. When Eastwood was doing research to mark the centenary of the start of the Great War, he discovered a story about an All Black named Andrew 'Son' White who was a survivor of several of the worst campaigns of the war.[311] He was eventually sent home with shell shock in 1918. Instead of going to a mental hospital, he returned to his family home in Invercargill and rebuilt his life through rugby. He played his first club match at the age of 25 in 1919, won his first cap for the All Blacks in 1921 and went on to become one of the star performers in the 'Invincibles' side captained by the legendary Cliff Porter.

Eastwood passed the story on to the All Blacks because one of the defining features of their team culture is the inspiration they draw from the players who have worn the jersey before them. This is how they reinforce their purpose and keep the sense of doing justice to the All Blacks shirt – by honouring those who have worn it in the past.

The British military also have lots of mottoes in order to define and create their culture:

- Be the best (Army).

- *Tenax Propositi* – tenacious of purpose (HMS *Bangor*).

- *Per ardua ad astra* – through adversity to the stars (Royal Air Force).

- I spread my wings and keep my promise (Royal Air Force – 14 Squadron).

- Serve to lead (Royal Military Academy Sandhurst).

- *Qui audet adipiscitur* – who dares wins (Special Air Service).

Challenge 6: Weaving Purpose

This challenge is about finding the best ways to weave your purpose into the life of your team. This will differ depending on your context, but here are some exercises to get you started.

Exercise 1: Write a 'Black Book'

Each time a new player joins the All Blacks, they are presented with a small black book, which is filled with pages of jerseys from the team's first tour in 1905 until the present day. It also includes statements about the values, principles, ethos and character of the team. The pages at the end of the book are blank, so each new player can add to the legacy. The questions below are to help you begin to create your own Black Book:

1   Think back to your purpose statement. What are the behaviours people need to live by in your team if that purpose is to be fulfilled?

2   Consider all the stakeholders who are impacted by your team (such as teachers, pupils, parents, managers and the wider community) and put them in order of importance.

3   Ask your team to suggest mottoes or catchphrases which summarise who they want to be as a team.

4   Gather stories about previous inspirational team members – what were they like? What made them awesome?

5   Try out your mottoes in meetings and conversations – see which resonate or stick. Note down your reflections and also write the mottoes that stick in your Black Book.

Exercise 2: Make Your Purpose Visible

You need to live out your purpose statement, but also make it visible so the whole organisation knows about it. Remember that you can't overdo this! Many of the most successful organisations go completely over the top – they are not subtle. They use visual aids, put photos of successful team members on the walls, make videos, paint quotes on the walls, tell stories about past team members and so on. Write down your ideas about how to make your purpose more visible.

Case Study: The Wright Brothers

We started by considering the difference purpose made to the All Blacks, and we are going to finish by telling the full story of the Wright brothers. At the turn of the twentieth century, at the height of the race to invent the first piloted aircraft, Samuel Pierpont Langley had everything going for him. The War Department awarded him US$50,000 and his employer, the Smithsonian, another US$20,000. He held a seat at Harvard and had great connections around the world. He hired the best minds that money could buy to join his team and was determined that he would achieve the first successful piloted flight.

Orville and Wilbur Wright, on the other hand, had only the proceeds from their bicycle shop and nobody on their team had a college education – not even Orville or Wilbur. And yet, on 17 December 1903, the Wright brothers beat Langley and became the first to achieve powered, sustained, controlled human flight. The Wright brothers went down in history; no one remembers Samuel Pierpont Langley.

Simon Sinek retells this moment in history in his book *Start with the Why* to remind us of the incredible importance of purpose.[312] The Wright brothers were driven by a sense of purpose. They believed that if they could solve the problem of piloted flight, they could change the world. Their belief inspired others and attracted a team of people around them who were also motivated to change the world. And with that intrinsic motivator of purpose their team worked for them with their blood, sweat and tears. The team members tell stories of how every time the Wright brothers went out they would have to bring five sets of parts because that's how many times they would crash before supper! Langley's team worked for the pay cheque and Langley himself wanted to be rich and famous. They were extrinsically motivated by the imagined rewards of their success. The day the Wright brothers took flight, Langley quit.

Conclusion

Having a clear sense of purpose doesn't make you infallible or guarantee you permanent success, as the All Blacks would attest after losing to England 7–19 in the 2019 World Cup semi-finals (the first match they have lost in a World Cup since 2007). But it makes an enormous difference. Other teams from around the world have tried to learn lessons from the success of the All Blacks. Connecting individuals' values to the wider team purpose and then to the bigger contribution the team makes to the world is a powerful motivator. As Dan Pink argues in *Drive*, we are fundamentally 'purpose maximisers', not 'profit maximisers'.[313]

Summary

- Find your unique 'why' as a team.

- What is your noble cause?

- Make that purpose visible.

- Connect individuals' roles to their purpose.

All men dream, but not equally. Those who dream by night in the dusty recesses of their minds, wake in the day to find that it was vanity: but the dreamers of the day are dangerous men, for they may act on their dreams with open eyes, to make them possible.

T. E. Lawrence[314]

Make a way out of no way.

Barack Obama [315]

Chapter 6

Lessons from Beneath the Water

Empowerment and Excellence in Schools

When Anthony Seldon took over Wellington College in 2005, it was described by the *Independent* newspaper as 'scandal-ridden, academically poor, stuck in its boys-only past',[316] and there had been a raft of tabloid stories about the school's bullying culture. Although much of this criticism was unfair, there was certainly a real challenge ahead for Seldon.

When he retired, after nearly ten years as master, he had taken the college up 256 places in the league tables[317] and overseen an enormous cultural change, making the school synonymous with well-being and happiness rather than bullying.[318] We interviewed him to find out what the key to successful cultural change had been.

Seldon described the key challenge as being about empowerment, efficacy and agency: 'The student body had a view of school authority as an enemy, a denier of their freedom, and of school as a place where policies and rules were inflicted on them from above.' He wanted to change that culture from one where the students saw things as being done 'to them' to one where things were done 'for them' – that is, where everybody would start taking responsibility for themselves and their futures.

In terms of bullying, there was a particularly dangerous cycle of boys feeling that because they had suffered from older year groups when they were younger, it was their turn to perpetuate that cycle of unkindness when they reached the top of the school. 'It did us no harm,' they said. 'It's the only way you get respect from younger years.'

Seldon initially considered going in with an entirely top-down solution, but then decided that he needed to find a way for students to own the change. He went through a process of setting clear expectations of what was not acceptable: 'I told the boys that if they bullied anyone else it would be the equivalent of bullying me and the consequences would be severe.' But he increasingly involved them in coming up with ideas about how to change behaviours and attitudes and create a vision for what they wanted the school to be like. When things went wrong the focus was on restorative justice and healing, not just on punishment.

It was a similar journey with improving grades. Rather than the school forcing and punishing students to be better, Seldon set high expectations and then encouraged the students to take responsibility for what they wanted from their lives and future. He didn't see them as 'passive widgets' in an academic machine but aimed to increase agency, making them the authors of their own narrative. Seldon felt that one key challenge was 'empowerment'. He approached this by focusing on changing the culture. One example of this was the increase in self-assessment, encouraging the students to take an honest look at where they were at that moment, where they wanted to be and then setting their own goals for which they would be held accountable. He said: 'The leadership challenge was about co-creating a vision that students and staff believed in, raising expectations and creating a culture of self-efficacy where individuals felt empowered to be active partners in helping to sculpt their own futures for themselves.'

From Power to Empower

Seldon believes that the main challenge in changing the culture of the school was to do with building self-efficacy, so that individuals felt empowered to help create their own futures. It was a shift from power being entirely top down to a partnership in which the students felt more empowered and committed to the vision.

We introduced you to Adam Grant in earlier chapters. He has spent a lot of time over the past few years studying the changing nature of power and has published a book called *Power Moves* based on interviews he conducted at the World Economic Forum in Davos in 2018.[319] He argues that the nature of power is changing. Whereas power used to be about hierarchy, respect and the physical goods which came with power, it is now much more about ideas, networks and influence. It has become easier to both gain power and lose it – influence is more fragile. Consider an Instagram vlogger with 15 million followers who can change the habits of a generation, or the impact that social media had in turning Greta Thunberg from an unknown teenager with a social conscience into a globally renowned eco-warrior.

A 'leader-follower' model has been dominant over centuries of human progress and has worked exceptionally well when work was mainly physical in nature. The model starts to fall apart in the modern context, where a lot of the emphasis is on cognitive abilities and less on manual work. Another problem with the leader-follower model is that success mainly hinges on one outstanding leader (or a small set of strong leaders); everybody else is treated like a follower, feels like a follower and acts like a follower. Decision-making authority does not percolate all the way down, and while followers may feel some ownership of parts of their work, there is little incentive for them to give work their full passion, energy and intellect. If you are mainly taking orders and getting things done, you are not functioning at 100% of your potential and are unlikely to feel inspired. It can lead to passive acceptance of orders and a lack of initiative.

We want to empower people through a leader-leader model.[320] This approach recognises that leadership isn't something a privileged few have bestowed upon them; instead, it asserts that we are all leaders, no matter what our title is, and we all influence those around us and create ripples in the lives of others. What makes us a leader is whether we accept that power and use it for good.

The main difference between a leader-leader and leader-follower system is how decisions are taken. For a leader-follower model, decisions are made and sent down. In a leader-leader system, whoever is best placed to make a decision can take it at the time.

> *Leadership is communicating to people their worth and potential so clearly that they are inspired to see it in themselves.*
>
> **Stephen Covey**[321]

Case Study: UK Manufacturing

In a study of over 300 UK manufacturing firms over two decades, researchers tracked the impact of management practices on productivity. What they found was that operation programmes such as just-in-time management, advanced manufacturing technology, supply chain partnering and total quality management didn't lead to any consistent gains in productivity.[322]

What did? Empowerment programmes. Productivity spiked when companies gave responsibility for operations to individuals and teams instead of leaving decisions to management. The effect was magnified when staff were given extensive training, leading to a 9% boost in value added per employee.[323] Why? Because employees were more likely to step up and fix mistakes, rather than saying, 'It's not my job'. Employees were also more disposed to prevent mistakes because they took the initiative to learn what caused them in the first place.

This links to the broader benefits of empowering your people:

- Builds self-efficacy – the belief that you can succeed.[324]

- Builds collective efficacy – the belief that your team or organisation can succeed.[325]

- Improves engagement.[326]

- Commitment to the organisation.[327]

- Lowers turnover.[328]

- Improves creativity.[329]

- Improves well-being and health.[330]

- Improves the bottom line and productivity.[331]

- Boosts morale.[332]

Lessons from Under the Sea – Empowerment

Captain L. David Marquet had trained for over a decade in the navy to reach the position of captain. He had put in the thousands of hours required to become an expert in military tactics, naval expertise and submarine knowledge. For the previous twelve months he had devoted himself to knowing every detail and nuance of the particular nuclear submarine he had been given to command. He flew out to Pearl Harbour and was ready to command, ready to lead it to excellence, ready to direct his team's every action and instil obedience.[333]

Then he received a last-minute change of instructions and was told he was needed to command the USS *Santa Fe* nuclear submarine instead. The *Santa Fe* was struggling: retention was the lowest in the US navy's fleet, the working environment was toxic, morale was low and an inspection was due shortly. Marquet's last year of studying was irrelevant – every nuclear submarine is different. He now had two weeks to learn the new sets of plans and handbooks. It was literally impossible for him to assimilate all the information required in time.

A submarine is a high-stress environment. The leader is constantly visible, it is crucial that everyone does their job and there is no margin for error. There was no way that Marquet could lead the crew in the same way he had led previous teams. He couldn't be the all-knowing leader who gave every command, because he didn't know the sub well enough – they would see straight through him.

*It is not the genius at
the top giving directions
that makes people great.
It is great people that
make the guy at the top
look like a genius.*

Simon Sinek[334]

One incident revealed this to him clearly and changed his view of leadership forever.[335] Marquet was running a simulation exercise to test the crew's ability to find and repair faults in combat conditions. They had shut down the reactor and the crew were responding in just the right way, shifting power to the auxiliary engine and coming shallow. Keen to make the simulation harder, to really test them – and also to improve his leadership credibility and not be seen as too 'soft' – he gave a command to increase speed from 'ahead 1/3' to 'ahead 2/3'.

Being a naval commander, Marquet was used to absolute obedience from his subordinates and they duly passed the order down the chain of command. But nothing happened. There was no increase in speed. Surprised by their lack of respect and instant obedience he turned to the helmsman, demanding to know why they weren't carrying out his order. There was no 2/3 speed setting on the auxiliary engine. Why hadn't they told him rather than the repeating and passing the impossible order down the chain of command? Because Marquet was the captain and he had given an order.

This changed everything for Marquet. He became determined to change the whole culture of the *Santa Fe* and his own leadership style and to stop giving unnecessary orders. No longer were submariners required to ask permission to take an action; instead they could say, 'I intend to ...' and a supervisor could say they approved it.[336] This phrase showed the crew that they were being actively involved in the running of their submarine and gave them permission to use all their knowledge and expertise to make the right decisions rather than blindly following orders.

The culture was different within twenty-four hours and the change was palpable, although it took a few years for the shift to be fully implemented. He trusted his people and gave them control. The only parameters were that decisions were (1) competent and (2) the right thing to do given their mission. The only decision he didn't delegate was the final order to launch a nuclear missile. That was his ethical and moral responsibility as the captain.

With decisions decentralised, it became even more critical that every crew member understood the submarine's purpose and values. On the *Santa Fe*, an announcement was made every time they passed a sunken submarine – a reminder of how important their role was in protecting and serving their country and how critical it was that they did their work excellently. Praise was also important, so any time a crew member made a great decision it was announced to their division as soon as possible afterwards. High standards, empowerment and gratitude. A powerful way to inspire your people to excellence.

Under Marquet's command, the *Santa Fe* went within one year from below average in inspections to receiving the highest inspection grade ever seen.

Challenge 1: Leader, Leader

1   For a week, look out for any time your team or colleagues say any of these disempowering phrases:

 - Can I ... ?

 - I'd like to ...

 - What should I do about?

 - Do you reckon we should ...?

 - Do you mind if ...?

 - May I try this?

Try to change the language so that people are free to make the decisions themselves and just tell you what they intend to do, rather than asking permission.

2   Try changing meetings for a fortnight so that rather than you telling people what you want them to do, you ask them:

 - What they want to achieve.

 - How it fits into the bigger purpose.

 - What support or information they need to achieve it.

Leadership should mean giving control rather than taking control and creating leaders rather than followers.

L. David Marquet[337]

How to Empower

The story of cultural change in Wellington College and the USS *Santa Fe*, combined with Adam Grant's interviews and research on power, have hopefully convinced you that in a world where many more jobs are dominated by cognitive tasks and everyone needs to make decisions, the leader-follower approach is ill-suited. We won't be able to inspire our people unless we empower them.

The key skills of empowerment are ones that you have learned already in this book:

- Active listening so that your team feel you are interested in their ideas and opinions.

- Asking effective questions rather than always providing the answers or telling everyone your ideas.

- Knowing your people's strengths and then crafting tasks in a way that plays to those strengths.

- Showing compassion and service in a way that will release oxytocin and enable your team to be their creative best.

- Creating psychological safety and having robust discussions so that your team are brave enough to share their ideas, take risks and challenge the status quo.

- Providing a clear sense of purpose so that your people are inspired to give their best to that vision.

Another specific action you can take to empower your people is to focus on developing them. One Gallup poll found that 87% of millennials (and 69% of non-millennials) view development as important in their jobs.[338] Assign new duties, rotate jobs, let the role grow, give people time to further their education and send them on training courses.

Case Study: Zappos

Zappos is an online clothing and shoes retailer. CEO Tony Hsieh joined the firm in 2000 and had two goals he wanted them to achieve by 2010: US$1 billion in sales and to be named as one of Fortune's 'best companies to work for'. He believed that the key to both of these was delivering outstanding customer service.

Recalling how he felt taking on the position, Hsieh says: 'It was about: What kind of company can we create where we all want to be there, including me? How can we create such a great environment, where employees get so much out of it they would do it for free?'[339]

To achieve this, he wanted to build a culture where all employees bought into this vision of outstanding customer service and felt happy and empowered. In 2004, they asked all their employees what Zappos meant to them and created an annual 'culture book' of testimonials. In 2006 they adopted ten core values, which Hsieh details in his book, *Delivering Happiness*:[340]

1   *Deliver WOW through service*

2   *Embrace and drive change*

3   *Create fun and a little weirdness*

4   *Be adventurous, creative and open-minded*

5   *Pursue growth and learning*

6   *Build open and honest relationships with communication*

7   *Build a positive team and family spirit*

8   *Do more with less*

9   *Be passionate and determined*

10 *Be humble*[341]

In 2008, Zappos reached their first goal of US$1 billion in gross merchandise sales (two years early) and in 2009 they made Forbes' best companies list.[342] Hsieh puts their success entirely down to the culture. Zappos employees are fiercely proud of their culture and there is incredibly low turnover of staff. Workers not only say they love their work in all the surveys, but also that they care deeply about others in the community – there are numerous heart-warming stories of the way employees have gone out of their way to look after customers. For example, one employee found out on a phone call that the pair of shoes being ordered was for a little girl going into hospital and sent a whole package of goodies to cheer her up along with the shoes.[343]

This links into one of the crucial aspects of the culture – employees feel empowered. In the Zappos call centre, reps aren't given a script to answer the phone (as most call centres do) and aren't rewarded on the basis of how many calls they take, but instead they are told to spend as much time as they want with each customer. Zappos want their reps to let their true personalities shine through during the calls and to be themselves. It is this freedom to spend as long as they deem right talking to customers which means that they get to know them so well, find out about their lives and end up both enjoying their work and delivering outstanding customer service. They are also empowered to be generous – a rep found out that a pair of shoes was for someone's dad who was learning to walk again after treatment and decided to upgrade delivery to overnight so they would be there for his first therapist appointment. The customer was blown away by the thoughtfulness and generosity of this gesture.[344]

This level of empowerment works so well because Zappos has such a clear sense of purpose that everyone buys into. Employees are motivated and inspired to give their best and then supported and set free to work hard at achieving it.

Challenge 2: Empowering Your Team

1   After reading about Zappos, what would you or your team like to change about your culture or environment?

2   How can you further empower your team?

3   Is there any further training, resources or support your team need in order to feel empowered?

Lessons from Beneath the Surface – Perseverance for Excellence

You're upside down. You've already been under water for twenty seconds. You've completed five 360-degree rotations. You're so dizzy you feel like you might vomit. Your muscles feel like they're being knifed with the burning stabs of lactic acid. Your lungs are about to burst. You really can't go on. But on you must go: you can't come up for breath for another twenty seconds and nor can your partner. When you do finally get some magical oxygen, you'll be back under again within ten seconds for more spinning and leg switching until you finally reach the end of your routine, four minutes later.

A synchronised swimming routine is a bit like running a mile at full speed, only much worse, as you only get to snatch ten-second breaths for one-quarter of your race. The training is brutal: swim as fast as you can for seventy-five metres under water, have a quick break and then do it again and again and again. Pool sessions are considered precious because of the cost of hiring a pool, and often last for five hours with only a break for the loo (although such breaks are not encouraged). Even at junior national level, training can be ten hours in one day (six or seven in the water and three or four on land), as it's hard to get the team together from across the country, and most national-level athletes will also train seven days a week. Synchronised swimmers are trained until they have a higher VO2 max (maximal oxygen uptake) than any other Olympic athlete other than cross-country skiers, and are more flexible than any Olympian other than the rhythmic gymnasts.

Katy is an ex-GB synchronised swimmer and says that nothing in her army training came close to her GB synchro training in terms of pain and exhaustion – an Ironman triathlon and GB age-group World and European sprint triathlons have been very straightforward in comparison! The forty hours (plus) a week of training leaves almost no time or energy for anything else, particularly not making money.

The current duet of Kate Shortman, 17, and Izzy Thorpe, 18, are a pair of human dynamos. They finished an impressive fourteenth at the 2019 World Championships as one of the very youngest pairs there, and they are well on their way to qualification for the Tokyo Olympics. They also achieved a wonderful fourth place at the 2019 European Junior Championships, showing how much they are progressing.

They have some serious resilience. It is not just that thousands of hours of practice are needed to perfect each second of a routine, but synchro is also more of a contact sport than you would imagine given the polished elegance of the final results. Broken bones are common from falling off lifts: Izzy has suffered three stress fractures in her ribs and Kate has broken two fingers, two toes and a thumb. A further break meant having a cast on her arm, making training incredibly tricky.

As leaders we would all love to have teams who are so dedicated to our vision that they are prepared to make sacrifices for it and persevere through the challenges and hard times to make it a reality. So what is it that keeps the synchro swimmers going? We asked the current GB team at their training base in Bristol, where they were squeezing forty athletes into two lanes of a swimming pool due to the high cost of water time.

What an amazingly optimistic and enthusiastic bunch! Despite being exhausted after their training session, they were full of smiles and hope. Katie Clark, a current GB coach and two-time Olympian, says that in order to stay motivated to put in the necessary work, they need 'to really, really believe that they can reach the top if they work hard enough'. Having incredibly high standards with relentless coaching and feedback helps to achieve this, as well as a focus on learning specific lessons from events. Their coaches (and therefore the athletes) are not primarily interested in the scores themselves, but rather they see every disappointment and success as an opportunity to learn.

Along with that relentless drive for excellence is the fact that the team feel cared for by their coaches, physios and team managers, who take great care to support the mental and physical well-being of all the athletes, making sure they are growing as people as well as athletes whatever their start point.

The GB team are not only committed to being the best they can be in terms of performance; they also want to make a wider positive impact on society. Hence Kate and Izzy performed their Olympic routine in a swimming pool full of plastic bottles to raise awareness of the problem of plastic in the ocean.[345] They had found their *ubuntu*, their connection to humanity, and are making ripples!

Putting in the Hard Work

The synchro swimming team are motivated and inspired to push through injury, persevere for thousands of hours of practice, and give their blood, sweat and tears for the chance of success. For a minor sport with insecure funding (there is very little money even at the top end) and low status in the sporting world, how did their leaders manage to motivate them?

- They have an ambitious goal of qualifying for the Olympic Games in 2021, as well as a higher purpose of raising awareness for the fight against plastic in the oceans.

- They have incredibly high standards with relentless coaching and feedback.

- They are full of hope – about the possibility of getting enough funding, of making it back after injury and of improving their performance.

- They are all cared for as people as well as athletes. Their coaches and managers take great interest in their lives outside the pool and gym.

- They work with the concept of 'we', not 'me' – it is about the group, not the individual, and there is a huge amount of joy from being part of that community.

- They also all just love synchro! They are doing what they are passionate about.

If you had to describe the quality that those synchronised swimmers possess in order to put in that many hours of practice and keep fighting injury, you might come up with the words perseverance, tenacity, stamina or grit. A kind of ferocious determination towards their goal. The only way they can continue to work so hard without giving up is because they believe that greatness is possible, that hard work pays off, that Olympic success in swimming is made up of many individual moves and that each move is possible with effort.

Growing Grit

So far in this book, we have laid the foundations of knowing and loving your people and considered the importance of having a clear vision for people to follow. Now we need to get our heads down and put in the hard work to make that vision a reality.

One of the most well-known researchers in this area is Angela Duckworth. Duckworth's research over the past two decades has changed the way we look at talent versus work ethic. Her key conclusion is that what really drives success is not talent but a unique combination of passion and perseverance towards long-term goals.[346]

This matters enormously for us as leaders because it implies that much of our success in leadership will be dependent on the hard work we put in to become great leaders, rather than being born a natural leader. It also matters for our teams because it suggests that their individual success and collective performance will be impacted as much by their perseverance as their talent.

Duckworth spent much of her adolescence bemoaning her own lack of talent and longing for more of it. Yet she is now a celebrated researcher and professor with a BA in neurobiology from Harvard, an MSc in neuroscience from Oxford and a PhD in psychology from the University of Pennsylvania, where she is now the Christopher H. Browne Distinguished Professor of Psychology.

Her early years in teaching raised real questions for her about why the most able and talented of the students she taught didn't necessarily do the best in the long run. This led to her choosing to work in the field of neuroscience and to research what leads to success. Duckworth studied children and adults in various different and challenging situations, such as teachers in failing schools, children in spelling bee competitions and army cadets in training. She was looking for patterns as to what determined who would succeed. The one characteristic that was the most significant predictor of success turned out to be grit.

Duckworth developed various psychometric tools to measure grit which she used to track whether grit was a significant predictor of success in other settings. The evidence was clear: grit matters for success in nearly every aspect of life. It is a predictor of the likelihood of graduation, performance in business and success in leadership.

A recent study gathered data on over 11,000 cadets going through the notoriously difficult West Point Military Academy and followed them through the initial training and for four years after graduation.[347] The researchers were looking to see what the main predictors of success would be: success was measured in terms of the cadets' military, academic and physical performance. It turned out that grit was the most important predictor of whether the cadets completed the basic seven-week training (known as 'Beast Barracks'). Both grit and physical ability were strong predictors of whether they graduated four years later. What was interesting is that while cognitive ability (test sores) predicted higher academic and military grades, they were not correlated with the final achievement of graduating from the academy. Overall, grit was a better predictor of which cadets would make it through West Point than either athletic ability or test scores.

Clearly, natural ability matters: some of us will never be tall enough to be professional basketball players or have the eyesight to become pilots. But for the vast majority of us, and our teams, we never get close to our own personal potential. Therefore, our focus should be on putting in the effort to become the best we can be, rather than worrying about how much innate talent we possess.

The optimum environment for growing grit is both demanding and supportive. It includes high expectations but is also psychologically safe enough to take risks and fail.

Leading for Grit

We are constantly discovering more about fostering resilience and grit, but there are some themes in the literature that are particularly helpful to us as leaders.

1. You Need to Believe Hard Work Pays Off

To have hope that you can achieve your purpose and vision, you need to believe that hard work pays off and that you can improve with effort. You need a growth mindset. You can increase your intelligence through reading and hard work, improve your swimming through practice or become a better leader through learning and trying out ideas. People with a growth mindset also embrace feedback (even negative feedback) because it is a chance to improve. This is very much how Gareth Southgate approached life. The attitude he has instilled in the England team includes embracing failure (as we discussed in Chapter 4). Gritty people have a growth mindset towards failure and interpret it as a cue to try harder. They stay positive. As Henry Ford (among others) reputedly said, 'Whether you believe you can do a thing or not, you are right.'

As we hinted at in Chapter 4, years of research have shown that the brain is not fixed and that if you deliberately practise something again and again your brain makes new neural pathways inside it and your brain actually changes.[348]

2. Optimism

Optimism is also very relevant to grit. Leaders need to be optimistic that their teams can achieve their vision. Warren Bennis, widely considered a pioneer of the contemporary field of leadership studies, tells us that optimism is one of the key things people need from their leaders in order to achieve positive results. 'Every exemplary leader that I have met,' writes Bennis, 'has what seems to be an unwarranted degree of optimism – and that helps generate the energy and commitment necessary to achieve results.'[349] This is closely aligned with the evidence on positivity we presented in Chapter 2.

3. Deliberate Practice

Deliberate practice involves a clearly defined stretch goal (a goal that is just beyond your reach at the moment but you could reach with enough effort), concentration and effort, immediate and informative feedback, and repetition with reflection and refinement. Model this perseverance and talk about it. Constantly remind your team that talent is largely a red herring; it's about qualitative improvements in skill and the accumulation of countless, perfectly executed yet mundane acts.

4. Purpose and Passion

We covered purpose and passion in Chapter 5. You need a compelling vision to help you push through the hard times and put in the work necessary to achieve it. If you want your team to do the same, it really helps if that purpose aligns with their own passion and values.

5. Attainable Goals

Your purpose is often lofty and long term but you also need smaller goals. You need to break down the big purpose into small achievable tasks, and then focus in even further so that your people know the exact next step to make. For example, if you were training for a marathon you would need to devise a training schedule which included gradual increases in distance as well as strength training and nutrition goals.

Duckworth did a random assigned study where teenagers were taught about breaking down their big goals into smaller and smaller tasks. The students really benefitted from this exercise and there were significant improvements in their academic performance. The biggest improvements came from those who broke down the goals into the smallest steps.[350]

Although vision is enormously important, its realisation is often outside of our control. Therefore, by also focusing on the process required to reach that vision we can focus on what is within our control, build the habits and create the daily mini goals that help us to reach the bigger purpose. This enables small wins that sustain your motivation.

6. Great Relationships

As we saw from the British synchro team, feeling cared for and being in positive relationships is enormously important for grit. During her master's research at Oxford, Katy looked at what was most significant in developing academic resilience and grit in students (measured by how long they were willing to persist with a task they were finding difficult). She found that the most important factor was whether the students perceived that their teachers cared about them.

It is pretty incredible that feeling cared for by a teacher is the most significant factor in how long students persevere at hard tasks. However, what is interesting is that this isn't just true in schools and for students. Katy also found this to be the case in the British Army: the more soldiers feel cared for by their leaders, the better they cope under pressure.

We spoke to Laura Reesby, an army helicopter pilot, who described to us a particularly dangerous operation in Iraq:

> *It was 11.15pm on 1 June 2007 and we had just climbed into bed when we received a call that one of our soldiers had been seriously injured during a mortar attack on an isolated British camp in Basra, southern*

Iraq. Their only chance of surviving was if we could launch an immedi-ate rescue mission by helicopter and fly them back for urgent medical treatment. The mission was perilous – flying in this area was extremely dangerous and intelligence reports suggested that a 'spectacular' attack on a helicopter was imminent.

We needed to land a large Merlin helicopter with a medical emergency response team on board in order to transport the casualty; our armed Lynx would provide protection for the Merlin and distract the enemy from our injured teammate's rescue.

Trying to ignore the risk, we prepared our helicopters as fast as we could. We took off into the night wearing night vision goggles, but faced with high levels of ambient light from urban glow and a clear night sky we had to adapt and swap goggle usage as the rescue unfolded. As we came closer to the location of the casualty, we found ourselves in the mid-dle of a firefight between the insurgents and British artillery fire, with explosions happening around us. Well aware of how much of a target we were – flying defensively at fifty feet above the rooftops, dodging mina-rets, towers and wires whilst trying to divert the insurgents' attention away from the vulnerable casualty and Merlin on the ground – we had to focus on our mission to evacuate the casualty. Incredibly, everyone survived that night, including our injured colleague, who made it to the field hospital.

The British Army is built on trust: trust that soldiers will always be rescued if in need, that no one will be left behind, that everyone will give their lives for one another. Without Reesby's team's bravery this casualty would certainly have died. But it's not easy to stay focused on a task when you and your team are in such extreme danger, so we asked Reesby how they coped. She told us:

There really isn't much training that can prepare you for the specific con-text of a firefight in these circumstances. Of course we had rehearsed the basics, but you can never be ready for that kind of situation, so I really put it down to our relationships. We were so tight as a team. We absolutely trusted each other and knew that whatever happened we were there for each other, we had each other's backs. We had built this trust through all the micro interactions we'd had working together over many months back in Germany and on previous operational tours of Iraq, through the mundane day-to-day training and maintenance tasks, to the adventure training and administrative work.

We had also spent a lot of time together socially both prior to and on tour, including the creation of a detachment cafe (comprising of a coffee grinder and a couple of broken chairs!) where we could gather together to unwind. In many ways you start to gel like a family – I even babysat for my aircraft commander's children before we deployed. This wasn't the case in all the teams I worked in and it really made a difference. When you are in a high-pressure situation where lives are at risk the most important questions are: can I trust my teammates? Do I know them well enough to know what their strengths and weaknesses are and how they are going to react? When you have that level of trust in your team, you can cope with the kind of night we had in Basra.

Laura's husband Keith, a former army helicopter pilot, agreed:

The relationships really matter for team resilience, and it's all the conversations you have that build the relationships. I really saw that when the team I was second in command of tragically experienced the death of the leader in a helicopter crash. It was the closeness of the relationships – how well everyone knew each other and therefore knew how to respond to each other – that allowed us to get through it. We stuck together and kept going together. We couldn't have done that without the investment before.

As leaders we need to remember that inspiring our teams to excellence and building grit will always be in the context of relationships. That is why we have to know and love our teams before we can really inspire them to give their best to an assignment. If you feel that your team are lacking grit, one of the key questions to ask yourself is: do my team feel cared for by me as their leader? Do they know I've got their back?

Magic Feedback

We started Lesson III with a question about how we motivate and inspire our teams. How do we lead them in such a way that, like the All Blacks, the Wright brothers or the GB synchro team, our people will give their best to the vision we are pursuing?

In 2013, some researchers in the United States looked at the impact of different types of feedback on student performance. Students were asked to write an essay and then teachers were asked to give different types of feedback. The results were fascinating. One type of feedback was far more effective than any other at motivating the students to go back and rewrite their essays and improve them. A simple phrase had a profound effect at inspiring them to excellence: 'I am giving you these comments because I have very high expectations and I know that you can reach them.'[351]

Obviously, this was a one-off increase in motivation for the student – the study isn't implying that one sentence will alter a student's work ethic forever – but it does give us a clue about some critical aspects of inspiring our teams. We need to have a clear purpose statement (as you hopefully developed in the previous chapter), high expectations, genuine hope that the expectations are achievable and then we need to empower people to get on with it.

Challenge 3: Growing Grit

1   Ask your team to share with each other times in their lives when hard work has paid off. How could they apply this to what they are trying to achieve now?

2   Reflect together on the purpose you co-created for your team. What impact is it having? Does your purpose need to be refined?

3   Ask your team, 'What attainable goals shall we set this week to bring us closer to our vision?'

4   What would 'magic feedback' – including high expectations, genuine optimism and belief in your people – look like in your context?

Question Time

There has been some rigorous academic debate about growth mindset and grit in the context of education and the extent to which it can be developed, so here are some questions we anticipate you might have as a leader.

Q.   *Is grit the only thing that matters for success?*

A.   No. As we have discussed throughout this book, the whole culture of your team is crucial to their success and that includes empathy, compassion, safety and purpose. But grit helps!

Q.   *Does being gritty and having a growth mindset mean that you should never give up?*

A.   No. There is such a thing as failure and you need judgement to decide when to give up. But our advice would be not to give up on a bad day or in a moment of emotional weakness; give up on a good day when you have clarity. If you are unsure, take advice from people you trust who care about you. Ask your best friend.

Q.   *Couldn't a growth mindset be very harsh because when people don't succeed it is entirely their own fault for not trying hard enough?*

A.   If you misuse growth mindset as a leader you could create that kind of culture of shame, which would be very negative and undermine psychological safety. There are many circumstances in life which are entirely beyond our control, and grit is not the only factor that determines success. As leaders, we need high expectations that inspire people to excellence but also to provide lots of support. You can't expect your team to work hard and succeed unless you, as a leader, provide the support and resources they need to achieve it. You need to find that magic balance of being deeply supportive and relentlessly challenging.

Grit in Healthcare

Cleveland Clinic (a non-profit academic medical centre and hospital in the United States) is a healthcare organisation which has really focused on building grit in order to achieve excellence, through encouraging passion and perseverance at an individual, team and organisational level.

Cleveland's CEO Toby Cosgrove is a great example of a leader who models grit personally and also works it through the culture.[352] Cosgrove had to work hard to become a surgeon, let alone a world-class surgeon. He struggled at school with dyslexia and had to work harder than all his contemporaries to get the same results. He was only accepted by one medical school.

During his surgical residency he was told that he was the least talented individual there, which just made him more determined to apply himself. He went all over the world trying to pick up tips on how to improve. He was told not to become a heart surgeon, but did so anyway. He has gone on to perform about 22,000 cardiac surgeries and invent new ways to minimise intrusion during valve surgery, gaining more than thirty patents and becoming a world-class surgeon.

When he became the CEO of Cleveland in 2004, he realised that he needed to bring the same passion and perseverance that he demonstrated in medicine to becoming a good leader. He knew that amazing clinicians do not automatically make amazing leaders, and he felt the burden of the 43,000 employees he now had to lead, so he resolved to learn everything he could about leadership. He read books, discussed ideas with experts and found a mentor. He poured over Cleveland's data and spoke to people who had been unhappy working there to see where things could be improved.

He understood that creating a gritty culture involves helping people to feel passionate about the bigger purpose they are working towards. Cleveland

Clinic has a clear purpose statement of 'putting patients' needs above all else', but Cosgrove wanted that to be more embedded in the culture. When he became CEO he therefore took the brave decision to give out lapel buttons to everyone saying 'Patients first'. He knew some people would think it was cheesy, but he was determined to keep the purpose central.

Another aspect of building a gritty culture is linking shorter term goals to the overall purpose. He helped staff to build a coherent hierarchy of goals, so that everyday tasks like cleaning the wards linked to broader goals, such as preventing infection, which linked to the higher purpose of putting patients first. This clear hierarchy of goals helps people to persevere with the day-to-day tasks.

Teams meet frequently to discuss ideas, review patients and set goals for improvement. This keeps them all aligned with their core purpose and helps them get to know each other (a key component for effective teams, as we already know!).

There is a constant, relentless drive to make things better. When a problem occurs – for example, the clinic found out that a delayed appointment had caused a patient to suffer for hours – they immediately trawled through processes and procedures to change things and prevent it happening again. It was about learning, not blame. Employees are recruited for grit and the annual professional reviews are all about providing support for improvement and learning. The assumption is that staff want to improve and be excellent at their work, and the clinic wants to back their efforts to get better and support them in this.

One of Cosgrove's staff came up with the idea of an 'appreciative inquiry' programme, where all the staff got together in small groups to spend a half-day discussing clinical cases they were proud of and where patient care had been excellent.[353] Nurses, doctors, cleaners and administrators were all involved, and they discussed what made the care outstanding in particular instances. It cost a lot of money, but was one of the most powerful ways that the clinic aligned people's individual passions and experiences with the overall mission.

Over Cosgrove's thirteen years as CEO, Cleveland Clinic moved from the bottom quartile in terms of patient experience to the top. Revenue increased, visits increased and every measure of patient outcomes improved.

Challenge 4: Appreciative Inquiry

1   What have we done in the last month that we feel proud of?

2   When have we been excellent as a team?

3   What enabled us to be excellent?

4   How can we make our purpose even more central and visible (e.g. lapel badges)?

Celebrate!

The concept of appreciative inquiry leads us to the end of this book with a final call to celebration.

If you, as a leader, have inspired your people to give their everything towards excellence and a higher purpose, you need to say thank you and you need to celebrate your people. Applaud their successes but also their progress and their story.

You see, gratitude isn't just an old-fashioned value or British quirk. In fact, it is one of the most reliable methods of increasing happiness, and as we saw earlier in the story about Zappos – happy teams produce amazing results.

Gratitude has been rigorously investigated, and we can confidently say that being grateful will improve your own well-being, help your team to flourish and create a powerful high-performing team culture. Scientifically speaking, regular grateful thinking can increase happiness by as much as 25%, while keeping a gratitude journal for as little as three weeks results in better sleep and more energy.[354] Here are some more benefits which researchers have found that people experience from practising gratitude.

Physical[355]

- Lower blood pressure.

- Exercise more and take better care of their health.

- Better quality and quantity of sleep.

- Stronger immune system.

- Less awareness of aches and pains.

- Fewer sick days.[356]

Psychological

- More well-being and happiness.[357]

- Increased feelings of optimism, joy, pleasure and enthusiasm.[358]

- Reduced anxiety and depression.[359]

- Increased resilience (research has shown that being grateful can help people to recover from trauma).[360]

- More alert, enthusiastic and determined.[361]

Social

- More outgoing.[362]

- Improved relationships.[363]

- People work harder for a more grateful boss.[364]

- Gratitude helps us to 'pay it forward' by making us more helpful, altruistic and compassionate.[365]

As a leader, you need to model gratitude and also create a culture of gratitude, where you regularly say thank you and celebrate people's effort, values and results. Adam Grant did some research in a call centre, where he found that when a manager visited staff on the call centre floor and explained how important what they were doing was and thanked them for their work, their productivity jumped by 50% (measured in terms of the number of calls they made). The research concluded that the reason for the increase in calls was that they felt more valued.[366] Various other surveys have confirmed these findings. In one poll for Glassdoor, 81% of employees said they were motivated to work harder when their boss showed appreciation for their work.[367]

Don't worry about gratitude making you or your staff complacent or more apathetic and less innovative. Research from the lab at University of California, Riverside has categorically concluded that gratitude is not just a sweet, fuzzy emotion that makes you accept your rubbish job and life as it is and feel thankful. In fact, it is an activating, energising force that can help us pursue our dreams and goals and be more actively socially engaged in improving the world.[369] So, congratulate your team, say thank you regularly, write them a card, throw a party, buy them a drink, get them a present – celebrate!

> *[Gratitude is] going to make your business more profitable, you're going to be more effective, your employees will be more engaged – but if that's the only reason you're doing it, your employees are going to think you're using them. You have to genuinely want the best for your people.*
>
> **Steve Foran, founder of Gratitude at Work**[368]

Challenge 5: Celebration and Gratitude

Gratitude can be grown. The following exercises are all scientifically proven to increase your gratitude and help you to reap its benefits.

1   Spend five to ten minutes at the end of each day writing in detail about three things that went well that day, large or small, and also describing why you think they happened. A 2005 study led by Martin

Seligman, founder of the Positive Psychology Center at the University of Pennsylvania, found that completing this exercise every day for one week led to increases in happiness that persisted for six months.[370]

2   Write a hand-written letter to someone saying thank you. It will have even more impact if you write it to someone important in your life who you have never properly thanked.

3   Say thank you to someone each day this week – either in person or write them a card.

4   Pick one way this week to celebrate something with your team.

5   Find a way to weave celebration into your regular routines. Discuss with your team: what are the events in your year which you could regularly celebrate? How do your team most enjoy celebrating?

Conclusion

We hope you have learned our lessons from beneath the water – that to inspire your people to put in the hard work necessary to turn your vision into a reality, you need to empower them, create a culture of grit and celebrate along the way. Be deeply supportive, relentlessly challenging and endlessly optimistic!

Summary

- Aim for excellence.
- Give your team the support and resources to reach this goal.
- Empower, don't direct.
- Believe they can improve.
- Model a growth mindset.
- Say thank you.

Remember to celebrate milestones as you prepare for the road ahead.

Nelson Mandela[371]

The first responsibility of a leader is to define reality. The last is to say thank you. In between the two, the leader must become a servant.

Max De Pree, former CEO of Herman Miller[372]

Conclusion

True Leadership

> *I know that true leadership – leadership that lifts families, leadership that sustains communities and transforms nations – that kind of leadership rarely starts in palaces or parliaments.*
>
> *That kind of leadership is not limited only to those of a certain age or status. And that kind of leadership is not just about dramatic events that change the course of history in an instant.*
>
> *Instead, true leadership often happens with the smallest acts, in the most unexpected places, by the most unlikely individuals.*
>
> Michelle Obama[373]

This book has presented a multitude of examples of true leadership – the kind of leadership that lifts families, sustains communities and organisations and transforms nations – and we have shown that this can come from anyone who has the courage to know, love and inspire their people.

We have taken you through three key lessons in true leadership, presenting you with compelling evidence on how to get the very best from people, whoever they are:

Lesson I: Know your people. As you think about knowing your people, remember you need to understand their values and strengths. You can do this through great listening, powerful questioning and empathy.

Lesson II: Love your people. To love your people, show them compassion, serve them and create psychological safety. You can do this through fearlessly loving, leading and communicating with your team.

Lesson III: Inspire your people. Inspiration comes when you give your team a clear sense of purpose. You can help them to achieve this purpose by empowering them and celebrating them with optimism and gratitude.

Leadership starts with *you*. It starts in all of the communities of which you are a part – from your family, to your neighbourhood, to your workplace.

Whatever our age or position, we must seize the opportunity to become the best leaders we can be. Stepping up is both a privilege and a duty. Accepting that challenge to make a positive difference in the lives of others and society is what makes us leaders.

Becoming Leaders – Join the Journey

We are aware that there are many stories out there of great leaders that we don't know about, particularly stories from women, young people, minorities, developing countries and less-connected communities, which don't get published and told as often as they should.

If you have a story of great leadership that you think should have been in this book, please do contact us – we would love to hear from you. You can also join the adventure on our website as we try to help and inspire one another to be the best leaders we can be. Leaders who enable others to flourish and make the world a better, happier place.

www.leaderknowloveinspire.com

Leadership lies in sacrifice, self-denial, love, fearlessness, and humility.

Vince Lombardi[374]

Endnotes

1 H. Tobar, Sixty-nine days: the ordeal of the Chilean miners. *New Yorker* (7 July 2014). Available at: https://www.newyorker.com/magazine/2014/07/07/sixty-nine-days.

2 K. Kristof, Chilean miners: leadership lessons from Luis Urzua. *CBS News* (14 October 2010). Available at: https://www.cbsnews.com/news/chilean-miners-leadership-lessons-from-luis-urzua.

3 L. Getlen, The untold story of how the buried Chilean miners survived. *New York Post* (11 October 2014). Available at: https://nypost.com/2014/10/11/how-the-chilean-miners-men-survived-for-69-days-beneath-the-earths-surface.

4 See http://www.mandela.gov.za/mandela_speeches/2002/020518_sisulu.htm.

5 Kristof, Chilean miners: leadership lessons from Luis Urzua.

6 See https://rework.withgoogle.com/print/guides/5721312655835136.

7 C. Duhigg, What Google learned from its quest to build the perfect team. *New York Times* (25 February 2016). Available at: https://www.nytimes.com/2016/02/28/magazine/what-google-learned-from-its-quest-to-build-the-perfect-team.html?smid=pl-share.

8 L. Delizonna, High-performing teams need psychological safety. Here's how to create it. *Harvard Business Review* (24 August 2017). Available at: https://hbr.org/2017/08/high-performing-teams-need-psychological-safety-heres-how-to-create-it.

9 A. W. Woolley, C. F. Chabris, A. Pentland, N. Hashmi and T. W. Malone, Evidence for a collective intelligence factor in the performance of human groups. *Science*, 330(6004) (2010), 686–688.

10 Calebjsaenz, Morning rehash: Popovich conducts a Wizards beatdown. *Pounding the Rock* (14 November 2013). Available at: https://www.poundingtherock.com/2013/11/14/5103402/morning-rehash-popovich-spurs-wizards-beatdown.

11 J. Turtel, Another victory for 'Pop'. Another show of leadership. *Fortune* (16 June 2014). Available at: https://fortune.com/2014/06/16/gregg-popovich-leadership.

12 C. Geoffreys, *Gregg Popovich: The Inspiring Life and Leadership Lessons of One of Basketball's Greatest Coaches* (Winter Park, FL: Calvintir Books, 2017).

13 Quoted in I. Boudway, The five pillars of Gregg Popovich. *Bloomberg Businessweek* (10 January 2018). Available at: https://www.bloomberg.com/news/features/2018-01-10/the-five-pillars-of-gregg-popovich.

14 B. Golliver, Gregg Popovich and the United Spurs of America. *Washington Post* (10 August 2019). Available at: https://www.washingtonpost.com/sports/2019/08/10/gregg-popovich-united-spurs-america/?noredirect=on.

15 J. M. Kouzes and B. Z. Posner, *The Leadership Challenge: How to Make Extraordinary Things Happen in Organizations*, 6th edn (Hoboken, NJ: John Wiley & Sons, 2017), p. 256.

16 Quoted in Boudway, The five pillars of Gregg Popovich.

17 Kouzes and Posner, *The Leadership Challenge*, p. 47.

18 Kouzes and Posner, *The Leadership Challenge*, p .41.

19 B. George and P. Sims, *True North: Discover Your Authentic Leadership* (San Francisco, CA: Jossey-Bass, 2007).

20 M. Gates, *Moment of Lift: How Empowering Women Changes the World* (London: Bluebird, 2019).

21 Gates, *Moment of Lift*, p. 215.

22 V. Lombardi Jr, *What It Takes to Be #1: Vince Lombardi on Leadership* (New York: McGraw-Hill, 2001); V. Lombardi Jr, *The Lombardi Rules: 26 Lessons from Vince Lombardi: The World's Greatest Coach* (New York: McGraw-Hill, 2003); J. Cavanaugh, *Giants Among Men: How Robustelli, Huff, Gifford, and the Giants Made New York a Football Town and Changed the NFL* (New York: Random House, 2008); F. Gifford and P. Richmond, *The Glory Game: How the 1958 NFL Championship Changed Football Forever* (New York: HarperCollins, 2008).

23 Quoted in J. Kerr, *Legacy: What the All Blacks Can Teach Us About the Business of Life* (London: Constable, 2013), p. 8.

24 Kerr, *Legacy*, p. 178.

25 From a speech delivered in Dayton, Ohio on 22 June 1970. Quoted in Lombardi, *What It Takes To Be #1*, p. 37.

26 Quoted in M. Zetlin, In just 9 minutes at Apple WWDC, Michelle Obama explains how to be a great leader. *Inc.com* (7 June 2017). Available at: https://www.inc.com/minda-zetlin/in-secret-appearance-at-apple-wwdc-michelle-obama-explains-how-to-be-a-great-lea.html. The other quotes in this section are from the same article.

27 *NPR*, Transcript: Michelle Obama's convention speech (August 25 2008). Available at: https://www.npr.org/templates/story/story.php?storyId=93963863.

28 *NPR*, Transcript: Michelle Obama's convention speech.

29 B. Machell, They're just wild about Harry Kane. *The Times* (3 June 2017).

30 *Marca*, The story behind Guardiola's decision to let Messi go to the 2008 Olympic Games (5 June 2019). Available at: https://www.marca.com/en/football/barcelona/2019/06/05/5cf818d5ca474149538b4622.html.

31 A. Forrest, I. Lawson, L. Chaput de Saintonge and M. Smith, *To Practise What We Preach: An Exploratory Survey of Values in Charities* (London: Cass Business School, 2012).

32 M. Ros, S. H. Schwartz and S. Surkiss, Basic individual values, work values, and the meaning of work. *Applied Psychology: An International Review*, 48(1) (1999), 49–71.

33 B. Brown, *Dare to Lead: Brave Work. Tough Conversations. Whole Hearts.* (London: Vermillion).

34 P. Lencioni, Make your values mean something. *Harvard Business Review* (July 2002). Available at: https://hbr.org/2002/07/make-your-values-mean-something.

35 B. Meglino, E. Ravlin and C. Adkins, A work values approach to corporate culture: a field test of the value congruence process and its relationship to individual outcomes. *Journal of Applied Psychology*, 74 (1989), 424–432.

36 B. Meglino and E. Ravlin, Individual values in organizations: concepts, controversies, and research. *Journal of Management*, 24(3) (1998), 351–389.

37 Personal communication with authors.

38 Adapted from George Reavis' fable which was originally written in the 1940s, during his time as assistant superintendent of the Cincinnati Public Schools.

39 B. Rigoni and J. Aspland, Strengths-based employee development: the business results. *Gallup Workplace* (10 July 2016). Available at: https://www.gallup.com/workplace/236297/strengths-based-employee-development-business-results.aspx.

40 P. Flade, J. Asplund and G. Elliot, Employees who use their strengths outperform those who don't. *Gallup Business Journal* (8 October 2015). Available at: https://www.gallup.com/workplace/236561/employees-strengths-outperform-don.aspx.

41 T. D. Hodges and D. O. Clifton, Strengths-based development in practice. In A. Linley and S. Joseph (eds), *Handbook of Positive Psychology in Practice* (Hoboken, NJ: John Wiley & Sons, 2004), pp. 256–268.

42 B. Brim and J. Asplund, Driving engagement by focusing on strengths. *Gallup Business Journal* (12 November 2009). Available at: https://news.gallup.com/businessjournal/124214/driving-engagement-focusing-strengths.aspx.

43 CAPP, Why Strengths? The Evidence (2010). Available at: http://emotionalintelligenceworldwide.com/wp-content/uploads/CAPP_Why_Strengths_The_Evidence.pdf.

44 M. E. P. Seligman, T. A. Steen, N. Park and C. Peterson, Positive psychology progress: empirical validation of interventions. *American Psychologist*, 60 (2005), 410–421; R. Govindji and P. A. Linley, Strengths use, self-concordance and well-being: implications for strengths coaching and coaching psychologists. *International Coaching Psychology Review*, 2(2) (2007), 143–153.

45 Govindji and Linley, Strengths use, self-concordance and well-being; C. Proctor, J. Maltby and P. A. Linley, Strengths use as a predictor of well-being and health-related quality of life. *Journal of Happiness Studies*, 10 (2009), 583–630.

46 G. Minhas, Developing realised and unrealised strengths: implications for engagement, self-esteem, life satisfaction and well-being. *Assessment and Development Matters,* 2 (2010), 12–16.

47 Govindji and Linley, Strengths use, self-concordance and well-being.

48 A. M. Wood, P. A. Linley, J. Maltby and R. Hurling, Using personal and psychological strengths leads to increases in well-being over time: a longitudinal study and the development of the strengths use questionnaire. *Personality and Individual Differences*, 50(1) (2010), 15–19.

49 CAPP, *Technical Manual and Statistical Properties for Realise2* (Coventry: CAPP, 2010).

50 P. A. Linley, K. M. Nielsen, A. M. Wood, R. Gillett and R. Biswas-Diener, Using signature strengths in pursuit of goals: effects on goal progress, need satisfaction, and well-being, and implications for coaching psychologists. *International Coaching Psychology Review*, 5(1) (2010), 8–17.

51 Corporate Leadership Council, *Performance Management Survey* (Washington, DC: Corporate Leadership Council, 2002).

52 J. K. Harter, F. L. Schmidt and T. L. Hayes, Business-unit-level relationship between employee satisfaction, employee engagement, and business outcomes: a meta-analysis. *Journal of Applied Psychology*, 87 (2002), 268–279.

53 K. M. Sheldon, T. Kasser, K. Smith and T. Share, Personal goals and psychological growth: testing an intervention to enhance goal-attainment and personality integration. *Journal of Personality*, 70, (2002), 5–31.

54 For more information, we recommend: https://ppc.sas.upenn.edu.

55 L. E. Waters, D. Loton and H. K. Jach, Does strength-based parenting predict academic achievement? The mediating effects of perseverance and engagement. *Journal of Happiness Studies*, 20(4) (2019), 1121–1140.

56 L. C. Hone, A. Jarden, S. Duncan and G. M. Schofield, Flourishing in New Zealand workers: associations with lifestyle behaviors, physical health, psychosocial, and work-related indicators. *Journal of Occupational and Environmental Medicine*, 57(9) (2015), 973–983.

57 S. Sorenson, How employees' strengths make your company stronger. *Gallup Workplace* (20 February 2014). Available at: https://www.gallup.com/workplace/231605/employees-strengths-company-stronger.aspx.

58 See http://www.viacharacter.org/
    character-strengths.
59 M. Buckingham, *Go Put Your Strengths to
    Work* (London: Simon & Schuster, 2007).
60 The psychologist Mihaly Csikszentmihalyi
    defines flow as total absorption in what you
    are doing: M. Csikszentmihalyi, *Flow: The
    Psychology of Optimal Experience* (New
    York: Harper & Row, 1990).
61 M. Farrer, 'This is England': nation unites
    to rejoice in Cricket World Cup final win.
    The Guardian (15 July 2019). Available at:
    https://www.theguardian.com/sport/2019/
    jul/15/this-is-england-nation-unites-to-
    rejoice-in-cricket-world-cup-win.
62 This section has been adapted from
    A. Strauss, *Driving Ambition: My
    Autobiography* (London: Hodder &
    Stoughton, 2014).
63 S. Hughes, Andrew Strauss was the
    'deputy's deputy' who became an
    exceptional leader of his England men. (29
    August 2012). Available at: https://www.
    telegraph.co.uk/sport/cricket/international/
    england/9507587/Andrew-Strauss-was-
    the-deputys-deputy-who-became-an-
    exceptional-leader-of-his-England-men.
    html.
64 Personal communication with authors.
65 L. M. Roberts, G. Spreitzer, J. E. Dutton,
    R. E. Quinn, E. D. Heaphy and B. Barker,
    How to play to your strengths. *Harvard
    Business Review* (January 2005).
    Available at: https://hbr.org/2005/01/
    how-to-play-to-your-strengths.
66 For more on this, we recommend: C. S.
    Dweck, *Mindset* (New York: Random
    House, 2006).
67 J. Kruger and D. Dunning, Unskilled and
    unaware of it: how difficulties in recognizing
    one's own incompetence lead to inflated
    self-assessments. *Journal of Personality
    and Social Psychology*, 77(6) (1999),
    1121–1134.
68 P. R. Clance and S. A. Imes, The impostor
    phenomenon in high achieving women:
    dynamics and therapeutic intervention.
    *Psychotherapy: Theory, Research &
    Practice*, 15(3) (1978), 241–247.
69 M. Buckingham and D. Clifton, *Now,
    Discover Your Strengths: How to Develop
    Your Talents and Those of the People
    You Manage* (London: Simon & Schuster,
    2004).
70 L. Morgan Roberts, G. Spreitzer, J.
    Dutton, R. Quinn, E. Heaphy and B.
    Barker, How to play to your strengths.
    Harvard Business Review (January 2005).
    Available at: https://hbr.org/2005/01/
    how-to-play-to-your-strengths.
71 See https://www.sc.com/en/about.
72 S. Bibb, *Strengths-Based Recruitment
    and Development: A Practical Guide to
    Transforming Talent Management Strategy
    for Business Results* (London: Kogan
    Page, 2016).
73 Quoted in K. Dempsey, Performance
    management: play to their strengths.
    Personnel Today (6 August 2007). Available
    at: https://www.personneltoday.com/hr/
    performance-management-play-to-their-
    strengths.
74 R. Huckman and G. Pisano, The firm
    specificity of individual performance.
    Management Science, 52 (2006), 473–488.
75 S. Covey, *The 7 Habits of Highly Effective
    People: Powerful Lessons in Personal
    Change* (London: Simon & Schuster, 1989),
    p. 239.
76 See https://www.centreforpeacefulsolutions.
    org.
77 H. Garlick, 'If I'd known, I might not
    have taken a life': can prisoners defuse
    their own disputes? *The Guardian* (10
    February 2018). Available at: https://www.
    theguardian.com/society/2018/feb/10/
    can-prisoners-resolve-disputes-dartmoor-
    mediation.
78 N. Singh Ospina, K. A. Phillips, R.
    Rodriguez-Gutierrez, A. Castaneda-
    Guarderas, M. R. Gionfriddo, M. E. Branda
    et al., Eliciting the patient's agenda:
    secondary analysis of recorded clinical
    encounters. *Journal of General Internal
    Medicine*, 34 (2019), 36–40.

79 *Financial Times*, Lunch with the FT: Daniel Goleman (5 January 2007). Available at: https://www.ft.com/content/acd3586e-9bc7-11db-9c9b-0000779e2340.

80 D. Goleman, Curing the common cold of leadership: poor listening. *LinkedIn* (2 May 2013). Available at: https://www.linkedin.com/pulse/20130502140433-117825785-curing-the-common-cold-of-leadership-poor-listening.

81 A. Mishra, The research on trust in leadership: the need for context. *Journal of Trust Research*, 3(1) (2013), 59–69.

82 F. F. Browne, *The Every-day Life of Abraham Lincoln: A Narrative and Descriptive Biography* (Chicago, IL: Browne & Howell, 1913), ch. 22. Available at: http://www.gutenberg.org/ebooks/14004.

83 N. Kline, *Time to Think: Listening to Ignite the Human Mind* (London: Cassell, 2002), p. 17.

84 J. Whitmore, *Coaching for Performance*, 4th edn (London: Nicholas Brealey Publishing, 2009), pp. 10–11.

85 J. McGovern, M. Lindemann, M. Vergara, S. Murphy, L. Barker and R. Warrenfeltz, Maximizing the impact of executive coaching: behavioral change, organizational outcomes, and return on investment. *Manchester Review*, 6(1) (2001), 3–11 at 7. Available at: https://www.perspect.ca/pdf/ExecutiveCoaching.pdf.

86 See *Cricketing Yorkshire*, Episode 1 [video]. *Sky Sports* (2015). Available at: https://www.skysports.com/watch/video/sports/cricket/9861800/cricketing-yorkshire-episode-1.

87 Quoted in D. McRae, Jason Gillespie: Trevor Bayliss was 100% the correct choice for England. *The Guardian* (8 April 2016). Available at: https://www.theguardian.com/sport/2016/apr/08/jason-gillespie-trevor-bayliss-yorkshire-coach-england.

88 M. Losada and E. Heaphy, The role of positivity and connectivity in the performance of business teams: a nonlinear model. *American Behavioral Scientist*, 47 (2004), 740–765.

89 For the geeks out there, you will be pleased to hear that the study used non-linear dynamics and Lorenz attractor diagrams, so causal directionality could be projected. We can say with confidence that it wasn't the high performance that was causing all the positive chat!

90 B. L. Fredrickson and M. F. Losada, Positive affect and the complex dynamics of human flourishing. *American Psychologist*, 60 (2005), 678–686.

91 S. Achor, *The Happiness Advantage: The Seven Principles of Positive Psychology* (New York: Random House, 2010), p. 60.

92 J. M. Gottman, *What Predicts Divorce? The Relationship Between Marital Processes and Marital Outcomes* (New York: Erlbaum, 1994).

93 Adapted from K. Cameron, *Positive Leadership* (Oakland, CA: Berrett-Koehler Publishers, 2011).

94 J. W. Pettit, J. P. Kline, T. Gencoz, F. Gencoz and T. E. Joiner, Are happy people healthier: the specific role of positive affect in predicting self-reported health symptoms. *Journal of Research in Personality*, 35, (2001) 521–536.

95 B. E. Kok, K. A. Coffey, M. A. Cohn, L. I. Catalino, T. Vacharkulksemsuk, S. B. Algoe et al., How positive emotions build physical health: perceived positive social connections account for the upward spiral between positive emotions and vagal tone. *Psychological Science*, 24(7) (2013), 1123–1132.

96 D. J. H. Deeg and R. J. Van Zonneveld, Does happiness lengthen life? The prediction of longevity in the elderly. In R. Veenhoven (ed.), *How Harmful Is Happiness? Consequences of Enjoying Life Or Not* (Rotterdam: Universitaire Pers Rotterdam, 1989), pp. 29–34; D. D. Danner, D. A. Snowdon and W. V. Friesen, Positive emotions in early life and longevity: findings from the nun study. *Journal of Personality and Social Psychology*, 80 (2001), 804–813.

97 S. M. Lamers, L. Bolier, G. J. Westerhof, F. Smit and E. T. Bohlmeijer, The impact of emotional well-being on long-term recovery and survival in physical illness: a meta-analysis. *Journal of Behavioral Medicine*, 35(5) (2012), 538–547.

98 Gottman, *What Predicts Divorce?*

99 A. L. Alden, J. A. Dale and D. E. DeGood, Interactive effects of the affect quality and directional focus of mental imagery on pain analgesia. *Applied Psychophysiology and Biofeedback*, 26 (2001), 117–126.

100 L. G. Aspinwall, Rethinking the role of positive affect in self-regulation. *Motivation and Emotion*, 22 (1998), 1–32.

101 D. Jundt and V. B. Hinsz, Are happier workers more productive workers? The impact of mood on self-set goals, self-efficacy, and task performance. Paper presented at the annual meeting of the Midwestern Psychological Association, Chicago, May 2001; S. Lyubomirsky, L. King and E. Diener, The benefits of frequent positive affect: does happiness lead to success? *Psychological Bulletin*, 131(6) (2005), 803–855.

102 Lyubomirsky et al., The benefits of frequent positive affect.

103 A. Rego, F. Sousa, C. Marques and M. P. Cunha, Optimism predicting employees' creativity: the mediating role of positive affect and the positivity ratio. *European Journal of Work and Organizational Psychology*, 21(2) (2012), 244–270.

104 A. M. Isen and B. Means, The influence of positive affect on decision-making strategy. *Social Cognition*, 2 (1983), 18 –31; A. M. Isen, Positive affect and decision making. In M. Lewis and J. M. Haviland-Jones (eds), *Handbook of Emotions*, 2nd edn (New York: Guilford Press, 2000), pp. 417–435.

105 G. Rowe, J. B. Hirsh and A. K. Anderson, Positive affect increases the breadth of attentional selection. *Proceedings of the National Academy of Sciences of the United States of America*, 104(1) (2007), 383–388.

106 L. Riolli, V. Savicki and E. Spain, Positive emotions in traumatic conditions: mediation of appraisal and mood for military personnel. *Military Psychology*, 22(2) (2010), 207–223.

107 D. Aderman, Elation, depression, and helping behavior. *Journal of Personality and Social Psychology*, 24(1) (1972), 91–101; L. I. Catalino and B. L. Fredrickson, A Tuesday in the life of a flourisher: the role of positive emotional reactivity in optimal mental health. *Emotion*, 11(4) (2011), 938–950.

108 B. L. Fredrickson, M. A. Cohn, K. A. Coffey, J. Pek and S. M. Finkel, Open hearts build lives: positive emotions, induced through loving-kindness meditation, build consequential personal resources. *Journal of Personality and Social Psychology*, 95 (2008), 1045–1062.

109 E. L. Garland, B. L. Fredrickson, A. M. Kring, D. P. Johnson, P. S. Meyer and D. L. Penn, Upward spirals of positive emotions counter downward spirals of negativity: insights from the broaden-and build theory and affective neuroscience on the treatment of emotion dysfunctions and deficits in psychopathology. *Clinical Psychology Review*, 30(7) (2010), 849–864; M. Diehl, E. L. Hay and K. M. Berg, The ratio between positive and negative affect and flourishing mental health across adulthood. *Aging and Mental Health*, 15(7) (2011), 882–893.

110 E. Diener, E. Sandvik and W. Pavot, Happiness is the frequency, not the intensity, of positive versus negative affect. In F. Strack, M. Argyle and N. Schwarz (eds), *Subjective Well-Being: An Interdisciplinary Perspective* (New York: Pergamon, 1991), pp. 119–139.

111 M. Métral, 7 things every manager should learn from Pep Guardiola. *LinkedIn* (23 September 2016). Available at: https://www.linkedin.com/pulse/7-thing-every-manager-should-learn-from-pep-guardiola-max-m%C3%A9tral.

112 G. Balague, *Pep Guardiola: Another Way of Winning: The Biography* (London: Weidenfeld & Nicolson, 2013), p. 122.

113 N. Collins, Be like Pep – the perfect leader. *Morgan McKinley* (29 January 2016). Available at: https://www.morganmckinley.ie/article/be-pep-perfect-leader.

114 Balague, *Pep Guardiola*, p. 218.

115 W. A. Gentry, T. J. Weber and G. Sadri, *Empathy in the Workplace: A Tool for Effective Leadership.* (Greensboro, NC: Center for Creative Leadership, 2007). Available at: https://www.ccl.org/wp-content/uploads/2015/04/EmpathyInTheWorkplace.pdf.

116 S. F. Young, E. M. Richard, R. G. Moukarzel, L. A. Steelman and W. A. Gentry, How empathic concern helps leaders in providing negative feedback: a two-study examination. *Journal of Occupational and Organizational Psychology*, 90(4) (2017), 535–558.

117 Brown, *Dare to Lead*, pp. 143–148.

118 Quoted in L. J. Colan and J. Davis-Colan, *The Power of Positive Coaching: The Mindset and Habits to Inspire Winning Results and Relationships* (New York: McGraw Hill Professional, 2018), p. 62.

119 J. Kabat-Zinn, Mindfulness-based interventions in context: past, present, and future. *Clinical Psychology: Science and Practice*, 10(2) (2003), 144–156 at 145.

120 J. Zenger and J. Folkman, What great listeners actually do. *Harvard Business Review* (14 July 2016). Available at: https://hbr.org/2016/07/what-great-listeners-actually-do.

121 T. Manfred, 55-year-old legend who quit his job to work for the Spurs explains why Gregg Popovich is a genius. *Business Insider* (5 December 2014). Available at: https://www.businessinsider.com/ettore-messina-on-gregg-popovich-2014-12?r=US&IR=T.

122 D. Coyle, How Gregg Popovich uses 'magical feedback' to inspire the San Antonio Spurs. *Time* (30 January 2018). Available at: https://time.com/5125421/gregg-popovich-san-antonio-spurs-success/#.

123 B. Burg and J. D. Mann, *The Go-Giver Leader* (London: Penguin Random House, 2016), p. 61.

124 D. L. Paulhus and K. M. Williams, The dark triad of personality: narcissism, Machiavellianism, and psychopathy. *Journal of Research in Personality*, 36(6) (2002), 556–563.

125 L. T. Brinke, A. Kish and D. Keltner, Hedge fund managers with psychopathic tendencies make for worse investors. *Personality and Social Psychology Bulletin*, 28 (2017), 484–495.

126 L. T. Brinke, C. C. Liu and D. Keltner, Virtues, vices, and political influence in the US Senate. *Psychological Science*, 27(1) (2015), 85–93.

127 This section has been adapted from R. Mason, *Gareth Southgate: Zero to Hero* [Kindle edn] (London: SJH Group, 2018).

128 Mason, *Gareth Southgate*, locs 1024, 1209.

129 C. Beesley, Robbie Fowler on why Gareth Southgate tops other England bosses. *MSN News* (9 July 2018). Available at: https://www.msn.com/en-gb/news/newsliverpool/robbie-fowler-on-why-gareth-southgate-tops-other-england-bosses/ar-AAzMCai.

130 Mason, *Gareth Southgate*, loc. 1687.

131 *New Statesman*, Gareth Southgate and the new progressive Englishness (4 July 2018). Available at: https://www.newstatesman.com/politics/sport/2018/07/gareth-southgate-and-new-progressive-englishness.

132 Mason, *Gareth Southgate*, loc. 1755.

133 A. Massiah, World Cup 2018: Gareth Southgate's compassion praised. *BBC News* (4 July 2018). Available at: https://www.bbc.co.uk/news/uk-44715244.

134 See https://www.premierleague.com/managers/2663/Jos%C3%A9-Mourinho/overview.

135 S. Gibson, Why is Jose Mourinho the special one? *The Telegraph*

(1 June 2016). https://www.
telegraph.co.uk/football/2016/06/01/
why-is-jose-mourinho-the-special-one.

136 B. Cotton, Jose Mourinho's sacking –
leadership lessons from the dismissal
of the 'special one'. *Business Leader* (1
January 2019). Available at: https://www.
businessleader.co.uk/jose-mourinhos-
sacking-leadership-lessons-from-the-
dismissal-of-the-special-one/57609.

137 J. Whaling, Jose Mourinho's most famous
quotes. *Irish Mirror* (17 December 2015).
Available at: https://www.irishmirror.ie/sport/
soccer/soccer-news/jose-mourinhos-most-
famous-quotes-7032648.

138 Z. Boswell, Jose Mourinho turning over
new leaf at Tottenham – 'It's not about
myself'. *Sky Sports* (21 November 2019).
Available at: https://www.skysports.
com/football/news/11675/11866411/
jose-mourinho-turning-over-new-leaf-at-
tottenham-its-not-about-myself.

139 L. Ginesi and R. Niescierowicz,
Neuroendocrinology and birth 2: the role of
oxytocin. *British Journal of Midwifery*, 6(12)
(1998), 791–796.

140 W. Jonas, L. M. Johansson, E. Nissen,
M. Ejdebäck, A. B. Ransjö-Arvidson and
K. Uvnäs-Moberg, Effects of intrapartum
oxytocin administration and epidural
analgesia on the concentration of plasma
oxytocin and prolactin, in response to
suckling during the second day postpartum.
Breastfeeding Medicine, 4(2) (2009),
71–82.

141 W. Harbaugh, U. Mayr and D. R.
Burghart, Neural responses to taxation
and voluntary giving reveal motives for
charitable donations. *Science*, 316 (2007),
1622–1623.

142 S. B. Algoe and B. M. Way, Evidence for
a role of the oxytocin system, indexed
by genetic variation in CD38, in the
social bonding effects of expressed
gratitude. *Social Cognitive and Affective
Neuroscience*, 9(12) (2014), 1855–1861.

143 E. Digitale, Oxytocin levels in blood,
cerebrospinal fluid are linked, study

finds. *Stanford Medicine News Center*
(4 November 2014). Available at: https://
med.stanford.edu/news/all-news/2014/11/
oxytocin-levels-in-blood-cerebrospinal-fluid-
are-linked-study-fi.html.

144 P. J. Zak, A. A. Stanton and S. Ahmadi,
Oxytocin increases generosity in humans.
PLOS ONE, 2(11) (2007), e1128.

145 J. Holt-Lunstad, W. A. Birmingham and
K. C. Light, Influence of a 'warm touch'
support enhancement intervention among
married couples on ambulatory blood
pressure, oxytocin amylase and cortisol.
Psychosomatic Medicine, 70 (2008),
976–985.

146 Holt-Lunstad et al., Influence of a 'warm
touch' support enhancement intervention.

147 Holt-Lunstad et al., Influence of a 'warm
touch' support enhancement intervention.

148 P. Gilbert, *The Compassionate Mind*
(London: Constable, 2013).

149 Gilbert, *The Compassionate Mind*.

150 Gilbert, *The Compassionate Mind*.

151 It appears that oxytocin may have several
roles to play in reducing the impact
of excessive fear or stress. Amygdala
activation is critical for signalling fear: D.
G. Amaral, The amygdala, social behavior,
and danger detection. *Annals of the New
York Academy of Sciences*, 1000 (2003),
337–347; R. Adolphs, F. Gosselin, T. W.
Buchanan, D. Tranel, P. Schyns and A.
R. Damasio, A mechanism for impaired
fear recognition after amygdala damage.
Nature, 433 (2005), 68–72. Labuschagne
and colleagues suggest that oxytocin
acts on the amygdala to reduce fear: I.
Labuschagne, K. L. Phan, A. Wood, M.
Angstadt, P. Chua, M. Heinrichs et al.,
Oxytocin attenuates amygdala reactivity to
fear in generalized social anxiety disorder.
Neuropsychopharmacology, 35(12) (2010),
2403–2413. Other researchers contend
that oxytocin modulates neural circuitry
for fear in humans: P. Kirsch, C. Esslinger,
Q. Chen, D. Mier, S. Lis, S. Siddhanti et
al., Oxytocin modulates neural circuitry
for social cognition and fear in humans.

Journal of Neuroscience, 25 (49) (2005), 11489–11493. This indicates that the impact of oxytocin on anxiety may be attributable to a combined effect on both amygdala activation and coupling to regions mediating fear response.

152 Digitale, Oxytocin levels in blood.

153 Zak et al., Oxytocin increases generosity in humans.

154 Zak et al., Oxytocin increases generosity in humans.

155 Zak et al., Oxytocin increases generosity in humans.

156 A. Seldon, Speech delivered at the 5th Ultimate Wellbeing in Education Conference, London, 17 October 2019.

157 T. Ben-Shahar and A. Ridgeway, *The Joy of Leadership: How Positive Psychology Can Maximize Your Impact (and Make You Happier) in a Challenging World* (Hoboken, NJ: John Wiley & Sons, 2017), p. 29.

158 A. Grant, J. Dutton and B. D. Rosso, Giving commitment: employee support programs and the prosocial sensemaking process, *Academy of Management Journal*, 51(5) (2017), 898–918.

159 J. E. Dutton, J. Lilius and J. Kanov, The transformative potential of compassion at work. In S. Piderit, R. Fry and D. Cooperrider (eds), *Handbook of Transformative Cooperation: New Designs and Dynamics* (Stanford, CA: Stanford University Press, 2007), pp. 107–126.

160 S. G. Barsade and O. A. O'Neill, What's love got to do with it? A longitudinal study of the culture of companionate love and employee and client outcomes in a long-term care setting. *Administrative Science Quarterly*, 59(4) (2014), 551–598.

161 D. Keltner, The Secrets of the Vagus Nerve [video]. *Greater Good Science Center* (2012). Available at: https://greatergood.berkeley.edu/video/item/secrets_of_the_vagus_nerve.

162 J. Haidt, *The Happiness Hypothesis: Finding Modern Truth in Ancient Wisdom* (New York: Basic Books, 2006).

163 R. Hougaard, J. Carter and J. Beck, Assessment: are you a compassionate leader? *Harvard Business Review* (15 May 2018). Available at: https://hbr.org/2018/05/assessment-are-you-a-compassionate-leader; S. Melwani, J. S. Mueller and J. R. Overbeck, Looking down: the influence of contempt and compassion on emergent leadership categorizations. *Journal of Applied Psychology*, 97(6) (2012), 1171–1185.

164 E. Seppälä, The best kept secret to happiness and health: compassion. *Psychology Today* (5 November 2012). Available at: https://www.psychologytoday.com/us/blog/feeling-it/201211/the-best-kept-secret-happiness-health-compassion.

165 *BBC*, #GarethSouthgateWould – England's manager takes social media by storm (4 July 2018). Available at: https://www.bbc.co.uk/sport/football/44718387.

166 Joe Bananas, Twitter post, 4 July 2018. Available at: https://twitter.com/joebananas80/status/1014635480183459840.

167 Georgia Gould, Twitter post, 11 July 2018. Available at: https://twitter.com/Georgia_Gould/status/1017162296601337856.

168 Transport for London, Twitter post, 11 July 2018. Available at: https://twitter.com/TfL/status/1017043498812563456.

169 Mason, *Gareth Southgate*.

170 *BBC*, World Cup 2018: England's Danny Rose reveals depression diagnosis (6 June 2018). Available at: https://www.bbc.co.uk/sport/football/44392337.

171 E. Saner, How the psychology of the England football team could change your life. *The Guardian* (10 July 2018). Available at: https://www.theguardian.com/football/2018/jul/10/psychology-england-football-team-change-your-life-pippa-grange.

172 Quoted in Lombardi, *What It Takes to Be #1*, p. 42.

173 D. Rakel, B. Barrett, Z. Zhang, T. Hoeft, B. Chewning, L. Marchand et al., Perception

of empathy in the therapeutic encounter: effects on the common cold. *Patient Education and Counseling*, 85(3) (2011), 390–397.

174 K. B. Zolnierek and M. R. Dimatteo, Physician communication and patient adherence to treatment: a meta-analysis. *Medical Care*, 47(8) (2009), 826–834.

175 S. Del Canale, D. Z. Louis, V. Maio, X. Wang, G. Rossi, M. Hojatet al., The relationship between physician empathy and disease complications: an empirical study of primary care physicians and their diabetic patients in Parma, Italy. *Academic Medicine*, 87(9) (2012), 1243–1249.

176 Del Canale et al., The relationship between physician empathy and disease complications.

177 L. D. Egbert and S. H. Jackson, Therapeutic benefit of the anesthesiologist–patient relationship. *Anesthesiology*, 119(6) (2013), 1465–1468.

178 Egbert and Jackson, Therapeutic benefit of the anesthesiologist–patient relationship.

179 C. M. Dahlin, J. M. Kelley, V. A. Jackson and J. S. Temel, Early palliative care for lung cancer: improving quality of life and increasing survival. *International Journal of Palliative Nursing*, 16(9) (2010), 420–423.

180 K. J. Kemper and H. A. Shaltout, Non-verbal communication of compassion: measuring psychophysiologic effects. *BMC Complementary and Alternative Medicine*, 11(132) (2011), 1–9.

181 J. M. Kelley, G. Kraft-Todd, L. Schapira, J. Kossowsky and H. Riess, The influence of the patient–clinician relationship on healthcare outcomes: a systematic review and meta-analysis of randomized controlled trials. *PLOS ONE*, 9(4) (2014): e101191.

182 Kelley et al., The influence of the patient–clinician relationship on healthcare outcomes.

183 C. P. West, M. M. Huschka, P. J. Novotny, J. A. Sloan, J. C. Kolars, T. M. Habermann et al., Association of perceived medical errors with resident distress and empathy: a prospective longitudinal study. *Journal*

of the American Medical Association, 296 (2006), 1071–1078.

184 S. Trzeciak and A. Mazzarelli, *Compassionomics: The Revolutionary Scientific Evidence That Caring Makes a Difference* (Pensacola, FL: Studer Group, 2018).

185 S. Trzeciak, How 40 Seconds of Compassion Could Save a Life [video]. *TEDx Talks* (5 June 2018). Available at: https://www.youtube.com/watch?v=elW69hyPUuI.

186 Kerr, *Legacy*, p. 7.

187 Personal communication with authors.

188 Quoted in S. Sinek, *Leaders Eat Last: Why Some Teams Pull Together and Others Don't* (London: Penguin, 2014), p. 65.

189 A. Grant, *Give and Take: A Revolutionary Approach to Success* [Kindle edn] (London: Weidenfeld & Nicholson, 2013).

190 F. Lievens, D. S. Ones and S. Dilchert, Personality scale validities increase throughout medical school. *Journal of Applied Psychology*, 94(6) (2009), 1514–1535; A. Grant and D. Barnes, Predicting sales revenue. Working paper (2011).

191 Grant, *Give and Take*, p. 55.

192 Grant, *Give and Take*, p. 219.

193 Grant, *Give and Take*, p. 195.

194 Grant, *Give and Take*, p. 202.

195 This case study has been adapted from D. Lee, Servant leadership lessons from a 17-year-old. *TLNT* (19 May 2017). Available at: https://www.tlnt.com/servant-leadership-lessons-from-a-17-year-old. The story is précised from J. Brubaker, *Stadium Status: Taking Your Business to the Big Time* (London: Bibliomotion, 2017).

196 This case study is based on D. Collins, *In Foreign Fields: Heroes of Iraq and Afghanistan in Their Own Words* [Kindle edn] (London: Monday Books, 2011), loc. 6292.

197 S. Sinek, How Great Leaders Inspire Action [video]. *TED.com* (4 May 2010). Available at: https://www.youtube.com/watch?v=qp0HIF3SfI4.

198 S. Sinek, Why Leaders Eat Last
[video]. *99U* (4 December 2013).
Available at: https://www.youtube.com/
watch?v=ReRcHdeUG9Y.

199 See https://www.army.mod.uk/who-we-are/
our-schools-and-colleges/rma-sandhurst.

200 Sinek, *Leaders Eat Last*, p. ix.

201 T. Roosevelt, Citizenship in a republic.
Speech delivered at the Sorbonne, Paris,
23 April 1910. Available at: https://www.
leadershipnow.com/tr-citizenship.html.

202 M. K. Gandhi, *Glorious Thoughts of Gandhi*
(New Delhi,: New Book Society of India,
1965), p. 168.

203 For more information, we recommend:
E. Shackleton, *South: The Endurance
Expedition* (London: Penguin, 2015) and
A. Lansing, *Endurance: Shackleton's
Incredible Voyage* (New York: Basic Books,
2014 [1959]).

204 See https://www.britannica.com/biography/
Ernest-Henry-Shackleton.

205 R. F. Scott, *Journals: Captain Scott's Last
Expedition* (Oxford: Oxford University
Press, 2006).

206 Lansing, *Endurance*.

207 E. Shackleton, A letter from Ernest
Shackleton to his wife, Emily (September
1916). Available at: https://www.
spri.cam.ac.uk/archives/shackleton/
articles/1537,2,32,15.html.

208 See https://makingscience.royalsociety.
org/s/rs/people/fst00000549. Priestley was
paraphrasing a line from the preface to
Apsley Cherry-Garrard's first-hand account
of Scott's expedition, *The Worst Journey in
the World* (London: Vintage, 2010 [1922]).

209 Duhigg, What Google learned from its
quest to build the perfect team.

210 L. Delizonna, High-performing teams need
psychological safety.

211 M. Wall, Space shuttle Columbia launched
on tragic mission 10 years ago. *Space.com*
(16 January 2013). Available at: https://
www.space.com/19283-shuttle-columbia-
tragedy-launch-10-years.html; E. Howell,
Columbia disaster: what happened, what
NASA learned. *Space.com* (1 February

2019). Available at: https://www.space.
com/19436-columbia-disaster.html.

212 J. Glanz and J. Schwartz, Dogged
engineer's effort to assess shuttle damage.
(26 September 2003). Available at:
https://www.nytimes.com/2003/09/26/us/
dogged-engineer-s-effort-to-assess-shuttle-
damage.html.

213 A. C. Edmondson, *The Fearless
Organization: Creating Psychological
Safety in the Workplace for Learning,
Innovation, and Growth* (Hoboken, NJ:
John Wiley & Sons, 2019).

214 *The Economist*, Companies will
perform better if employees are
not cowed into silence (12 January
2019). Available at: https://www.
economist.com/business/2019/01/12/
companies-will-perform-better-if-
employees-are-not-cowed-into-silence.

215 In her book, Amy Edmondson draws
on a number of case studies about the
Tenerife crash: U. Schafer, J. Hagen and
C. Burger, Mr KLM (A): Jacob Veldhuyzen.
Case Study. ESMT No. 411-0117 (Berlin:
European School of Management and
Technology, 2011); U. Schafer, J. Hagen
and C. Burger. Mr KLM (B): Captain van
Zanten. Case Study. ESMT No. 411-0118
(Berlin: European School of Management
and Technology, 2011); and U. Schafer, J.
Hagen and C. Burger, Mr KLM (C): Jaap.
Case Study. ESMT No. 411-0119.(Berlin:
European School of Management and
Technology, 2011).

216 D. Coyle, *The Culture Code: The Secrets
of Highly Successful Groups* (London:
Random House Business, 2018), p. 21.

217 Edmondson, *The Fearless Organization*,
summarised in ch. 2.

218 The research team expected to find higher
error rates with lower mean scores on
perceived unit performance, quality of
unit relationships and nurse manager
behaviour, including coaching. They
found exactly the opposite. See A. C.
Edmondson, Learning from mistakes
is easier said than done: group and

organizational influences on the detection and correction of human error. *Journal of Applied Behavioral Science*, 32(1) (1996), 5–28.

219 A. C. Edmondson, Psychological safety and learning behavior in work teams. *Administrative Science Quarterly*, 44(2) (1999), 350–383.

220 Edmondson, Psychological safety and learning behavior in work teams, at 350.

221 M. Syed, *Black Box Thinking* (New York: Portfolio/Penguin, 2015), p. 296.

222 Gallup, *State of the American Workforce Report* (2017), p. 112. Available at: https://www.gallup.com/workplace/238085/state-american-workplace-report-2017.aspx.

223 P. J. Zak and S. Knack, Trust and growth. *Economic Journal*, 111(470) (2001), 295–321.

224 P. Zak, The neuroscience of trust. *Harvard Business Review* (January–February 2017). Available at: https://hbr.org/2017/01/the-neuroscience-of-trust.

225 D. A. Garvin. How Google sold its engineers on management. *Harvard Business Review* (December 2013). Available at: https://hbr.org/2013/12/how-google-sold-its-engineers-on-management.

226 These points have been adapted from: Edmondson, *The Fearless Organization*, ch. 2; C. Nickisch, Creating psychological safety in the workplace [interview with Amy Edmondson]. *Harvard Business Review* (4 July 2019). Available at: https://hbr.org/ideacast/2019/01/creating-psychological-safety-in-the-workplace; and A. Edmondson, How fearless organizations succeed. *Strategy+Business* (14 November 2018). Available at: https://www.strategy-business.com/article/How-Fearless-Organizations-Succeed?gko=63131.

227 Nickisch, Creating psychological safety in the workplace [interview with Amy Edmondson].

228 Edmondson, *The Fearless Organization*, summarised in ch. 8

229 B. L. Fredrickson, The role of positive emotions in positive psychology: the broaden-and-build theory of positive emotions. *American Psychologist*, 56 (2001), 218–226.

230 E. Alderman, Owen Farrell's ref chat backfires, *The Times* (24 December 2014).

231 D. Tiluck, Remembering Zinedine Zidane's headbutt and the 2006 World Cup Final. *Bleacher Report* (9 July 2015). Available at: https://bleacherreport.com/articles/2514359-remembering-zinedine-zidanes-headbutt-and-the-2006-world-cup-final.

232 J. K. Rowling, The fringe benefits of failure, and the importance of imagination. Harvard commencement speech delivered on 5 June 2008. Available at: https://news.harvard.edu/gazette/story/2008/06/text-of-j-k-rowling-speech.

233 Rowling, The fringe benefits of failure.

234 See https://www.changemakers.com/users/myshkin-ingawale.

235 M. Ingawale and L. Espiau, A 20 second blood test without bleeding. *TEDx Talks* (8 February 2013). Available at: https://www.youtube.com/watch?v=RyeQt0GodsE.

236 Quoted in J. Stibel, Branson: a profile in failure. *LinkedIn* (30 October 2014). Available at: https://www.linkedin.com/pulse/20141030172700-461078-richard-branson-a-profile-in-failure.

237 Stibel, Branson.

238 Interestingly, Branson is highlighted in Grant's book *Give and Take* as being a 'giver'. We know that relationships are crucial to resilience, so from the research it looks like loving your people is a great way to build your own resilience and theirs!

239 M. Pickford, Why not try God?, *St. Petersburg Times* (25 January 1936), sect. 2, p. 3. Available at: https://news.google.com/newspapers?id=SQxPAAAAIBAJ&sjid=500DAAAAIBAJ&pg=4725,3554118&dq=pickford+not-the-falling-down&hl=en.

240 R. Felloni, GM CEO Mary Barra said the recall crisis of 2014 forever changed her leadership style. *Business Insider*

(14 November 2018). Available at: https://www.businessinsider.com/gm-mary-barra-recall-crisis-leadership-style-2018-11?r=US&IR=T. All the quotes from Barra in this section appear in Felloni's article.

241 Felloni, GM CEO Mary Barra said the recall crisis of 2014 forever changed her leadership style.

242 Saner, How the psychology of the England football team could change your life.

243 A. C. Edmondson, Strategies for learning from failures. *Harvard Business Review* (April 2011). Available at: https://hbr.org/2011/04/strategies-for-learning-from-failure.

244 Edmondson, Strategies for learning from failures.

245 I. M. Nembhard and A. C. Edmondson, Making it safe: the effects of leader inclusiveness and professional status on psychological safety and improvement efforts in health care teams. *Journal of Organizational Behavior*, 27(7) (2006), 941–966.

246 C. S. Dweck, *Mindset: The New Psychology of Success*, updated edn (New York: Ballantine Books, 2007).

247 K. De Castella, P. Goldin, H. Jazaieri, M. Ziv, C. S. Dweck and J. J. Gross, Beliefs about emotion: links to emotion regulation, well-being, and psychological distress. *Basic and Applied Social Psychology*, 35(6) (2013), 497–505; V. Job, G. M. Walton, K. Bernecker and C. S. Dweck, Implicit theories about willpower predict self-regulation and grades in everyday life. *Journal of Personality and Social Psychology*, 108(4) (2015), 637–647; S. Claro, D. Paunesku and C. S. Dweck, Growth mindset tempers the effects of poverty on academic achievement. *Proceedings of the National Academy of Sciences of the United States of America*, 113(31), (2016), 8664–8668; K. Haimovitz and C. S. Dweck, What predicts children's fixed and growth intelligence mind-sets? Not their parents' views of intelligence but

their parents' views of failure. *Psychological Science*, 27(6) (2016), 859–869.

248 C. S. Lewis, *The Magician's Nephew* (London: Grafton, 2002), p. 116.

249 See Nickisch, Creating psychological safety in the workplace [interview with Amy Edmondson].

250 B. Kenny and A. C. Edmondson, How a new leader broke through a culture of accuse, blame and criticize [podcast]. *Harvard Business Review* (17 September 2019). Available at: https://hbr.org/podcast/2019/09/how-a-new-leader-broke-through-a-culture-of-accuse-blame-and-criticize.

251 See https://daretolead.brenebrown.com.

252 Brown, *Dare to Lead*, p. 6.

253 Please see Chapter 2 for more information on asking coaching questions and the research on the impact of coaching on performance.

254 Brown, *Dare to Lead*, p. 44.

255 Brown, *Dare to Lead*, p. 198.

256 Sinek, *Leaders Eat Last*, p. 14.

257 D. Ariely, U. Gneezy, G. Lowenstein and N. Mazar, Large Stakes and Big Mistakes. Federal Reserve Bank of Boston Working Paper No. 05-11 (2005), as cited in D. Pink, *Drive: The Surprising Truth About What Motivates Us* (Edinburgh: Canongate Books, 2011).

258 E. L. Deci, R. M. Ryan and R. Koestner, A meta-analytic review of experiments examining the effects of extrinsic rewards on intrinsic motivation. *Psychological Bulletin*, 125(6) (1999), 627–668.

259 C. Piekema, Does money really motivate people? *BBC Future* (18 November 2014). Available at: http://www.bbc.com/future/story/20120509-is-it-all-about-the-money.

260 D. Pink, Drive: The Surprising Truth About What Motivates Us [video]. *RSA Animate* (2010). Available at: https://www.youtube.com/watch?v=u6XAPnuFjJc.

261 See https://www.allblacks.com/teams/all-blacks.

262 J. Kerr, The All Blacks guide to being successful (off the field). *The Telegraph* (14

November 2013). Available at: https://www. telegraph.co.uk/men/active/10427619/ The-All-Blacks-guide-to-being-successful-off-the-field.html.

263 Kerr, *Legacy*, p. 14.

264 Kerr, *Legacy*, p. 33.

265 Kerr, *Legacy*.

266 R. Leider, *The Power of Purpose: Find Meaning, Live Longer, Better* (London: Berrett-Koehler, 1997), p. 1.

267 LinkedIn and Imperative, *Purpose at Work: 2016 Workforce Purpose Index* (2016). Available at: https://www.ciphr. com/wp-content/uploads/2016/10/Global_ Purpose_Index_2016.pdf.

268 Quoted in R. L. Daft, *The Leadership Experience*, 7th edn (Boston: Cengage Learning, 2018), p. 408.

269 C. D. Ryff, B. H Singer and G. D. Love, Positive health: connecting well-being with biology. *Philosophical Transactions of the Royal Society B: Biological Sciences*, 359(1449) (2004), 1383–1394; C. Rush, S. Hooker, K. Ross, A. Frers, J. Peters, K. Masters et al., Brief report: meaning in life is mediated by self-efficacy in the prediction of physical activity. *Journal of Health Psychology* (2019). DOI: 10.1177/1359105319828172.

270 P. A. Boyle, L. L. Barnes, A. S. Buchman and D. A. Bennett, Purpose in life is associated with mortality among community-dwelling older persons. *Psychosomatic Medicine*, 71(5) (2009), 574–579.

271 Ryff et al., Positive health.

272 Ryff et al., Positive health; Boyle et al., Purpose in life is associated with mortality among community-dwelling older persons.

273 P. L. Hill and N. A. Turiano, Purpose in life as a predictor of mortality across adulthood. *Psychological Science*, 25(7) (2004), 1482–1486.

274 K. A. Arnold, N. Turner, J. Barling, E. Kelloway and M. C. McKee, Transformational leadership and psychological well-being: the mediating role of meaningful work. *Journal of*

Occupational Health Psychology, 12(3) (2007), 193–203.

275 Imperative, *Purpose at Work: 2019 Workforce Purpose Index* (2019), p. 19. Available at: https://www.2019wpi.com.

276 *Harvard Business Review, The Business Case for Purpose* (2015). Available at: https://www.ey.com/ Publication/vwLUAssets/ey-the-business-case-for-purpose/$FILE/ ey-the-business-case-for-purpose.pdf.

277 D. S. Yeager, M. Henderson, S. D'Mello, D. Paunesku, G. M. Walton, B. J. Spitzer et al., Boring but important: a self-transcendent purpose for learning fosters academic self-regulation. *Journal of Personality and Social Psychology*, 107 (2014), 559–580.

278 Center for Generational Kinetics, *Unlocking Millennial Talent 2015: Brand New Insights for Employing the Fastest Growing Generation in the Workplace* (2015). Available at: https://genhq. com/wp-content/uploads/2015/06/ Unlocking-Millennial-Talent-c-2015-The-Center-for-Generational-Kinetics.pdf.

279 The text in this section is adapted from R. Quin and A. Thakor, Creating a purpose-driven organisation. *Harvard Business Review* (July–August 2018). Available at: https://hbr.org/2018/07/creating-a-purpose-driven-organization.html.

280 DTE Energy, *DTE Energy Way: Code of Conduct* (2016), p. i. Available at: https://newlook.dteenergy. com/wps/wcm/connect/5ffb7155-2b3e-4981-a3a2-d6dc0bb66197/ dteEnergyWayCodeOfConduct. pdf?MOD=AJPERES.

281 Gallup, The 2019 Gallup Great Workplace Award Recipients (28 March 2019). Available at: https://www.gallup.com/ workplace/248105/2019-gallup-great-workplace-award-recipients.aspx

282 See https://www.un.org/ sustainabledevelopment/ sustainable-development-goals.

283 Kouzes and Posner, *The Leadership Challenge.*

284 S. Sinek, *Start with Why: How Great Leaders Inspire Everyone to Take Action* (London: Penguin, 2011).

285 H. Gardner, M. Csikszentmihalyi and W. Damon, *Good Work: When Excellence and Ethics Meet* (New York: Basic Books, 2008), p. ix.

286 LinkedIn and Imperative, *Purpose at Work: 2016.*

287 See https://www.forbes.com/profile/indra-nooyi/#3a1608eb5d6f.

288 D. Wiener-Bronner, How Indra Nooyi built Pepsi for the future. *CNN* (7 August 2018). Available at: https://money.cnn.com/2018/08/07/news/companies/indra-nooyi-legacy/index.html.

289 J. Tang, Four ways PepsiCo CEO motivates her employees. *LinkedIn* (16 August 2017). Available at: https://business.linkedin.com/talent-solutions/blog/employee-retention/2017/4-ways-pepsico-ceo-motivates-her-employees.

290 Tang, Four ways PepsiCo CEO motivates her employees.

291 Tang, Four ways PepsiCo CEO motivates her employees.

292 R. Umoh, PepsiCo CEO Indra Nooyi: 5 powerful career habits that drove her success. *CNBC* (2 October 2019). Available at: https://www.cnbc.com/2018/10/02/pepsico-ceo-indra-nooyis-last-day-5-habits-that-drove-her-success.html.

293 See http://pathways.shc.edu/wp-content/uploads/2016/12/Bricklayers-ParableActivity.pdf.

294 A. C. Edmondson, R. M. Bohmer and G. P. Pisano, Disrupted routines: team learning and new technology implementation in hospitals. *Administrative Science Quarterly*, 46(4) (2001), 685–716.

295 Yeager et al., Boring but important.

296 See https://mgmt.wharton.upenn.edu/profile/grantad.

297 J. M. Berg, A. Wrzesniewski and J. E. Dutton, Perceiving and responding to challenges in job crafting at different ranks: when proactivity requires adaptivity. *Journal of Organizational Behavior*, 31 (2010), 158–186.

298 A. Wrzesniewski, Engage in job crafting. In J. E. Dutton and G. Spreitzer (eds), *How to Be a Positive Leader: Small Actions, Big Impact* (San Francisco, CA: Berrett-Koehler, 2014), pp. 65–77.

299 A. Wrzesniewski, J. E. Dutton and G. Debebe, Interpersonal sensemaking and the meaning of work. In R. Kramer and B. Staw (eds), *Research in Organizational Behavior*, vol. 25 (Oxford: Elsevier, 2003), pp. 93–135.

300 K. M. Sheldon, P. Jose, T. Kashdan and A. Jarden, Personality, effective goal-striving, and enhanced well-being: comparing 10 candidate personality strengths. *Personality and Social Psychology Bulletin*, 41(4) (2015), 575–585.

301 A. Wrzesniewski and J. Dutton, Crafting a job: revisioning employees as active crafters of their work. *Academy of Management Review,* 26(2) (2001), 179–201.

302 C. Wilson, Team culture expert Owen Eastwood gets ramped-up role as All Whites aim to shift mindset. *Stuff* (5 March 2017) Available at: https://www.stuff.co.nz/sport/football/nz-teams/90006153/team-culture-expert-owen-eastwood-gets-rampedup-role-as-all-whites-aim-to-shift-mindset.

303 Elite Performance Partners, Performance culture expert and South African cricket star join guests at leadership forum (8 May 2018). Available at: https://eppartners.co.uk/news-blog/performance-culture-expert-and-south-african-cricket-star-join-guests-at-leadership-forum.

304 Kerr, *Legacy*, p. 41.

305 F. Nietzsche, *Twilight of the Idols* (Oxford: Oxford University Press, 1998 [1889]), p. 6.

306 Elite Performance Partners, Performance culture expert and South African cricket star join guests at leadership forum.

307 Quoted in H. J. Brown Jr, *Life's Instructions for Wisdom, Success, and Happiness*

(Nashville, TN: Rutledge Hill Press, 2000), p. 132.

308 B. N. Pfau, How an accounting firm convinced its employees they could change the world. *Harvard Business Review* (6 October 2015). Available at: https://hbr.org/2015/10/how-an-accounting-firm-convinced-its-employees-they-could-change-the-world.

309 Coyle, *The Culture Code*, pp. 207–208.

310 Coyle, *The Culture Code*, p. 229.

311 G. Mairs, How the All Blacks drew inspiration from First World War soldier's ordeal. *The Telegraph* (10 November 2014). Available at: https://www.telegraph.co.uk/sport/rugbyunion/international/newzealand/11221948/How-the-All-Blacks-drew-inspiration-from-First-World-War-soldiers-ordeal.html.

312 Sinek, *Start with Why*, pp. 97–99.

313 Pink, *Drive*, p. 32.

314 T. E. Lawrence, *Seven Pillars of Wisdom* (Ware: Wordsworth Editions, 1997 [1935]), p. 7.

315 B. Obama, *The Audacity of Hope: Thoughts on Reclaiming the American Dream* (New York: Crown, 2006), p. 206.

316 T. Walker, Superhead Anthony Seldon and his challenge to improve Wellington College. *The Independent* (6 October 2005). Available at: https://www.independent.co.uk/news/education/education-news/superhead-anthony-seldon-and-his-challenge-to-improve-wellington-college-317608.html.

317 Interview with the authors, 24 October 2019.

318 I. Hunt, Sir Anthony Seldon: the value of a good head. *The Telegraph* (30 June 2015). Available at: https://www.telegraph.co.uk/education/educationopinion/11705706/Sir-Anthony-Seldon-the-value-of-a-good-head.html.

319 A. Grant, *Power Moves: Lessons from Davos* [audio] (Newark, NJ: Audible, 2019).

320 The subject of L. D. Marquet, *Turn the Ship Around! A True Story of Turning Followers into Leaders* (London: Penguin, 2015).

321 S. Covey, foreword to Marquet, *Turn the Ship Around!*, pp. xiii–xiv.

322 K. Birdi, C. Clegg, M. Patterson, A. Robinson, C. B. Stride, T. Wall et al., The impact of human resource and operational management practices on company productivity: a longitudinal study. *Personnel Psychology*, 61(4) (2008), 467–501.

323 Birdi et al., The impact of human resource and operational management practices on company productivity, p. 490.

324 E. L. Deci and R. M. Ryan, *Intrinsic Motivation and Self-Determination in Human Behavior* (New York: Springer, 1985).

325 G. L. Stewart, A meta-analytic review of relationships between team design features and team performance. *Journal of Management*, 32 (2006), 29–55.

326 G. Chen, B. L. Kirkman, R. Kanfer, D. Allen and B. Rosen, A multilevel study of leadership, empowerment, and performance in teams. *Journal of Applied Psychology*, 92 (2007), 331–346.

327 A. L. Kristof-Brown, R. D. Zimmerman and E. C. Johnson, Consequences of individuals' fit at work: a meta-analysis of person-job, person-organization, person-group, and person-supervisor fit. *Personnel Psychology*, 58 (2005), 281–342.

328 R. W. Griffeth, P. W. Hom and S. Gaertner, A meta-analysis of antecedents and correlates of employee turnover: update, moderator tests, and research implications for the next millennium. *Journal of Management*, 26 (2000), 463–488.

329 G. M. Spreitzer, Psychological empowerment in the workplace: construct definition, measurement, and validation. *Academy of Management Journal*, 38 (1995), 1442–1465.

330 G. M. Spreitzer, M. Kizilos and S. Nason, A dimensional analysis of the relationship between psychological empowerment and effectiveness, satisfaction, and strain. *Journal of Management*, 23 (1997), 679–704.

331 A. D. Stajkovic and F. Luthans, Self-efficacy and work-related performance: a meta-analysis. *Psychological Bulletin*, 124 (1998), 240–261; S. E. Seibert, G. Wang and S. H. Courtright, Antecedents and consequences of psychological and team empowerment in organizations: a meta-analytic review. *Journal of Applied Psychology*, 96(5) (2011), 981–1003.

332 Society for Human Resource Management, *2016 Employee Job Satisfaction and Engagement: Revitalizing a Changing Workforce* (2016). Available at: https://www.shrm.org/hr-today/trends-and-forecasting/research-and-surveys/Pages/Job-Satisfaction-and-Engagement-Report-Revitalizing-Changing-Workforce.aspx.

333 This section has been adapted from Marquet, *Turn the Ship Around!*

334 Sinek, *Leaders Eat Last*, p. 18.

335 Marquet, *Turn the Ship Around!*, pp. 85–90.

336 Marquet, *Turn the Ship Around!*, p. 84.

337 L. David Marquet, Twitter post, 30 September 2016. Available at: https://twitter.com/ldavidmarquet/status/781960562619981824.

338 A. Adkins and B. Rigoni, Millennials want jobs to be development opportunities. *Gallup Workplace* (30 June 2016). Available at: https://www.gallup.com/workplace/236438/millennials-jobs-development-opportunities.aspx.

339 A. Jacobs, Happy feet: inside the online shoe utopia. *The New Yorker* (7 September 2009). Available at: https://www.newyorker.com/magazine/2009/09/14/happy-feet.

340 T. Hsieh, *Delivering Happiness: A Path to Profits, Passion and Purpose* (New York: Business Plus, 2010).

341 See https://www.zappos.com/about/what-we-live-by.

342 R. J. Thomas and Y. Silverstone, *Empowering Employees at Zappos*. Outlook Case Study: Workforce of the Future (Boston, MA: Accenture, 2015), p. 3. Available at: https://www.accenture.com/t20151015t042910__w__/us-en/_acnmedia/accenture/conversion-assets/outlook/documents/2/accenture-outlook-zappos-web-pdf.pdf.

343 S. G. Leslie and J. Aaker, Zappos: happiness in a box. Stanford Graduate School of Business – Case M-333 (23 August 2010), p. 20. Available at: https://innovaservicios.weebly.com/uploads/3/3/6/8/3368095/zappos_stanford_gsb.pdf.

344 Leslie and Aaker, Zappos: happiness in a box, p. 21.

345 Their protest made the BBC website and you can watch it on YouTube: https://www.youtube.com/watch?v=ccJuBYc6azs.

346 See, for example, A. L. Duckworth, *Grit: Why Passion and Persistence Are the Secrets to Success* (London: Vermilion Life Essentials, 2019) and Grit: The Power of Passion and Perseverance [video]. *TED.com* (April 2013). Available at: https://www.ted.com/talks/angela_lee_duckworth_grit_the_power_of_passion_and_perseverance/transcript?language=en.

347 A. L. Duckworth, A. Quirk, R. Gallop, R. H. Hoyle, D. R. Kelly and M. D. Matthews, Cognitive and noncognitive predictors of success. *Proceedings of the National Academy of Sciences of the United States of America*, 116(47) (2019), 23499–23504.

348 N. Doidge, *The Brain That Changes Itself: Stories of Personal Triumph from the Frontiers of Brain Science* (New York: Viking, 2007).

349 W. Bennis, The leadership advantage. *Leader to Leader*, No. 12 (spring 1999), p. 5. Available at: http://www.prodaio.com/uploads/1/1/4/8/11482976/the_leadership_advantage_-_warren_bennis.pdf.

350 L. Fessler, How to cultivate grit in your employees. *Advisory Board* (7 May 2018). Available at: https://www.advisory.com/daily-briefing/2018/05/07/duckworth-grit.

351 D. S. Yeager, V. Purdie-Vaughns, J. Garcia, N. Apfel, P. Brzustoski, A. Master et al., Breaking the cycle of mistrust: wise interventions to provide critical feedback across the racial divide. *Journal of*

Experimental Psychology: General, 143 (2013), 804–824 at 809.

352 This section has been adapted from T. H. Lee and A. L. Duckworth, Organizational grit. *Harvard Business Review* (September–October 2018). Available at: https://hbr.org/2018/09/organizational-grit. See also J. I. Merlino and A. Raman, Health care's service fanatics. *Harvard Business Review* (May 2013). Available at: https://hbr.org/2013/05/health-cares-service-fanatics.

353 Appreciative inquiry was developed by Case Western Reserve University's Department of Organizational Behavior and is a model that aims to engage stakeholders in finding their strengths and using these to drive improvements. See D. L. Cooperrider and D. Whitney, *Appreciative Inquiry: A Positive Revolution in Change* (San Francisco, CA: Berrett Koehler, 2005).

354 R. Emmons, Pay it forward. *Greater Good Magazine* (2007). Available at: https://greatergood.berkeley.edu/article/item/pay_it_forward.

355 Emmons, Pay it forward.

356 S. Kaplan, J. C. Bradley-Geist, A. Ahmad, A. Anderson, A. Hargrove and A. Lindsey, A test of two positive psychology interventions to increase employee well-being. *Journal of Business and Psychology*, 29 (2013), 367–380. https://doi.org/10.1007/s10869-013-9319-4.

357 P. C. Watkins, K. Woodward, T. Stone and R. L. Kolts, Gratitude and happiness: development of a measure of gratitude and subjective wellbeing. *Social Behavior and Personality*, 31(5) (2003), 431–451.

358 J. J. Froha, W. J. Sefick and R. A. Emmons, Counting blessings in early adolescents: an experimental study of gratitude and subjective well-being. *Journal of School Psychology*, 46(2) (2008), 213–233.

359 N. Petrocchi and A. Couyoumdjian, The impact of gratitude on depression and anxiety: the mediating role of criticizing, attacking, and reassuring the self. *Self and Identity*, 15(2) (2016), 191–205.

360 J. Vieselmeyer, J. Holguin and A. Mezulis, The role of resilience and gratitude in posttraumatic stress and growth following a campus shooting. *Psychological Trauma: Theory, Research, Practice, and Policy*, 9(1) (2017), 62–69.

361 D. W. Chan, Gratitude, gratitude intervention and subjective well-being among Chinese school teachers in Hong Kong. *Educational Psychology*, 30(2) (2010), 139–153.

362 R. Emmons and R. Stern, Gratitude as a psychotherapeutic intervention. *Journal of Clinical Psychology*, 69(8) (2013), 846–855.

363 M. Y. Bartlett and D. DeSteno, Gratitude and prosocial behavior: helping when it costs you. *Psychological Science*, 17(4), (2006), 319–325.

364 J. Smith, Five ways to cultivate gratitude at work. *Greater Good Magazine* (16 May 2015). Available at: https://greatergood.berkeley.edu/article/item/five_ways_to_cultivate_gratitude_at_work.

365 Emmons, Pay it forward.

366 A. Grant and F. Gino, A little thanks goes a long way: explaining why gratitude expressions motivate prosocial behavior. *Journal of Personality and Social Psychology*, 98(6) (2010), 946–955.

367 J. Smith, How to show appreciation and get better results from your employees this holiday season. *Forbes* (13 November 2013). Available at: https://www.forbes.com/sites/jacquelynsmith/2013/11/13/how-to-show-appreciation-and-get-better-results-from-your-employees-this-holiday-season.

368 Quoted in K. Newman, How gratitude can transform your workplace. *Greater Good Magazine* (6 September 2017). Available at: https://greatergood.berkeley.edu/article/item/how_gratitude_can_transform_your_workplace.

369 R. Emmons and A. Mishra, Why gratitude enhances well-being: what we know, what

we need to know. In K. M. Sheldon, T. B. Kashdan and M. F. Steger (eds), *Designing Positive Psychology: Taking Stock and Moving Forward* (New York: Oxford University Press, 2010), pp. 248–264 at p. 254.

370 Research summarised in S. Lyubomirsky, *The How of Happiness: A New Approach to Getting the Life You Want* (New York: Penguin, 2007), p. 92.

371 Quoted at https://www.virgin.com/richard-branson/my-top-10-quotes-celebrating.

372 Quoted in P. J. Zak, The neuroscience of trust. *Harvard Business Review* (January–February 2017). Available at: https://hbr.org/2017/01/the-neuroscience-of-trust.

373 M. Obama, Remarks by the First Lady during keynote address at Young African Women Leaders Forum (22 June 2011). Available at: https://obamawhitehouse.archives.gov/the-press-office/2011/06/22/remarks-first-lady-during-keynote-address-young-african-women-leaders-fo.

374 Quoted in Lombardi, *What It Takes to Be #1*, p. 37.

Bibliography

Achor, S. (2010) *The Happiness Advantage: The Seven Principles of Positive Psychology* (New York: Random House).

Aderman, D. (1972) Elation, depression, and helping behavior. *Journal of Personality and Social Psychology*, 24(1), 91–101.

Adkins, A. and Rigoni, B. (2016) Millennials want jobs to be development opportunities. *Gallup Workplace* (30 June). Available at: https://www.gallup.com/workplace/236438/millennials-jobs-development-opportunities.aspx.

Adolphs, R., Gosselin, F., Buchanan, T. W., Tranel, D., Schyns, P. and Damasio, A. R. (2005) A mechanism for impaired fear recognition after amygdala damage. *Nature*, 433, 68–72.

Alden, A. L., Dale, J. A. and DeGood, D. E. (2001) Interactive effects of the affect quality and directional focus of mental imagery on pain analgesia. *Applied Psychophysiology and Biofeedback*, 26, 117–126.

Alderman, E. (2014) Owen Farrell's ref chat backfires. *The Times* (24 December).

Algoe, S. B. and Way, B. M. (2014) Evidence for a role of the oxytocin system, indexed by genetic variation in CD38, in the social bonding effects of expressed gratitude. *Social Cognitive and Affective Neuroscience*, 9(12), 1855–1861.

Amaral, D. G. (2003) The amygdala, social behavior, and danger detection. *Annals of the New York Academy of Sciences*, 1000, 337–347.

Anderson, M. C. and MetrixGlobal LLC (2001) Executive briefing: case study on the return on investment of executive coaching (2 November). Available at: https://researchportal.coachfederation.org/Document/Pdf/abstract_681.

Ariely, D., Gneezy, U., Lowenstein, G. and Mazar, N. (2005) Large Stakes and Big Mistakes. Federal Reserve Bank of Boston Working Paper No. 05–11.

Arnold, K. A., Turner, N., Barling, J., Kelloway, E. and McKee M. C. (2007) Transformational leadership and psychological well-being: the mediating role of meaningful work. *Journal of Occupational Health Psychology*, 12(3), 193–203.

Aspinwall, L. G. (1998) Rethinking the role of positive affect in self-regulation. *Motivation and Emotion*, 22, 1–32.

Balague, G. (2013) *Pep Guardiola: Another Way of Winning: The Biography* (London: Weidenfeld & Nicolson).

Barsade, S. G. and O'Neill, O. A. (2014) What's love got to do with it? A longitudinal study of the culture of companionate love and employee and client outcomes in a long-term care setting. *Administrative Science Quarterly*, 59(4), 551–598.

Bartlett, M. Y. and DeSteno, D. (2006) Gratitude and prosocial behavior: helping when it costs you. *Psychological Science*, 17(4), 319–325.

BBC (2018a) #GarethSouthgateWould – England's manager takes social media by storm (4 July). Available at: https://www.bbc.co.uk/sport/football/44718387.

BBC (2018b) World Cup 2018: England's Danny Rose reveals depression diagnosis (6 June). Available at: https://www.bbc.co.uk/sport/football/44392337.

Beesley, C. (2018) Robbie Fowler on why Gareth Southgate tops other England bosses. *MSN News* (9 July). Available at: https://www.msn.com/en-gb/news/newsliverpool/robbie-fowler-on-why-gareth-southgate-tops-other-england-bosses/ar-AAzMCai.

Bennis, W. (1999) The leadership advantage. *Leader to Leader*, No. 12 (spring). Available at: http://www.prodaio.com/uploads/1/1/4/8/11482976/the_leadership_advantage_-_warren_bennis.pdf.

Ben-Shahar, T. and Ridgeway, A. (2017) *The Joy of Leadership: How Positive Psychology Can Maximize Your Impact (and Make You Happier) in a Challenging World* (Hoboken, NJ: John Wiley & Sons).

Berg, J. M., Wrzesniewski, A. and Dutton, J. E. (2010) Perceiving and responding to challenges in job crafting at different ranks: when proactivity requires adaptivity. *Journal of Organizational Behavior*, 31, 158–186.

Bibb, S. (2016) *Strengths-Based Recruitment and Development: A Practical Guide to Transforming Talent Management Strategy for Business Results* (London: Kogan Page).

Birdi, K., Clegg, C., Patterson, M., Robinson, A., Stride, C. B., Wall, T. et al. (2008). The impact of human resource and operational management practices on company productivity: a longitudinal study. *Personnel Psychology*, 61, 467–501.

Boswell, Z. (2019) Jose Mourinho turning over new leaf at Tottenham – 'It's not about myself'. *Sky Sports* (21 November). Available at: https://www.skysports.com/football/news/11675/11866411/jose-mourinho-turning-over-new-leaf-at-tottenham-its-not-about-myself.

Boudway, I. (2018) The five pillars of Gregg Popovich. *Bloomberg Businessweek* (10 January). Available at: https://www.bloomberg.com/news/features/2018-01-10/the-five-pillars-of-gregg-popovich.

Boyle, P. A., Barnes, L. L., Buchman, A. S. and Bennett, D. A. (2009) Purpose in life is associated with mortality among community-dwelling older persons. *Psychosomatic Medicine*, 71(5), 574–579.

Brim, B. and Asplund, J. (2009) Driving engagement by focusing on strengths. *Gallup Business Journal* (12 November). Available at: https://news.gallup.com/businessjournal/124214/driving-engagement-focusing-strengths.aspx.

Brinke, L. T., Kish, A. and Keltner, D. (2017) Hedge fund managers with psychopathic tendencies make for worse investors. *Personality and Social Psychology Bulletin*, 28, 484–495.

Brinke, L. T., Liu, C. C. and Keltner, D. (2015) Virtues, vices, and political influence in the US Senate. *Psychological Science*, 27(1), 85–93.

Brown, B. (2018) *Dare to Lead: Brave Work. Tough Conversations. Whole Hearts.* (London: Vermillion).

Brown Jr, H. J. (2000) *Life's Instructions for Wisdom, Success, and Happiness* (Nashville, TN: Rutledge Hill Press).

Browne, F. F. (1913) *The Every-day Life of Abraham Lincoln: A Narrative and Descriptive Biography* (Chicago, IL: Browne & Howell). Available at: http://www.gutenberg.org/ebooks/14004.

Brubaker, J. (2017) *Stadium Status: Taking Your Business to the Big Time* (London: Bibliomotion).

Buckingham, M. (2007). *Go Put Your Strengths to Work* (London: Simon & Schuster).

Buckingham, M. and Clifton, D. (2004). *Now, Discover Your Strengths: How to Develop Your Talents and Those of the People You Manage* (London: Simon & Schuster).

Burg, B. and Mann, J. D. (2016) *The Go-Giver Leader* (London: Penguin Random House).

Calebjsaenz (2013) Morning rehash: Popovich conducts a Wizards beatdown. *Pounding the Rock* (14 November). Available at: https://www.poundingtherock.com/2013/11/14/5103402/morning-rehash-popovich-spurs-wizards-beatdown.

Cameron, K. (2011) *Positive Leadership* (Oakland, CA: Berrett-Koehler Publishers).

CAPP (2010a) *Technical Manual and Statistical Properties for Realise2* (Coventry: CAPP).

CAPP (2010b) Why Strengths? The Evidence. Available at: http://emotionalintelligenceworldwide.com/wp-content/uploads/CAPP_Why_Strengths_The_Evidence.pdf.

Catalino, L. I. and Fredrickson, B. L. (2011) A Tuesday in the life of a flourisher: the role of positive emotional reactivity in optimal mental health. *Emotion*, 11(4), 938–950.

Cavanaugh, J. (2008) *Giants Among Men: How Robustelli, Huff, Gifford, and the Giants Made New York a Football Town and Changed the NFL* (New York: Random House).

Center for Generational Kinetics (2015) *Unlocking Millennial Talent 2015: Brand New Insights for Employing the Fastest Growing Generation in the Workplace*. Available at: https://genhq.com/wp-content/uploads/2015/06/Unlocking-Millennial-Talent-c-2015-The-Center-for-Generational-Kinetics.pdf.

Chan, D. W. (2010) Gratitude, gratitude intervention and subjective well-being among Chinese school teachers in Hong Kong. *Educational Psychology*, 30(2), 139–153.

Chen, G., Kirkman, B. L., Kanfer, R., Allen, D. and Rosen, B. (2007) A multilevel study of leadership, empowerment, and performance in teams. *Journal of Applied Psychology*, 92, 331–346.

Cherry-Garrard, A. (2010 [1922]) *The Worst Journey in the World* (London: Vintage).

Clance, P. R. and Imes, S. A. (1978) The impostor phenomenon in high achieving women: dynamics and therapeutic intervention. *Psychotherapy: Theory, Research & Practice*, 15(3), 241–247.

Claro, S., Paunesku, D. and Dweck, C. S. (2016) Growth mindset tempers the effects of poverty on academic achievement. *Proceedings of the National Academy of Sciences of the United States of America*, 113(31), 8664–8668.

Colan, L. J. and Davis-Colan, J. (2018) *The Power of Positive Coaching: The Mindset and Habits to Inspire Winning Results and Relationships* (New York: McGraw Hill Professional).

Collins, D. (2011) *In Foreign Fields: Heroes of Iraq and Afghanistan in Their Own Words* [Kindle edn] (London: Monday Books).

Collins, N. (2016) Be like Pep – the perfect leader. *Morgan McKinley* (29 January). Available at: https://www.morganmckinley.ie/article/be-pep-perfect-leader.

Cooperrider, D. and Whitney, D. (2005) *Appreciative Inquiry: A Positive Revolution in Change* (San Francisco, CA: Berrett Koehler).

Corporate Leadership Council (2002) *Performance Management Survey* (Washington, DC: Corporate Leadership Council).

Cotton, B. (2019) Jose Mourinho's sacking – leadership lessons from the dismissal of the 'special one'. *Business Leader* (1 January). Available at: https://www.businessleader.co.uk/jose-mourinhos-sacking-leadership-lessons-from-the-dismissal-of-the-special-one/57609.

Covey, S. (1989) *The 7 Habits of Highly Effective People: Powerful Lessons in Personal Change* (London: Simon & Schuster).

Coyle, D. (2018) *The Culture Code: The Secrets of Highly Successful Groups* (London: Random House Business).

Coyle, D. (2018) How Gregg Popovich uses 'magical feedback' to inspire the San Antonio Spurs. *Time* (30 January). Available at: https://time.com/5125421/gregg-popovich-san-antonio-spurs-success/#.

Cricketing Yorkshire (2015) Episode 1 [video]. *Sky Sports*. Available at: https://www.skysports.com/watch/video/sports/cricket/9861800/cricketing-yorkshire-episode-1.

Csikszentmihalyi, M. (1990) *Flow: The Psychology of Optimal Experience* (New York: Harper & Row).

Daft, R. L. (2018) *The Leadership Experience*, 7th edn (Boston, MA: Cengage Learning).

Dahlin, C. M., Kelley, J. M., Jackson, V. A. and Temel, J. S. (2010) Early palliative care for lung cancer: improving quality of life and increasing survival. *International Journal of Palliative Nursing*, 16(9), 420–423.

Danner, D. D., Snowdon, D. A. and Friesen, W. V. (2001) Positive emotions in early life and longevity: findings from the nun study. *Journal of Personality and Social Psychology*, 80, 804–813.

De Castella, K., Goldin, P., Jazaieri, H., Ziv, M., Dweck, C. S. and Gross, J. J. (2013) Beliefs about emotion: links to emotion regulation, well-being, and psychological distress. *Basic and Applied Social Psychology*, 35(6), 497–505.

Deci, E. L. and Ryan, R. M. (1985) *Intrinsic Motivation and Self-Determination in Human Behavior* (New York: Springer).

Deci, E. L., Ryan, R. M. and Koestner, R. (1999) A meta-analytic review of experiments examining the effects of extrinsic rewards on intrinsic motivation. *Psychological Bulletin*, 125(6), 627–668.

Deeg, D. J. H. and Van Zonneveld, R. J. (1989) Does happiness lengthen life? The prediction of longevity in the elderly. In R. Veenhoven (ed.), *How Harmful Is Happiness? Consequences of Enjoying Life or Not* (Rotterdam: Universitaire Pers Rotterdam), pp. 29–34.

Del Canale, S., Louis, D. Z., Maio, V., Wang, X., Rossi, G., Hojat, M. et al. (2012) The relationship between physician empathy and disease complications: an empirical study of primary care physicians and their diabetic patients in Parma, Italy. *Academic Medicine*, 87(9), 1243–1249.

Delizonna, L. (2017) High performing teams need psychological safety. Here's how to create it. *Harvard Business Review* (24 August). Available at: https://hbr.org/2017/08/high-performing-teams-need-psychological-safety-heres-how-to-create-it.

Dempsey, K. (2007) Performance management: play to their strengths. *Personnel Today* (6 August). Available at: https://www.personneltoday.com/hr/performance-management-play-to-their-strengths.

Diehl, M., Hay, E. L. and Berg, K. M. (2011) The ratio between positive and negative affect and flourishing mental health across adulthood. *Aging and Mental Health*, 15(7), 882–893.

Diener, E., Sandvik, E. and Pavot, W. (1991) Happiness is the frequency, not the intensity, of positive versus negative affect. In F. Strack, M. Argyle and N. Schwarz (eds), *Subjective Well-being: An Interdisciplinary Perspective* (New York: Pergamon), pp. 119–139.

Digitale, E. (2014) Oxytocin levels in blood, cerebrospinal fluid are linked, study finds. *Stanford Medicine News Center* (4 November). Available at: https://med.stanford.edu/news/all-news/2014/11/oxytocin-levels-in-blood-cerebrospinal-fluid-are-linked-study-fi.html.

Doidge, N. (2007) *The Brain That Changes Itself: Stories of Personal Triumph from the Frontiers of Brain Science* (New York: Viking).

DTE Energy (2016) *DTE Energy Way: Code of Conduct*. Available at: https://newlook.dteenergy.com/wps/wcm/connect/5ffb7155-2b3e-4981-a3a2-d6dc0bb66197/dteEnergyWayCodeOf Conduct.pdf?MOD=AJPERES.

Duckworth, A. L. (2013) Grit: The Power of Passion and Perseverance [video]. *TED.com* (April). Available at: https://www.ted.com/talks/angela_lee_duckworth_grit_the_power_of_passion_and_perseverance/transcript?language=en.

Duckworth, A. L. (2019) *Grit: Why Passion and Persistence Are the Secrets to Success* (London: Vermilion Life Essentials).

Duckworth, A. L., Quirk, A., Gallop, R., Hoyle, R. H., Kelly, D. R. and Matthews, M. D. (2019) Cognitive and noncognitive predictors of success. *Proceedings of the National Academy of Sciences of the United States of America*, 116(47), 23499–23504.

Duhigg, C. (2016) What Google learned from its quest to build the perfect team. *New York Times* (25 February). Available at: https://www.nytimes.com/2016/02/28/magazine/what-google-learned-from-its-quest-to-build-the-perfect-team.html.

Dutton, J. E., Lilius, J. and Kanov, J. (2007) The transformative potential of compassion at work. In S. Piderit, R. Fry and D. Cooperrider (eds), *Handbook of Transformative Cooperation: New Designs and Dynamics* (Stanford, CA: Stanford University Press), pp. 107–126.

Dweck, C. S. (2006) *Mindset* (New York: Random House).

Dweck, C. S. (2007) *Mindset: The New Psychology of Success*, updated edn (New York: Ballantine Books).

Economist, The (2019) Companies will perform better if employees are not cowed into silence (12 January). Available at: https://www.economist.com/business/2019/01/12/

companies-will-perform-better-if-employees-are-not-cowed-into-silence.

Edmondson, A. C. (1996) Learning from mistakes is easier said than done: group and organizational influences on the detection and correction of human error. *Journal of Applied Behavioral Science*, 32(1), 5–28.

Edmondson, A. C. (1999) Psychological safety and learning behavior in work teams. *Administrative Science Quarterly*, 44(2), 350–383.

Edmondson, A. C. (2011) Strategies for learning from failures. *Harvard Business Review* (April). Available at: https://hbr.org/2011/04/strategies-for-learning-from-failure.

Edmondson, A. C. (2015) The kinds of teams health care needs. *Harvard Business Review* (16 December). Available at: https://hbr.org/2015/12/the-kinds-of-teams-health-care-needs.

Edmondson, A. C. (2018) How fearless organizations succeed. *Strategy+Business* (14 November). Available at: https://www.strategy-business.com/article/How-Fearless-Organizations-Succeed?gko=63131.

Edmondson, A. C. (2019) *The Fearless Organization: Creating Psychological Safety in the Workplace for Learning, Innovation, and Growth* (Hoboken, NJ: John Wiley & Sons).

Edmondson, A. C., Bohmer, R. M. and Pisano, G. P. (2001) Disrupted routines: team learning and new technology implementation in hospitals. *Administrative Science Quarterly*, 46(4), 685–716.

Egbert, L. D. and Jackson, S. H. (2013) Therapeutic benefit of the anesthesiologist–patient relationship. *Anesthesiology*, 119(6), 1465–1468.

Elite Performance Partners (2018) Performance culture expert and South African cricket star join guests at leadership forum (8 May). Available at: https://eppartners.co.uk/news-blog/performance-culture-expert-and-south-african-cricket-star-join-guests-at-leadership-forum.

Emmons, R. (2007) Pay it forward. *Greater Good Magazine* (1 June). Available at: https://greatergood.berkeley.edu/article/item/pay_it_forward.

Emmons, R. and Mishra, A. (2010) Why gratitude enhances well-being: what we know, what we need to know. In K. M. Sheldon, T. B. Kashdan and M. F. Steger (eds), *Designing Positive Psychology: Taking Stock and Moving Forward* (New York: Oxford University Press), pp. 248–264.

Emmons, R. and Stern, R. (2013) Gratitude as a psychotherapeutic intervention. *Journal of Clinical Psychology*, 69(8), 846–855.

Eurosport (2019) Jose Mourinho: 'The nice manager, after three months, is a puppet' (15 May). Available at: https://www.eurosport.com/football/premier-league/2018-2019/jose-mourinho-the-nice-manager-after-three-months-is-a-puppet_sto7273119/story.shtml.

Farrer, M. (2019) 'This is England': nation unites to rejoice in Cricket World Cup final win. *The Guardian* (15 July). Available at: https://www.theguardian.com/sport/2019/jul/15/this-is-england-nation-unites-to-rejoice-in-cricket-world-cup-win.

Felloni, R. (2018) GM CEO Mary Barra said the recall crisis of 2014 forever changed her leadership style. *Business Insider* (14 November). Available at: https://www.businessinsider.com/

gm-mary-barra-recall-crisis-leadership-style-2018-11?r=US&IR=T.

Fessler, L. (2018) How to cultivate grit in your employees. *Advisory Board* (7 May). Available at: https://www.advisory.com/daily-briefing/2018/05/07/duckworth-grit.

Financial Times (2007) Lunch with the FT: Daniel Goleman (5 January). Available at: https://www.ft.com/content/acd3586e-9bc7-11db-9c9b-0000779e2340.

Flade, P., Asplund J. and Elliot, G. (2015) Employees who use their strengths outperform those who don't. *Gallup Business Journal* (8 October). Available at: https://www.gallup.com/workplace/236561/employees-strengths-outperform-don.aspx.

Forrest, A., Lawson, I., Chaput de Saintonge, L. and Smith, M. (2012) *To Practise What We Preach: An Exploratory Survey of Values in Charities* (London: Cass Business School).

Foster Wallace, D. (2006) *Consider the Lobster: Essays and Arguments* (London: Hachette).

Fredrickson, B. L. (2001) The role of positive emotions in positive psychology: the broaden-and-build theory of positive emotions. *American Psychologist*, 56, 218–226.

Fredrickson, B. L., Cohn, M. A., Coffey, K. A., Pek, J. and Finkel, S. M. (2008) Open hearts build lives: positive emotions, induced through loving-kindness meditation, build consequential personal resources. *Journal of Personality and Social Psychology*, 95, 1045–1062.

Fredrickson, B. L. and Losada, M. F. (2005) Positive affect and the complex dynamics of human flourishing. *American Psychologist*, 60, 678–686.

Froha, J. J., Sefick, W. J. and Emmons, R. A. (2008) Counting blessings in early adolescents: an experimental study of gratitude and subjective well-being. *Journal of School Psychology*, 46(2), 213–233.

Gallup (2017) *State of the American Workforce Report*. Available at: https://www.gallup.com/workplace/238085/state-american-workplace-report-2017.aspx.

Gallup (2019) The 2019 Gallup Great Workplace Award Recipients (28 March). Available at: https://www.gallup.com/workplace/248105/2019-gallup-great-workplace-award-recipients.aspx.

Gandhi, M. K. (1965) *Glorious Thoughts of Gandhi* (New Delhi: New Book Society of India).

Gardner, H., Csikszentmihalyi, M. and Damon, W. (2008) *Good Work: When Excellence and Ethics Meet* (New York: Basic Books).

Garland, E. L., Fredrickson, B. L., Kring, A. M., Johnson, D. P., Meyer, P. S. and Penn, D. L. (2010) Upward spirals of positive emotions counter downward spirals of negativity: insights from the broaden-and-build theory and affective neuroscience on the treatment of emotion dysfunctions and deficits in psychopathology. *Clinical Psychology Review*, 30(7), 849–864.

Garlick, H. (2018) 'If I'd known, I might not have taken a life': can prisoners defuse their own disputes? *The Guardian* (10 February). Available at: https://www.theguardian.com/society/2018/feb/10/can-prisoners-resolve-disputes-dartmoor-mediation.

Garvin, D. A. (2013) How Google sold its engineers on management. *Harvard Business Review* (December). Available at: https://hbr.org/2013/12/how-google-sold-its-engineers-on-management.

Gates, M. (2019) *Moment of Lift: How Empowering Women Changes the World* (London: Bluebird).

Gentry, W. A., Weber, T. J. and Sadri, G. (2007) *Empathy in the Workplace: A Tool for Effective Leadership* (Greensboro, NC: Center for Creative Leadership). Available at: https://www.ccl.org/wp-content/uploads/2015/04/EmpathyInTheWorkplace.pdf.

Geoffreys, C. (2017) *Gregg Popovich: The Inspiring Life and Leadership Lessons of One of Basketball's Greatest Coaches* (Winter Park, FL: Calvintir Books).

George, B. and Sims, P. (2007) *True North: Discover Your Authentic Leadership* (San Francisco, CA: Jossey-Bass).

Getlen, L. (2014) The untold story of how the buried Chilean miners survived. *New York Post* (11 October). Available at: https://nypost.com/2014/10/11/how-the-chilean-miners-men-survived-for-69-days-beneath-the-earths-surface.

Gibson, S. (2016) Why is Jose Mourinho the special one? *The Telegraph* (1 June). https://www.telegraph.co.uk/football/2016/06/01/why-is-jose-mourinho-the-special-one.

Gifford, F. and Richmond, P. (2008) *The Glory Game: How the 1958 NFL Championship Changed Football Forever* (New York: HarperCollins).

Gilbert, P. (2013) *The Compassionate Mind* (London: Constable).

Ginesi, L. and Niescierowicz, R. (1998) Neuroendocrinology and birth 2: the role of oxytocin. *British Journal of Midwifery*, 6(12), 791–796.

Glanz, J. and Schwartz, J. (2003) Dogged engineer's effort to assess shuttle damage. *New York Times* (26 September). Available at: https://www.nytimes. com/2003/09/26/us/dogged-engineer-s-effort-to-assess-shuttle-damage.html.

Goleman, D. (2013) Curing the common cold of leadership: poor listening. *LinkedIn* (2 May). Available at: https://www.linkedin.com/pulse/20130502140433-117825785-curing-the-common-cold-of-leadership-poor-listening.

Golliver, B. (2019) Gregg Popovich and the United Spurs of America. *Washington Post* (10 August). Available at: https://www.washingtonpost.com/sports/2019/08/10/gregg-popovich-united-spurs-america/?noredirect=on.

Goodwin, D. K. (2009) *Team of Rivals: The Political Genius of Abraham Lincoln* (London: Penguin).

Gottman, J. M. (1994) *What Predicts Divorce? The Relationship Between Marital Processes and Marital Outcomes* (New York: Erlbaum).

Govindji, R. and Linley, P. A. (2007) Strengths use, self-concordance and well-being: implications for strengths coaching and coaching psychologists. *International Coaching Psychology Review*, 2(2), 143–153.

Grant, A. (2013) *Give and Take: A Revolutionary Approach to Success* [Kindle edn] (London: Weidenfeld & Nicholson).

Grant, A. (2019) *Power Moves: Lessons from Davos* [audio] (Newark, NJ: Audible).

Grant, A. and Barnes, D. (2011). Predicting sales revenue. Working paper.

Grant, A., Dutton, J. and Rosso, B. D. (2017) Giving commitment: employee support programs and the prosocial sensemaking process. *Academy of Management Journal*, 51(5), 898–918.

Grant, A. and Gino, F. (2010) A little thanks goes a long way: explaining why gratitude expressions motivate prosocial behavior. *Journal of Personality and Social Psychology*, 98(6), 946–955.

Griffeth, R. W., Hom, P. W. and Gaertner, S. (2000) A meta-analysis of antecedents and correlates of employee turnover: update, moderator tests, and research implications for the next millennium. *Journal of Management*, 26, 463–488.

Haidt, J. (2006) *The Happiness Hypothesis: Finding Modern Truth in Ancient Wisdom* (New York: Basic Books).

Haimovitz, K. and Dweck, C. S. (2016) What predicts children's fixed and growth intelligence mind-sets? Not their parents' views of intelligence but their parents' views of failure. *Psychological Science*, 27(6), 859–869.

Harbaugh, W., Mayr, U. and Burghart, D. R. (2007) Neural responses to taxation and voluntary giving reveal motives for charitable donations. *Science*, 316, 1622–1623.

Harter, J. K., Schmidt, F. L. and Hayes, T. L. (2002) Business-unit-level relationship between employee satisfaction, employee engagement, and business outcomes: a meta-analysis. *Journal of Applied Psychology*, 87, 268–279.

Harvard Business Review (2015) *The Business Case for Purpose*. Available at: https://www.ey.com/Publication/vwLUAssets/ey-the-business-case-for-purpose/$FILE/ey-the-business-case-for-purpose.pdf.

Hill, P. L. and Turiano, N. A. (2004) Purpose in life as a predictor of mortality across adulthood. *Psychological Science*, 25(7), 1482–1486.

Hodges, T. D. and D. O. Clifton (2004) Strengths-based development in practice. In A. Linley and S. Joseph (eds), *Handbook of Positive Psychology in Practice* (Hoboken, NJ: John Wiley & Sons), pp. 256–268.

Holt-Lunstad, J., Birmingham, W. A. and Light, K. C. (2008) Influence of a 'warm touch' support enhancement intervention among married couples on ambulatory blood pressure, oxytocin amylase and cortisol. *Psychosomatic Medicine*, 70, 976–985.

Hone, L. C., Jarden, A., Duncan, S. and Schofield, G. M. (2015) Flourishing in New Zealand workers: associations with lifestyle behaviors, physical health, psychosocial, and work-related indicators. *Journal of Occupational and Environmental Medicine*, 57(9), 973–983.

Hougaard, R., Carter, J. and Beck, J. (2018) Assessment: are you a compassionate leader? *Harvard Business Review* (15 May). Available at: https://hbr.org/2018/05/assessment-are-you-a-compassionate-leader.

Howell, E. (2019) Columbia disaster: what happened, what NASA learned. *Space.com* (1 February). Available at: https://www.space.com/19436-columbia-disaster.html.

Hsieh, T. (2010) *Delivering Happiness: A Path to Profits, Passion and Purpose* (New York: Business Plus).

Huckman, R. and Pisano, G. (2006) The firm specificity of individual performance. *Management Science*, 52, 473–488.

Hughes, S. (2012) Andrew Strauss was the 'deputy's deputy' who became an exceptional leader of his England men. *The Telegraph* (29 August). Available at: https://www.telegraph.co.uk/sport/cricket/international/england/9507587/Andrew-Strauss-was-the-deputys-deputy-who-became-an-exceptional-leader-of-his-England-men.html.

Hunt, I. (2015) Sir Anthony Seldon: the value of a good head. *The Telegraph* (30 June). Available at: https://

www.telegraph.co.uk/education/
educationopinion/11705706/Sir-Anthony-
Seldon-the-value-of-a-good-head.html.

Imperative (2019) *Purpose at Work: 2019
Workforce Purpose Index*. Available at:
https://www.2019wpi.com.

Ingawale, M. and Espiau, L. (2013) A
20 second blood test without bleeding.
TEDx Talks (8 February). Available
at: https://www.youtube.com/
watch?v=RyeQt0GodsE.

Isen, A. M. (2000) Positive affect and
decision making. In M. Lewis and J. M.
Haviland-Jones (eds), *Handbook of
Emotions*, 2nd edn (New York: Guilford
Press), pp. 417–435.

Isen, A. M. and Means, B. (1983) The
influence of positive affect on decision-
making strategy. *Social Cognition*, 2,
18–31.

Jacobs, A. (2009) Happy feet: inside the
online shoe utopia. *The New Yorker* (7
September). Available at: https://www.
newyorker.com/magazine/2009/09/14/
happy-feet.

Job, V., Walton, G. M., Bernecker, K. and
Dweck, C. S. (2015) Implicit theories about
willpower predict self-regulation and grades
in everyday life. *Journal of Personality and
Social Psychology*, 108(4), 637–647.

Jonas, W., Johansson, L. M., Nissen, E.,
Ejdebäck, M., Ransjö-Arvidson, A. B.
and Uvnäs-Moberg, K. (2009) Effects of
intrapartum oxytocin administration and
epidural analgesia on the concentration
of plasma oxytocin and prolactin, in
response to suckling during the second day
postpartum. *Breastfeeding Medicine*, 4(2),
71–82.

Jundt, D. and Hinsz, V. B. (2001) Are
happier workers more productive workers?
The impact of mood on self-set goals,
self-efficacy, and task performance. Paper
presented at the annual meeting of the
Midwestern Psychological Association,
Chicago, May.

Kabat-Zinn, J. (2003) Mindfulness-based
interventions in context: past, present, and
future. *Clinical Psychology: Science and
Practice*, 10(2), 144–156.

Kaplan, S., Bradley-Geist, J. C., Ahmad, A.,
Anderson, A., Hargrove, A. and Lindsey,
A. (2013) A test of two positive psychology
interventions to increase employee well-
being. *Journal of Business and Psychology*,
29, 367–380. https://doi.org/10.1007/
s10869-013-9319-4.

Kelley, J. M., Kraft-Todd, G., Schapira,
L., Kossowsky, J. and Riess, H. (2014)
The influence of the patient–clinician
relationship on healthcare outcomes: a
systematic review and meta-analysis of
randomized controlled trials. *PLOS ONE*,
9(4): e101191.

Kelly, M. (2004) *The Rhythm of Life:
Living Every Day with Passion and
Purpose* (New York: Simon & Schuster).

Keltner, D. (2012) The Secrets of the
Vagus Nerve [video]. *Greater Good
Science Center*. Available at: https://
greatergood.berkeley.edu/video/item/
secrets_of_the_vagus_nerve.

Kemper, K. J. and Shaltout, H. A. (2011)
Non-verbal communication of compassion:
measuring psychophysiologic effects. *BMC
Complementary and Alternative Medicine*,
11(132), 1–9.

Kenny, B. and Edmondson, A. C.
(2019) How a new leader broke
through a culture of accuse, blame and
criticize [podcast]. *Harvard Business
Review* (17 September). Available at:
https://hbr.org/podcast/2019/09/
how-a-new-leader-broke-through-a-
culture-of-accuse-blame-and-criticize.

Kerr, J. (2013a) The All Blacks guide to being successful (off the field). *The Telegraph* (14 November). Available at: https://www.telegraph.co.uk/men/active/10427619/The-All-Blacks-guide-to-being-successful-off-the-field.html.

Kerr, J. (2013b) *Legacy: What the All Blacks Can Teach Us About the Business of Life* (London: Constable).

Kirsch, P., Esslinger, C., Chen, Q., Mier, D., Lis, S., Siddhanti, S. et al. (2005) Oxytocin modulates neural circuitry for social cognition and fear in humans. *Journal of Neuroscience*, 25(49), 11489–11493.

Kline, N. (2002) *Time to Think: Listening to Ignite the Human Mind* (London: Cassell).

Kok, B. E., Coffey, K. A., Cohn, M. A., Catalino, L. I., Vacharkulksemsuk, T., Algoe, S. B. et al. (2013) How positive emotions build physical health: perceived positive social connections account for the upward spiral between positive emotions and vagal tone. *Psychological Science*, 24(7), 1123–1132.

Kouzes, J. M. and Posner, B. Z. (2017) *The Leadership Challenge: How to Make Extraordinary Things Happen in Organizations*, 6th edn (Hoboken, NJ: John Wiley & Sons).

Kristof, K. (2010) Chilean miners: leadership lessons from Luis Urzua. *CBS News* (14 October). Available at: https://www.cbsnews.com/news/chilean-miners-leadership-lessons-from-luis-urzua.

Kristof-Brown, A. L., Zimmerman, R. D. and Johnson, E. C. (2005) Consequences of individuals' fit at work: a meta-analysis of person-job, person-organization, person-group, and person-supervisor fit. *Personnel Psychology*, 58, 281–342.

Kruger, J. and Dunning, D. (1999) Unskilled and unaware of it: how difficulties in recognizing one's own incompetence lead to inflated self-assessments. *Journal of Personality and Social Psychology*, 77(6), 1121–1134.

Labuschagne, I., Phan, K. L., Wood, A., Angstadt, M., Chua, P., Heinrichs, M. et al. (2010) Oxytocin attenuates amygdala reactivity to fear in generalized social anxiety disorder. *Neuropsychopharmacology*, 35(12), 2403–2413.

Lamers, S. M., Bolier, L., Westerhof, G. J., Smit, F. and Bohlmeijer, E. T. (2012) The impact of emotional well-being on long-term recovery and survival in physical illness: a meta-analysis. *Journal of Behavioral Medicine*, 35(5), 538–547.

Lansing, A. (2014 [1959]) *Endurance: Shackleton's Incredible Voyage* (New York: Basic Books).

Lawrence, T. E. (1997 [1935]) *Seven Pillars of Wisdom* (Ware: Wordsworth Editions).

Lee, D. (2017) Servant leadership lessons from a 17-year-old. *TLNT* (19 May). Available at: https://www.tlnt.com/servant-leadership-lessons-from-a-17-year-old.

Lee, T. H. and Duckworth, A. L. (2018) Organizational grit. *Harvard Business Review* (September–October). Available at: https://hbr.org/2018/09/organizational-grit.

Leider, R. (1997) *The Power of Purpose: Find Meaning, Live Longer, Better* (London: Berrett-Koehler Publishers).

Lencioni, P. (2002) Make your values mean something. *Harvard Business Review* (July). Available at: https://hbr.org/2002/07/make-your-values-mean-something.

Leslie, S. G. and Aaker, J. (2010) Zappos: happiness in a box. Stanford

Graduate School of Business – Case M-333 (23 August). Available at: https://innovaservicios.weebly.com/uploads/3/3/6/8/3368095/zappos_stanford_gsb.pdf.

Lewis, C. S. (2002 [1955]) *The Magician's Nephew* (London: Grafton).

Lievens, F., Ones, D. S. and Dilchert, S. (2009) Personality scale validities increase throughout medical school. *Journal of Applied Psychology*, 94(6), 1514–1535.

LinkedIn and Imperative (2016) *Purpose at Work: 2016 Workforce Purpose Index*. Available at: https://www.ciphr.com/wp-content/uploads/2016/10/Global_Purpose_Index_2016.pdf.

Linley, P. A., Nielsen, K. M., Wood, A. M., Gillett, R. and Biswas-Diener, R. (2010) Using signature strengths in pursuit of goals: effects on goal progress, need satisfaction, and well-being, and implications for coaching psychologists. *International Coaching Psychology Review*, 5(1), 8–17.

Lombardi Jr, V. (2001) *What It Takes to Be #1: Vince Lombardi on Leadership* (New York: McGraw Hill).

Lombardi Jr, V. (2003) *The Lombardi Rules: 26 Lessons from Vince Lombardi: The World's Greatest Coach* (New York: McGraw-Hill).

Losada, M. and Heaphy, E. (2004) The role of positivity and connectivity in the performance of business teams: a nonlinear model. *American Behavioral Scientist*, 47, 740–765.

Lyubomirsky, S. (2007) *The How of Happiness: A New Approach to Getting the Life You Want* (New York: Penguin).

Lyubomirsky, S., King, L. and Diener, E. (2005) The benefits of frequent positive affect: does happiness lead to success? *Psychological Bulletin*, 131(6), 803–855.

McGovern, J., Lindemann, M., Vergara, M., Murphy, S., Barker, L. and Warrenfeltz, R. (2001) Maximizing the impact of executive coaching: behavioral change, organizational outcomes, and return on investment. *Manchester Review*, 6(1), 3–11. Available at: https://www.perspect.ca/pdf/ExecutiveCoaching.pdf.

Machell, B. (2017). They're just wild about Harry Kane. *The Times* (3 June).

McRae, D. (2016) Jason Gillespie: Trevor Bayliss was 100% the correct choice for England. *The Guardian* (8 April). Available at: https://www.theguardian.com/sport/2016/apr/08/jason-gillespie-trevor-bayliss-yorkshire-coach-england.

Mairs, G. (2014) How the All Blacks drew inspiration from First World War soldier's ordeal. *The Telegraph* (10 November). Available at: https://www.telegraph.co.uk/sport/rugbyunion/international/newzealand/11221948/How-the-All-Blacks-drew-inspiration-from-First-World-War-soldiers-ordeal.html.

Manfred, T. (2014) 55-year-old legend who quit his job to work for the Spurs explains why Gregg Popovich is a genius. *Business Insider* (5 December). Available at: https://www.businessinsider.com/ettore-messina-on-gregg-popovich-2014-12?r=US&IR=T.

Marca (2019) The story behind Guardiola's decision to let Messi go to the 2008 Olympic Games (5 June). Available at: https://www.marca.com/en/football/barcelona/2019/06/05/5cf818d5ca474149538b4622.html.

Marquet, L. D. (2015) *Turn the Ship Around! A True Story of Turning Followers into Leaders* (London: Penguin).

Mason, R. (2018) *Gareth Southgate: Zero to Hero* [Kindle edn] (London: SJH Group).

Massiah, A. (2018) World Cup 2018: Gareth Southgate's compassion praised. *BBC News* (4 July). Available at: https://www.bbc.co.uk/news/uk-44715244.

Meglino, B. and Ravlin, E. (1998) Individual values in organizations: concepts, controversies, and research. *Journal of Management*, 24(3), 351–389.

Meglino, B., Ravlin, E. and Adkins, C. (1989) A work values approach to corporate culture: a field test of the value congruence process and its relationship to individual outcomes. *Journal of Applied Psychology*, 74, 424–432.

Melwani, S., Mueller, J. S. and Overbeck, J. R. (2012) Looking down: the influence of contempt and compassion on emergent leadership categorizations. *Journal of Applied Psychology*, 97(6), 1171–1185.

Merlino, J. I. and Raman, A. (2013) Health care's service fanatics. *Harvard Business Review* (May). Available at: https://hbr.org/2013/05/health-cares-service-fanatics.

Messina, E. (2014) What the Spurs are all about. *Sports.ru*. Available at: https://m.sports.ru/tribuna/blogs/messina/710302.html.

Métral, M. (2016) 7 things every manager should learn from Pep Guardiola. *LinkedIn* (23 September). Available at: https://www.linkedin.com/pulse/7-thing-every-manager-should-learn-from-pep-guardiola-max-m%C3%A9tral.

Minhas, G. (2010) Developing realised and unrealised strengths: implications for engagement, self-esteem, life satisfaction and well-being. *Assessment and Development Matters*, 2, 12–16.

Mishra, A. (2013) The research on trust in leadership: the need for context. *Journal of Trust Research*, 3(1), 59–69.

Morgan Roberts, L., Spreitzer, G., Dutton, J., Quinn, R., Heaphy, E. and Barker, B. (2005) How to play to your strengths. *Harvard Business Review* (January). Available at: https://hbr.org/2005/01/how-to-play-to-your-strengths.

Nembhard, I. M. and Edmondson, A. C. (2006) Making it safe: the effects of leader inclusiveness and professional status on psychological safety and improvement efforts in health care teams. *Journal of Organisational Behaviour*, 27(7), 941–966.

Newman, K. (2017) How gratitude can transform your workplace. *Greater Good Magazine* (6 September). Available at: https://greatergood.berkeley.edu/article/item/how_gratitude_can_transform_your_workplace.

New Statesman (2018) Gareth Southgate and the new progressive Englishness (4 July). Available at: https://www.newstatesman.com/politics/sport/2018/07/gareth-southgate-and-new-progressive-englishness.

Nickisch, C. (2019) Creating psychological safety in the workplace [interview with Amy Edmondson]. *Harvard Business Review* (4 July). Available at: https://hbr.org/ideacast/2019/01/creating-psychological-safety-in-the-workplace.

Nietzsche, F. (1998 [1889]) *Twilight of the Idols* (Oxford: Oxford University Press).

NPR (2008) Transcript: Michelle Obama's convention speech (August 25). Available at: https://www.npr.org/templates/story/story.php?storyId=93963863.

Obama, B. (2006) *The Audacity of Hope: Thoughts on Reclaiming the American Dream* (New York: Crown).

Obama, M. (2011) Remarks by the First Lady during keynote address at Young African Women Leaders Forum (22 June). Available at: https://obamawhitehouse.

archives.gov/the-press-office/2011/06/22/
remarks-first-lady-during-keynote-address-
young-african-women-leaders-fo.

Paulhus, D. L. and Williams, K. M. (2002)
The dark triad of personality: narcissism,
Machiavellianism, and psychopathy. *Journal
of Research in Personality*, 36(6), 556–563.

Petrocchi, N. and Couyoumdjian, A. (2016)
The impact of gratitude on depression and
anxiety: the mediating role of criticizing,
attacking, and reassuring the self. *Self and
Identity*, 15(2), 191–205.

Pettit, J. W., Kline, J. P., Gencoz, T.,
Gencoz, F. and Joiner, T. E. (2001) Are
happy people healthier? The specific role
of positive affect in predicting self-reported
health symptoms. *Journal of Research in
Personality*, 35, 521–536.

Pfau, B. N. (2015) How an accounting
firm convinced its employees they
could change the world. *Harvard
Business Review* (6 October).
Available at: https://hbr.org/2015/10/
how-an-accounting-firm-convinced-its-
employees-they-could-change-the-world.

Pickford, M. (1936) Why not try God? *St.
Petersburg Times* (25 January). Available
at: https://news.google.com/newspapers?i
d=SQxPAAAAIBAJ&sjid=500DAAAA
IBAJ&pg=4725,3554118&dq=pickford+
not-the-falling-down&hl=en.

Piekema, C. (2014) Does money really
motivate people? *BBC Future* (18
November). Available at: http://www.bbc.
com/future/story/20120509-is-it-all-
about-the-money.

Pink, D. (2010). Drive: The Surprising
Truth About What Motivates Us [video].
RSA Animate. Available at: https://www.
youtube.com/watch?v=u6XAPnuFjJc.

Pink, D. (2011) *Drive: The Surprising
Truth About What Motivates Us*
(Edinburgh: Canongate Books).

Proctor, C., Maltby, J. and Linley, P. A.
(2009) Strengths use as a predictor of
well-being and health-related quality of life.
Journal of Happiness Studies, 10, 583–630.

Quin, R. and Thakor, A. (2018) Creating
a purpose-driven organisation. *Harvard
Business Review* (July–August). Available
at: https://hbr.org/2018/07/creating-a-
purpose-driven-organization.html.

Rakel, D., Barrett, B., Zhang, Z., Hoeft, T.,
Chewning, B., Marchand L. et al. (2011)
Perception of empathy in the therapeutic
encounter: effects on the common cold.
Patient Education and Counseling, 85(3),
390–397.

Reavis, G. (1999 [1940]) *The Animal
School* (Peterborough, NH: Crystal Spring
Books).

Rego, A., Sousa, F., Marques, C. and
Cunha, M. P. (2012) Optimism predicting
employees' creativity: the mediating
role of positive affect and the positivity
ratio. *European Journal of Work and
Organizational Psychology*, 21(2),
244–270.

Rigoni, B. and Aspland, J. (2016)
Strengths-based employee development:
the business results. *Gallup Workplace* (10
July). Available at: https://www.gallup.
com/workplace/236297/strengths-based-
employee-development-business-results.
aspx.

Riolli, L., Savicki, V. and Spain, E. (2010)
Positive emotions in traumatic conditions:
mediation of appraisal and mood for
military personnel. *Military Psychology*,
22(2), 207–223.

Roberts, L. M., Spreitzer, G., Dutton, J. E.,
Quinn, R. E., Heaphy, E. D. and Barker,
B. (2005) How to play to your strengths.
Harvard Business Review (January).
Available at: https://hbr.org/2005/01/
how-to-play-to-your-strengths.

Roosevelt, T. (1910) Citizenship in a republic. Speech delivered at the Sorbonne, Paris, 23 April. Available at: https://www.leadershipnow.com/tr-citizenship.html.

Ros, M., Schwartz, S. H. and Surkiss, S. (1999) Basic individual values, work values, and the meaning of work. *Applied Psychology: An International Review*, 48(1), 49–71.

Rowe, G., Hirsh, J. B. and Anderson, A. K. (2007) Positive affect increases the breadth of attentional selection. *Proceedings of the National Academy of Sciences of the United States of America*, 104(1), 383–388.

Rowling, J. K. (2008) The fringe benefits of failure, and the importance of imagination. Harvard commencement speech delivered on 5 June. Available at: https://news.harvard.edu/gazette/story/2008/06/text-of-j-k-rowling-speech.

Rush, C., Hooker, S., Ross, K., Frers, A., Peters, J., Masters, K. et al. (2019) Brief report: meaning in life is mediated by self-efficacy in the prediction of physical activity. *Journal of Health Psychology*. DOI: 10.1177/1359105319828172.

Ryff, C. D., Singer, B. H. and Love, G. D. (2004) Positive health: connecting well-being with biology. *Philosophical Transactions of the Royal Society B: Biological Sciences*, 359(1449), 1383–1394.

Saner, E. (2018) How the psychology of the England football team could change your life. *The Guardian* (10 July). Available at: https://www.theguardian.com/football/2018/jul/10/psychology-england-football-team-change-your-life-pippa-grange.

Schafer, U., Hagen, J. and Burger, C. (2011a) Mr KLM (A): Jacob Veldhuyzen. Case Study. ESMT No. 411-0117 (Berlin: European School of Management and Technology).

Schafer, U., Hagen, J. and Burger, C. (2011b) Mr KLM (B): Captain van Zanten. Case Study. ESMT No. 411-0118 (Berlin: European School of Management and Technology).

Schafer, U., Hagen, J. and Burger, C. (2011c) Mr KLM (C): Jaap. Case Study. ESMT No. 411-0119.(Berlin: European School of Management and Technology).

Scott, R. F. (2006) *Journals: Captain Scott's Last Expedition* (Oxford: Oxford University Press).

Seibert, S. E., Wang, G. and Courtright, S. H. (2011) Antecedents and consequences of psychological and team empowerment in organizations: a meta-analytic review. *Journal of Applied Psychology*, 96(5), 981–1003.

Seldon, A. (2019) Speech delivered at the 5th Ultimate Wellbeing in Education Conference, London, 17 October.

Seligman, M. E. P., Steen, T. A., Park, N. and Peterson, C. (2005) Positive psychology progress: empirical validation of interventions. *American Psychologist*, 60, 410–421.

Seppälä, E. (2012) The best kept secret to happiness and health: compassion. *Psychology Today* (5 November). Available at: https://www.psychologytoday.com/us/blog/feeling-it/201211/the-best-kept-secret-happiness-health-compassion.

Shackleton, E. (2015) *South: The Endurance Expedition* (London: Penguin).

Shackleton, E. (1916) A letter from Ernest Shackleton to his wife, Emily (September). Available at: https://www.spri.cam.ac.uk/archives/shackleton/articles/1537,2,32,15.html.

Shariatmadari, D. (2019) Cancelled for sadfishing: the top 10 words of 2019. *The Guardian* (14 October). Available at: https://www.theguardian.com/science/2019/oct/14/cancelled-for-sadfishing-the-top-10-words-of-2019.

Sheldon, K. M., Jose, P., Kashdan, T. and Jarden, A. (2015) Personality, effective goal-striving, and enhanced well-being: comparing 10 candidate personality strengths. *Personality and Social Psychology Bulletin*, 41(4), 575–585.

Sheldon, K. M., Kasser, T., Smith, K. and Share, T. (2002) Personal goals and psychological growth: testing an intervention to enhance goal-attainment and personality integration. *Journal of Personality*, 70, 5–31.

Sinek, S. (2010) How Great Leaders Inspire Action [video]. *TED.com* (4 May). Available at: https://www.youtube.com/watch?v=qp0HIF3SfI4.

Sinek, S. (2011) *Start with Why: How Great Leaders Inspire Everyone to Take Action* (London: Penguin).

Sinek, S. (2013) Why Leaders Eat Last [video]. *99U* (4 December). Available at: https://www.youtube.com/watch?v=ReRcHdeUG9Y.

Sinek, S. (2014) *Leaders Eat Last: Why Some Teams Pull Together and Others Don't* (London: Penguin).

Singh Ospina, N., Phillips, K. A., Rodriguez-Gutierrez, R., Castaneda-Guarderas, A., Gionfriddo, M. R., Branda, M. E. et al. (2019) Eliciting the patient's agenda: secondary analysis of recorded clinical encounters. *Journal of General Internal Medicine*, 34, 36–40.

Smith, J. (2013) How to show appreciation and get better results from your employees this holiday season. *Forbes* (13 November). Available at: https://www.forbes.com/sites/jacquelynsmith/2013/11/13/how-to-show-appreciation-and-get-better-results-from-your-employees-this-holiday-season.

Smith, J. (2015) Five ways to cultivate gratitude at work. *Greater Good Magazine* (16 May). Available at: https://greatergood.berkeley.edu/article/item/five_ways_to_cultivate_gratitude_at_work.

Society for Human Resource Management (2016) *2016 Employee Job Satisfaction and Engagement: Revitalizing a Changing Workforce*. Available at: https://www.shrm.org/hr-today/trends-and-forecasting/research-and-surveys/Pages/Job-Satisfaction-and-Engagement-Report-Revitalizing-Changing-Workforce.aspx.

Sorenson, S. (2014) How employees' strengths make your company stronger. *Gallup Workplace* (20 February). Available at: https://www.gallup.com/workplace/231605/employees-strengths-company-stronger.aspx.

Spreitzer, G. M. (1995) Psychological empowerment in the workplace: construct definition, measurement, and validation. *Academy of Management Journal*, 38, 1442–1465.

Spreitzer, G. M., Kizilos, M. and Nason, S. (1997) A dimensional analysis of the relationship between psychological empowerment and effectiveness, satisfaction, and strain. *Journal of Management*, 23, 679–704.

Stajkovic, A. D. and Luthans, F. (1998) Self-efficacy and work-related performance: a meta-analysis. *Psychological Bulletin*, 124, 240–261.

Stewart, G. L. (2006) A meta-analytic review of relationships between team design features and team performance. *Journal of Management*, 32, 29–55.

Stibel, J. (2014) Branson: a profile in failure. *LinkedIn* (30 October).

Available at: https://www.linkedin.com/ pulse/20141030172700-461078-richard-branson-a-profile-in-failure.

Strauss, A. (2014) *Driving Ambition: My Autobiography* (London: Hodder & Stoughton).

Syed, M. (2015) *Black Box Thinking* (New York: Portfolio/Penguin).

Tang, J. (2017) Four ways PepsiCo CEO motivates her employees. *LinkedIn* (16 August). Available at: https://business. linkedin.com/talent-solutions/blog/ employee-retention/2017/4-ways-pepsico-ceo-motivates-her-employees.

Thomas, R. J. and Silverstone, Y. (2015) *Empowering Employees at Zappos.* Outlook Case Study: Workforce of the Future (Boston, MA: Accenture). Available at: https://www.accenture. com/t20151015t042910__w___/us-en/_ acnmedia/accenture/conversion-assets/ outlook/documents/2/accenture-outlook-zappos-web-pdf.pdf.

Tiluck, D. (2015) Remembering Zinedine Zidane's headbutt and the 2006 World Cup Final. *Bleacher Report* (9 July). Available at: https://bleacherreport.com/ articles/2514359-remembering-zinedine-zidanes-headbutt-and-the-2006-world-cup-final.

Tobar, H. (2014) Sixty-nine days: the ordeal of the Chilean miners. *New Yorker* (7 July). Available at: https://www. newyorker.com/magazine/2014/07/07/ sixty-nine-days.

Trzeciak, S. (2018) How 40 Seconds of Compassion Could Save a Life [video]. *TEDx Talks* (5 June). Available at: https://www.youtube.com/ watch?v=elW69hyPUuI.

Trzeciak, S. and Mazzarelli, A. (2018) *Compassionomics: The Revolutionary*

Scientific Evidence That Caring Makes a Difference (Pensacola, FL: Studer Group).

Turtel, J. (2014) Another victory for 'Pop'. Another show of leadership. *Fortune* (16 June). Available at: https://fortune.com/2014/06/16/ gregg-popovich-leadership.

Umoh, R. (2019) PepsiCo CEO Indra Nooyi: 5 powerful career habits that drove her success. *CNBC* (2 October). Available at: https://www.cnbc.com/2018/10/02/ pepsico-ceo-indra-nooyis-last-day-5-habits-that-drove-her-success.html.

Vieselmeyer, J., Holguin, J. and Mezulis, A. (2017) The role of resilience and gratitude in posttraumatic stress and growth following a campus shooting. *Psychological Trauma: Theory, Research, Practice, and Policy*, 9(1), 62–69.

Walker, T. (2005) Superhead Anthony Seldon and his challenge to improve Wellington College. *The Independent* (6 October). Available at: https://www. independent.co.uk/news/education/ education-news/superhead-anthony-seldon-and-his-challenge-to-improve-wellington-college-317608.html.

Wall, M. (2013) Space shuttle Columbia launched on tragic mission 10 years ago. *Space.com* (16 January). Available at: https://www.space.com/19283-shuttle-columbia-tragedy-launch-10-years.html;

Waters, L. E., Loton, D. and Jach, H. K. (2019) Does strength-based parenting predict academic achievement? The mediating effects of perseverance and engagement. *Journal of Happiness Studies*, 20(4), 1121–1140.

Watkins, P. C., Woodward, K., Stone, T. and Kolts, R. L. (2003) Gratitude and happiness: development of a measure of gratitude and relationships with subjective wellbeing. *Social Behavior and Personality*, 31(5), 431–451.

West, C. P., Huschka, M. M., Novotny, P. J., Sloan, J. A., Kolars, J. C., Habermann, T. M. et al. (2006) Association of perceived medical errors with resident distress and empathy: a prospective longitudinal study. *Journal of the American Medical Association*, 296, 1071–1078.

Whaling, J. (2015) Jose Mourinho's most famous quotes. *Irish Mirror* (17 December). Available at: https://www. irishmirror.ie/sport/soccer/soccer-news/jose-mourinhos-most-famous-quotes-7032648.

Whitmore, J. (2009) *Coaching for Performance*, 4th edn (London: Nicholas Brealey Publishing).

Wiener-Bronner, D. (2018) How Indra Nooyi built Pepsi for the future. *CNN* (7 August). Available at: https://money.cnn. com/2018/08/07/news/companies/indra-nooyi-legacy/index.html.

Williams, P. (2002) *The Paradox of Power: A Transforming View of Leadership* (New York: Warner Books).

Wilson, C. (2017) Team culture expert Owen Eastwood gets ramped-up role as All Whites aim to shift mindset. *Stuff* (5 March). Available at: https://www.stuff. co.nz/sport/football/nz-teams/90006153/ team-culture-expert-owen-eastwood-gets-rampedup-role-as-all-whites-aim-to-shift-mindset.

Wood, A. M., Linley, P. A., Maltby, J. and Hurling, R. (2010) Using personal and psychological strengths leads to increases in well-being over time: a longitudinal study and the development of the strengths use questionnaire. *Personality and Individual Differences* 50(1), 15–19.

Woolley, A. W., Chabris, C. F., Pentland, A., Hashmi, N. and Malone, T. W. (2010) Evidence for a collective intelligence factor in the performance of human groups. *Science*, 330(6004), 686–688.

Wrzesniewski, A. (2014) Engage in job crafting. In J. E. Dutton and G. Spreitzer (eds), *How to Be a Positive Leader: Small Actions, Big Impact* (San Francisco, CA: Berrett-Koehler), pp. 65–77.

Wrzesniewski, A. and Dutton, J. E. (2001) Crafting a job: revisioning employees as active crafters of their work. *Academy of Management Review*, 26(2), 179–201.

Wrzesniewski, A., Dutton, J. E. and Debebe, G. (2003) Interpersonal sensemaking and the meaning of work. In R. Kramer and B. Staw (eds), *Research in Organizational Behavior*, vol. 25 (Oxford: Elsevier), pp. 93–135.

Yeager, D. S., Henderson, M., D'Mello, S., Paunesku, D., Walton, G. M., Spitzer, B. J. et al. (2014) Boring but important: a self-transcendent purpose for learning fosters academic self-regulation. *Journal of Personality and Social Psychology*, 107, 559–580.

Yeager, D. S., Purdie-Vaughns, V., Garcia, J., Apfel, N., Brzustoski, P., Master, A. et al. (2013) Breaking the cycle of mistrust: wise interventions to provide critical feedback across the racial divide. *Journal of Experimental Psychology: General*, 143, 804–824.

Young, S. F., Richard, E. M., Moukarzel, R. G., Steelman, L. A. and Gentry, W. A. (2017) How empathic concern helps leaders in providing negative feedback: a two-study examination. *Journal of Occupational and Organizational Psychology*, 90(4), 535–558.

Zak, P. J. (2017) The neuroscience of trust. *Harvard Business Review* (January–February). Available at: https://hbr. org/2017/01/the-neuroscience-of-trust.

Zak, P. J. and Knack, S. (2001) Trust and growth. *Economic Journal*, 111(470), 295–321.

Zak, P. J., Stanton, A. A. and Ahmadi, S. (2007) Oxytocin increases generosity in humans. *PLOS ONE*, 2(11): e1128.

Zenger, J. and Folkman, J. (2016) What great listeners actually do. *Harvard Business Review* (14 July). Available at: https://hbr.org/2016/07/what-great-listeners-actually-do.

Zetlin, M. (2017) In just 9 minutes at Apple WWDC, Michelle Obama explains how to be a great leader. *Inc.com* (7 June). Available at: https://www.inc.com/minda-zetlin/in-secret-appearance-at-apple-wwdc-michelle-obama-explains-how-to-be-a-great-lea.html.

Zolnierek, K. B. and Dimatteo, M. R. (2009) Physician communication and patient adherence to treatment: a meta-analysis. *Medical Care*, 47(8), 826–834.

Join the authors to learn more:

We'd love to welcome you to join the Global Social Leaders (GSL) movement here: www.globalsocialleaders.com.

We'd also love you to participate in our online course, which is free of charge and was co-created with The Oxford Character Project and the Human Flourishing Program at Harvard University's Institute for Quantitative Social Science. Please visit: http://leaderknowloveinspire.com and click on 'Learn more'.